"PEDLAR IN DIVINITY"

"PEDLAR IN DIVINITY"

GEORGE WHITEFIELD AND THE TRANSATLANTIC REVIVALS, 1737–1770

Frank Lambert

PRINCETON UNIVERSITY PRESS   PRINCETON, NEW JERSEY

Copyright © 1994 by Princeton University Press
Published by Princeton University Press, 41 William Street,
Princeton, New Jersey 08540
In the United Kingdom: Princeton University Press, 3 Market Place,
Woodstock, Oxfordshire OX20 1SY
All Rights Reserved

Second printing, and first paperback printing, 2003
Paperback ISBN 0-691-09616-3

*The Library of Congress has cataloged the cloth edition of this
book as follows*

Lambert, Frank, 1943–
"Pedlar in divinity" : George Whitefield and the transatlantic
revivals, 1737–1770 / Frank Lambert.
p. cm.
Includes bibliographical references and index.
ISBN 0-691-03296-3
1. Whitefield, George, 1714–1770. 2. Evangelists—Biography.
3. Revivals—Great Britain—History—18th century. 4. Great
Awakening. 5. Evangelical Revival. 6. Preaching—History—18th
century. 7. Revivals—North America—History—18th century.
I. Title.
BX9225.W4L35 1993
269.2'092—dc20
[B] 93-1345

British Library Cataloging-in-Publication Data is available

This book has been composed in Baskerville

Printed on acid-free paper. ∞

www.pupress.princeton.edu

Printed in the United States of America

3 5 7 9 10 8 6 4 2

For Beth

Contents

Illustrations

Acknowledgments

FOR MUCH of his ministry, George Whitefield was indebted to creditors who financed his transatlantic enterprises. His private correspondence expresses the evangelist's fervent hope to settle all arrears, a desire fulfilled only just before his death in 1770. Like Whitefield, I have accumulated a lifetime of debts to many persons who have provided invaluable criticism, counsel, and encouragement.

Throughout this project, T. H. Breen has been a constant source of constructive criticism, offering thoughtful suggestions for transforming a dissertation into a book. In the process, I learned to appreciate him as both a fine scholar and a good friend. Others read parts or all of the manuscript. I have benefited particularly from the astute observations and helpful evaluations of Jim Oakes, Bob Wiebe, Bill Heyck, Harold Perkin, Dee Andrews, Christine Leigh Heyrman, and John Murrin.

A number of librarians demonstrated not only competence but kindness and patience in the search for manuscripts. R. Russell Maylone, Director of the Rare Books Collection at Northwestern University, and David K. Himrod, Director of Reader Services at Garrett Evangelical Theological Seminary, provided invaluable assistance, especially in the early stages of research. I wish also to thank the fine staffs at the British Library, the National Library of Wales, the University of Manchester Libraries, the New York Public Library, the Massachusetts Historical Society, the Library Company of Philadelphia, the American Philosophical Society, the Houghton Library at Harvard, the Firestone Library at Princeton, the Newberry Library, and the Library of Congress—Manuscripts Division.

Portions of the book have appeared in substantially different form as journal articles. Part of chapter 2 appeared as " 'Pedlar in Divinity': George Whitefield and the Great Awakening, 1737–1745," *Journal of American History* 77 (December 1990): 812–837. Sections of chapter 3 were first developed in "Subscribing for Profits and Piety: The Friendship of Benjamin Franklin and George Whitefield," *William and Mary Quarterly* 50 (July 1993). And part of chapter 5 appeared as "The Great Awakening as Artifact: George Whitefield and the Construction of Intercolonial Revival, 1739–1745," *Church History* 60 (June 1991): 223–246. I appreciate the readers and editors of those journals who helped me work out ideas that became central to this volume.

In the process of preparing the manuscript for publication, I learned to appreciate the hard work and professionalism of the editorial staff at Princeton University Press. In particular, Lauren Osborne skillfully guided the project through evaluation, production, and publication.

Finally, I am deeply grateful to Beth, Talley, and Will, who bore the entire project with love, patience, encouragement, and good humor.

"PEDLAR IN DIVINITY"

IN THE mid-eighteenth-century Anglo-American world, George Whitefield enjoyed immense power and standing, especially among evangelicals. His preaching triggered religious revivals on both sides of the Atlantic. After his graduation from Pembroke College, Oxford, in 1736, until his death at Newburyport, Massachusetts, in 1770, Whitefield preached an estimated eighteen thousand sermons to hundreds of thousands of men and women throughout Britain and the American colonies. In London, crowds of more than thirty thousand gathered in public parks to hear the revivalist proclaim his message of a spiritual new birth. Even in the much smaller colonial cities of Philadelphia and Boston, attendance at Whitefield's services exceeded twenty thousand auditors. Crisscrossing England, Wales, Scotland, and Ireland on preaching tours, the itinerant ignored national and ecclesiastical boundaries to convey the gospel to young and old, rich and poor, aristocrat and vagrant. His journeys included fifteen preaching tours in Scotland, three in Ireland, and seven in America where he exhorted such diverse audiences as the throngs of New Englanders on Boston Common and a handful of slaves in rural South Carolina.[1]

Contemporaries and historians alike have acknowledged Whitefield as a man who had tremendous, though ill-defined, impact on colonial society. Describing the alteration in Philadelphians' manners after Whitefield's arrival in 1739, Benjamin Franklin noted that "it seem'd as if all the World were growing Religious."[2] Other assessments were less flattering. In 1745, an association of Connecticut ministers denounced the confusion and disorder following Whitefield's uninvited appearances in their parishes, claiming "that religion is now in a far worse state than it was [before Whitefield visited]."[3] Likewise, scholars have offered a variety of interpretations. Some have viewed Whitefield as a bit player in a series of local revivals of little lasting significance. Others have cast him as leader of a transatlantic evangelical movement that altered religious and political authority. We continue to search for the

[1] Cited in James Downey, *The Eighteenth Century Pulpit: A Study of the Sermons of Butler, Bradley, Secker, Sterne, Whitefield, and Wesley* (Oxford, 1969), 156.

[2] J. A. Leo Lemay and P. M. Zall, eds., *The Autobiography of Benjamin Franklin: A Genetic Text* (Knoxville, Tenn., 1981), 103.

[3] *The Declaration of the Association of the County of New Haven in Connecticut, Conven'd at New-Haven, February 19, 1744–45, Concerning the Rev. Mr. George Whitefield, His Conduct, and the State of Religion at this Day* (Boston, 1745), 6.

1. "Dr. Squintum." Portrait of Whitefield.

man who did so much—at once reviled and revered. And, like Sartre's Antoine Roquentin, who sought to understand the merchant and deputy Olivier Blevigne through studying his portrait, we turn first to Whitefield's visual image.[4]

In 1737, at the outset of his ministry, Whitefield sat for his portrait. The artist, one J. Cochran, captured the twenty-two-year-old preacher's likeness in a half-length pose. Dressed in clerical robe, Whitefield appears to be gesturing with his upturned right hand extended across his breast, while his left hand rests on his lap. He is not speaking. He stares ahead in an unfocused gaze, his left eye rolled inward, fixing the viewer's attention on the defect that prompted detractors to call him "Dr. Squintum." A wig seems to fit on the back half of his head, covering what appears to be a bald pate.[5]

Subsequent renderings by better-known portraitists were no more flattering. In 1742, John Wollaston, a popular artist who took commissions throughout the empire, depicted the revivalist standing in a pulpit, arms stretched stiffly in front of his body. Again, the left eye is turned in while his right eye peers straight ahead. His large, sharp nose and full lips make this an altogether unattractive piece. The next year Francis Kyte, a mezzotint-engraver and portrait-painter for whom such notables as George Frideric Handel sat, completed what Whitefield's admirer and editor, John Gillies, called "the best resemblance of him in his younger days, before he became corpulent." However, this full-length painting highlights the same features as did the earlier works, especially the remarkable crossed eyes.[6]

The portraits raise questions about the creation of images. They invite viewers to ask whose Whitefield they are viewing and why the evangelist agreed to sit for at least three different paintings within a short span of time. The fact that Whitefield advertised his portraits for sale suggests that they represented more than private acts announcing, for instance, his arrival or success. The portraits were those of a *public* person, more than an ordinary preacher, indeed, a living symbol of a successful revival of "true religion." Whitefield seemed to recognize that these paintings were "texts," and he sought to fashion editions which people would "read" in the way he desired.[7] More concerned

---

[4] Jean-Paul Sartre, *Nausea*, trans. Lloyd Alexander (Cambridge, Mass., 1959), 91–92.

[5] See Arnold A. Dallimore, *George Whitefield: The Life and Times of the Great Evangelist of the Eighteenth-Century Revival*, 2 vols. (London, 1980). For portraits, see frontispieces to both volumes. Also see 1:145.

[6] Ibid.

[7] For discussion of the cultural constructions of meaning, see John E. Toews, "Intellectual History after the Linguistic Turn: The Autonomy of Meaning and the Irre-

about making a theological than an aesthetic statement, the evangelist settled for what appears to be an unflattering portrait. Indeed, his decision to sit for the first painting was an effort to combat what he considered a misrepresentation by his opponents. Some detractors had portrayed him leaning on a cushion with a bishop looking very enviously over his shoulder. A caption, "Mitred Drones," made explicit the suggestion that Whitefield was enriching himself through his ministry.[8] To combat this caricature, Whitefield posed as an unsmiling, severe figure—a sober, orthodox Anglican priest in traditional clerical vestments.

Yet in the spreading consumer market of the mid-1700s, his renditions competed with others offering a far different account of the evangelist and his message. The famous artist William Hogarth mocked Whitefield in two engravings presenting the revivalist as a religious fanatic who held sway over the superstitious lower orders. In the second, Hogarth introduced a cherub in the form of a post-boy, delivering a message to "St. Money-Trap," insinuating that Whitefield raised large sums of money not for charity but for himself.[9] Throughout his ministry, Whitefield's attempts to shape his public image faced competition in a market offering multiple interpretations of the itinerant. In the end, consumers decided the issue, creating images of the revivalist that neither he nor his opposers fully anticipated.

Whitefield's portraits were also commodities, reproduced, advertised, and sold in British and American marketplaces—goods in what has been termed a "consumer revolution." Within the past ten years historians have presented a rich, textured account of the consumer revolution in the mid-eighteenth-century English Atlantic world. Most scholars agree on its nature: proliferation of consumer goods produced in English workshops and homes; a new, more elastic view of demand extending beyond the affluent sort to the middling and lesser folk; innovations in merchandising and advertising exploiting the new, inexpensive newspapers spanning Britain and America.[10] These new market conceptions and strategies not only revolutionized the sale of manufactured goods; they offered far-reaching possibilities for propa-

---

ducibility of Experience," *American Historical Review* 92 (October 1987): 879–907. See also Dominick LaCapra, *History and Criticism* (Ithaca, 1985).

[8] [Banner of Truth Trust], *George Whitefield's Journals* (London, 1960), 91.

[9] Joseph Burke and Colin Caldwell, eds., *Hogarth: The Complete Engravings* (New York, n.d.), 253.

[10] The term "consumer revolution" as applied to the mid-eighteenth-century commercial revolution was coined by Neil McKendrick, John Brewer, and J. H. Plumb, eds., *The Birth of a Consumer Society: The Commercialization of Eighteenth-Century England* (Bloomington, 1982).

gating ideas. This study explores how one group, evangelical revivalists, appropriated and adapted new commercial techniques to promote transatlantic revivalism.

By the late 1730s, the consumer revolution had introduced possibilities for redefining audiences in ways unimaginable in the mid-1600s. Seventeenth-century divines had largely conceived of their audiences as private bodies, defined by parish, sect, or denomination. With the introduction of inexpensive popular print, especially newspapers, evangelicals could now think of addressing a new, much broader public. Indeed the word *public* assumed new meaning. The emerging public was not the court and courtiers. It was private persons operating outside such private settings as churches and acting as arbiters of "public opinion" through the exercise of independent reason.[11] It was at this new public—a mass audience that transcended denominational, national, and even continental boundaries—that George Whitefield and other revivalists, as well as their opponents, aimed their messages.

Most scholars of the Great Awakening, the American phase of the revivals, have noted almost in passing Whitefield's appropriation of commercial means for advance publicity.[12] But there has been little analysis of how he and his associates organized, publicized, and funded the revivals. While we know a great deal about the revivalists' message and oratorical skills, we know little about how they promoted their preaching services and how they attracted crowds numbering in the tens of thousands. And though much has been suggested about why men and women responded to revivalism, we know far less about how evangelists exploited demand for "experimental religion," the term that distinguished faith expressed in a conversion experience from that reflected in subscription to a particular creed. This work examines closely the process by which Whitefield and others borrowed merchandising means to attain their evangelistic ends. In particular it explores the innovative use of print to publicize, deliver, and reinforce the gos-

[11] For discussion of public opinion, especially as expressed in an emerging "religious public sphere," see chapter 5.

[12] Inattention to the role of print is especially evident in older standard treatments such as Edwin S. Gaustad, *The Great Awakening in New England* (New York, 1957); Charles Maxson, *The Great Awakening in the Middle Colonies* (Chicago, 1920); Wesley Gewehr, *The Great Awakening in Virginia, 1740–1790* (Durham, N.C., 1930). While Harry Stout minimized the role of print in "Religion, Communications, and the Ideological Origins of the American Revolution," *William and Mary Quarterly* 34 (October 1977): 519–541, his more recent biography, though continuing to focus on Whitefield's pulpit performances, acknowledges the importance of print in publicizing the evangelist's services. See Harry Stout, *The Divine Dramatist: George Whitefield and the Rise of Modern Evangelicalism* (Grand Rapids, Mich., 1991).

pel. Newspapers on both sides of the Atlantic constitute a particularly rich body of evidence for this study.

Throughout his ministry, Whitefield exhibited ambivalence toward the spreading consumer market. He presented himself as both backward-looking, fearing the market's erosion of Christian values, and forward-thinking—adapting commercial strategies for his own ends. Opposed to the rationalism of the mid-eighteenth-century Anglican clergy, Whitefield fought against any attempt to elevate human understanding above divine sovereignty. To the revivalist, the market of his day represented the "world" and should be viewed with suspicion. He preferred the past and its cries against the world for inspiration: the works of Jesus, the Reformers, and "almost all the writers a century ago."[13] While advocating an otherworldly message, Whitefield confessed that evangelicals should use the world to propagate the gospel. He contended that "the devotion and business of a Methodist go hand in hand," adding that the rationalization of the countinghouse should extend to the meetinghouse.[14]

Whitefield's ambiguous self-presentation is seen most clearly in his views concerning consumption. His sermonic pronouncements against luxuries echo those of Puritan divines a century earlier. He was unsparing in his criticism of those who placed pursuit of earthly gain above concern for eternal salvation. In a representative warning, Whitefield cautioned, "When you are called from hence, then all riches and grandeur will be over; the grave will make no distinction; great estates will be of no signification in the other world." He added that on Judgment Day all would be called to account "for the use to which [they] had put the abundance of the things of this life." More than the churches that preached what he considered false doctrine, the consumer market was emerging as Whitefield's greatest competitor for the attention of his audiences.[15]

Yet Whitefield was a pioneer in the commercialization of religion, discovering within the market the very strategies and language to attack its excesses. He faced a problem similar to that of the new merchants: how to reach an ever-expanding audience of anonymous strangers, most of whom he could not reach face-to-face. Similar problems led to similar solutions and a parallel turning to print. To fund and promote his religious enterprises, Whitefield forged a new, volun-

---

[13] John Gillies, ed., *The Works of the Rev. George Whitefield, M.A. Late of Pembroke College, Oxford, and Chaplain to the Rt. Hon. the Countess of Huntingdon, Containing All His Sermons and Tracts Which Have Been Already Published With a Selected Collection of Letters*, 6 vols. (London, 1771), 2:206.

[14] George Whitefield, *Sermons on Important Subjects* (London, 1825), 654.

[15] Ibid., 87, 176, 478–486.

tary transatlantic organization along the lines established by commercial innovators. He developed a reliable system of contacts through which he circulated information about his revival successes, solicited funds for his missionary work, and instructed ministers on the practice of revivalism.[16] Whitefield and his associates developed a pervasive publicity campaign featuring endorsements, testimonials, and controversy in newspapers, magazines, and pamphlets. And they exploited the demand among evangelicals for his revival publications through such merchandising devices as quantity discounts, prepayment incentives, serial publication, convenience packaging, and home delivery. Hence, the Grand Itinerant proclaimed a message not of the market but in the market.

Although biographical, this is not a biography of George Whitefield. Rather, Whitefield provides a window into the cultural ramifications of the consumer revolution, a case study of the commercialization of religion. Such a study has more than one protagonist. While much attention is focused on Whitefield, other people play important roles. Printers mediated the revivalist's message. Even when audiences assembled to hear Whitefield preach, they attended and listened with preconceptions shaped by extensive newspaper coverage. And readers were far from being mere consumers of messages; they produced their own meanings, often in conflict with the evangelist's intentions. Revivalism, then, is understood in a matrix of evangelists, printers, and audience.

Some of the tawdriness characteristic of late twentieth-century commercialized religion demands a clarification of focus. It is true that Whitefield faced charges that have a modern ring: persistent accusations concerning misappropriation of funds and intermittent suggestions of sexual misconduct. However, this study is not intended as a quest for the origins of abuses culminating in televangelist scandals. Rather, the intent is to explore how he redefined his conception and practice of ministry through market tropes and strategies. It would be reductionist to suggest that the medium was the message of the evangelical revivals, but a commercial context and language did invest the revivalists' message with new meaning.

While this is an exercise in microhistory, it does illuminate larger issues of the mid-eighteenth-century Atlantic world. Chapter 1 looks at Whitefield's spiritual conversion within the context of the consumer revolution, exploring how the spreading market enabled the evangelist to redefine his mission and imagine a mass audience. Chapter 2 exam-

---

[16] For operation of evangelical communications, see Susan O'Brien, "A Transatlantic Community of Saints: The Great Awakening and the First Evangelical Network, 1735–1755," *American Historical Review* 91 (December 1986): 811–832.

ines important changes in the nature and extent of the English consumer market, specifically for marketing and distributing ideas. Chapter 3 describes how Whitefield linked previously unconnected, local American awakenings into a national movement before there was a nation. In chapter 4 the focus is on Whitefield's audiences: not only consumers of revivalism, they became producers of meanings as they interpreted his message through their own daily experiences. Chapter 5 looks at the emergence of a religious public sphere as supporters and opponents of the revivals debated revivalism, largely in newspapers and pamphlets, and attempted to persuade readers. And chapter 6 suggests that print served as a direct link between the Great Awakening and the American Revolution as evangelical experiences with Anglican arbitrariness reinforced fears of imperial tyranny. An epilogue views Whitefield as the father of modern revivalism whose innovations influenced evangelists from Charles Grandison Finney to Billy Graham.

CHAPTER 1

Eighteenth-Century Transformations: Whitefield's New Birth and the Consumer Revolution

IN 1740, at the age of twenty-six, George Whitefield published an account of his spiritual conversion, tracing his transformation from an aspiring shopkeeper to a transatlantic revivalist. In his widely circulated autobiography, the evangelical revivalist recorded that eight years earlier, during his first year at Pembroke College, Oxford, he had come under the influence of a group of pious students whose teaching challenged the young scholar to examine his own faith. Consequently, Whitefield sought salvation through various routes including extreme asceticism, a period of fasting that resulted in such a weakened physical condition that in 1735 he withdrew from school for six months to regain his strength. Then, at John Wesley's encouragement, he discovered the devotional works of seventeenth-century Puritans. While perusing Henry Scougal's *The Life of God Within the Soul of Man* (1677), Whitefield realized that what the author described as "falsely placed religion" applied to his own conception: "going to church, doing hurt to no one, being constant in the duties of the closet [prayer], and now and then reaching out . . . to give alms to . . . poor neighbours." Whitefield discovered that "true religion was [nothing less than] union of the soul with God, and Christ formed within." He testified that as he read those words, "a ray of Divine light . . . instantaneously darted upon my soul, and from that moment, but not till then, did I know that I must be a new creature."[1]

As viewed within the context of evangelical Christianity, Whitefield's conversion account confirms the widely held view among contemporaries and historians alike that the revivalist's theology was backward-looking.[2] Pursuing John and Charles Wesley's reading program of Puritan texts, Whitefield studied such works as Joseph Alleine's *Alarm to the Unconverted* (1673), Richard Baxter's *Call to the Unconverted* (1658),

---

[1] *Whitefield's Journals*, 46–47.

[2] For a representative view of Whitefield as a backward-looking preacher, see the interpretation in Perry Miller, *Jonathan Edwards* (New York, 1949).

and Joseph Hall's *Contemplations on the New Testament* (1617).[3] Reflecting the derivative nature of his theology, Whitefield later preached and published familiar Puritan themes lifted from his reading: original sin, predestination, imputed righteousness, and perseverance. Topics and even titles of many of his works illustrate the degree of Whitefield's borrowing from his spiritual forefathers. Throughout his ministry, Whitefield proclaimed his preference for Puritan writings over all others. Recommending suitable authors to a young convert in the 1740s, Whitefield stated his preference for the works of seventeenth-century Dissenters. Approving the Puritan theology embraced by another follower, the Grand Itinerant wrote, "The doctrines you now preach are no new doctrines; you are now got into the good old way."[4] Considered within a religious context, Whitefield's writings are linked by obvious textual similarities to the seventeenth-century Puritans.

However, Whitefield's life also unfolded in another context, one strikingly different from that of the mid-1600s, enabling the young evangelical to express his religious convictions in ways unavailable to his spiritual forebears. The beginning of Whitefield's transatlantic evangelism coincided with a commercial transformation in the Atlantic world. Driven by demand for the consumer goods pouring out of thousands of households and shops throughout the English countryside, per capita consumption in England and America exploded.[5] In their competition for business in an expanding consumer market, mer-

---

[3] Joseph Alleine, *An Alarme to Unconverted Sinners . . . Whereunto are annexed divers practical cases of Conscience Judiciously Resolved* (London, 1673). Richard Baxter, *A Call to the Unconverted to Turn and Live* (London, 1658). Joseph Hall, *Contemplations Upon the Principle Passages of the Holy Storie* (London, 1617).

[4] Gillies, *Works of Whitefield*, 2:206.

[5] Literature on the emerging consumer society is extensive. In addition to McKendrick, Brewer, and Plumb, *Birth of a Consumer Society*, see T. H. Breen, "An Empire of Goods: The Anglicization of Colonial America, 1690–1776," *Journal of British Studies* 25 (October 1986): 467–499, and " 'Baubles of Britain': The American and Consumer Revolutions of the Eighteenth Century," *Past and Present* 119 (May 1980): 73–104; Ralph Davis, *A Commercial Revolution: English Overseas Trade in the Seventeenth and Eighteenth Centuries* (London, 1967); John J. McCusker and Russell Menard, *The Economy of British America, 1607–1789* (Chapel Hill, 1985); Edwin Perkins, *The Economy of Colonial America*, 2d ed. (New York, 1988); Jacob M. Price, *Capital and Credit in the British Overseas Trade: The View from the Chesapeake, 1700–1776* (Cambridge, Mass., 1980); James F. Shepherd and Gary M. Walton, *Shipping, Maritime Trade, and the Economic Development of Colonial North America* (Cambridge, Eng., 1972); Charles H. Wilson, *England's Apprenticeship, 1603–1763*, (Cambridge, Eng., 1965); Roy Porter, *English Society in the Eighteenth Century* (New York, 1982); Joan Thirsk, *Economic Policy and Projects: The Development of a Consumer Society in Early Modern England* (Oxford, 1978); Lorna Weatherill, "A Possession of One's Own: Women and Consumer Behavior in England, 1660–1740," *Journal of British Studies* 25 (April 1986): 131–156, and "Toward a History of the Standard of Living in British North America," *William and Mary Quarterly* 45 (January 1988): 116–170.

chants changed the way they sold their goods. Rather than "remain[ing] at home and let[ting] the orders come to them," by midcentury they "travel[ed] the whole island to promote the sale," a practice that one contemporary observed "would have astounded our forefathers."[6] By the middle of the eighteenth century enterprising merchants had employed innovative merchandising strategies to break the "cosseted constraints" of class and geography that had long restricted their sales.[7] They began to see the lower and middling sorts in America as well as the highborn in London as consumers of their wares.

In addition to supplying merchants with many new products for expanding markets, the fast-growing print trade provided them with powerful means for promoting all kinds of merchandise. A reciprocal relationship developed between exploding consumer demand and publishing innovations: accelerated demand prompted new forms of advertising, which in turn further fueled demand. For instance, merchants demanded a vehicle for providing accurate information about prices and demand in ports throughout the Atlantic world and a forum for publicizing their wares to distant strangers. The response was a newspaper network emanating from London and extending through the English provinces and on to the American colonies. In the opinion of one student of the eighteenth-century Atlantic market, "newspapers were by far the most powerful and extensive public communications innovation that developed within the English Atlantic empire between 1675 and 1740, . . . mak[ing] news available to a wide audience."[8] Newspaper advertising along with magazines and serial publications expanded the means of promoting ideas as well as merchandise.[9] Indeed, Whitefield discovered that ideas could be treated as commodities.

The publication history of Whitefield's autobiography illustrates the link between his spiritual conversion and the commercial transformation of the 1700s. Whitefield's printed testimony circulated as a consumer good within the expanding Atlantic market, advertised in newspapers on both sides of the ocean. Having made a conversion experience central to his message, Whitefield published an account of his new birth in 1740 to establish his own spiritual credentials for proclaiming experimental religion. Hence the autobiography became an important element in the revivalist's advance publicity that prepared

---

[6] William Hutton, *An History of Birmingham to the End of the Year 1780* (Birmingham, 1781), 70.

[7] McKendrick, Brewer, and Plumb, *Birth of Consumer Society*, 198.

[8] Ian Steele, *The English Atlantic, 1675–1740: An Exploration of Communication and Community* (New York, 1986), 113–114.

[9] J. H. Plumb, *The Commercialisation of Leisure in Eighteenth-Century England* (Reading, 1973), 8.

Americans for his arrival. Aboard the *Elizabeth* en route to the colonies in August 1739, Whitefield penned *A Short Account of God's Dealings with the Reverend Mr. George Whitefield.* Noting that God had called him to a public work, the revivalist "thought His children would be glad to know how [he] was trained up for it."[10]

Crafting his spiritual autobiography for a mass audience, Whitefield disseminated the volume extensively in the Atlantic world. Publishing the work in 1740 in both America and Britain, the itinerant authorized ten editions: four in London, one in Edinburgh, three in Boston, and two in Philadelphia. Printers directed the book toward the widest audience, offering it for sale in three different sizes including one in sextodecimo, a compact volume that even the poor could afford.[11] American readers eagerly purchased Whitefield's autobiography. The Boston printer and bookseller Daniel Henchman published two different runs of fifteen hundred volumes each—a large number for an age when the "more successful writing sold 1500" in the print capital of London.[12] By widely circulating his account of God's calling him to preach the necessity of the new birth, Whitefield sought to strengthen the bond between message and messenger.

The conjunction of Whitefield's conversion and the mid-eighteenth-century commercial transformation shaped the revivalist's interpretation of the Great Commission to proclaim the gospel to every creature. Like the rest of us, the evangelist constructed his social reality with the elements at hand, and by the 1740s, commercial language and techniques abounded, affording him new ways of organizing, promoting, and explaining his evangelical mission.[13]

The spreading market enabled him to conceive of organizing a revival spanning the Atlantic, making "the whole world [his] parish."[14] Improvements in marketing organization and practices provided the means of relieving the suffering of "strangers at a distance," transforming mere awareness of distant needs into a moral imperative to

---

[10] George Whitefield, *A Short Account of God's Dealings with the Reverend Mr. George Whitefield* (Philadelphia, 1740). For an account of Whitefield's writing his autobiography, see *Whitefield's Journals*, 35 and 332–333.

[11] For the various editions of Whitefield's works, see Roland Austin, "Bibliography of the Works of George Whitefield," *Proceedings of the Wesley Historical Society* 10 (1916): 173.

[12] See "Publishing in Boston, 1726–57: The Accounts of Daniel Henchman," *Proceedings of the American Antiquarian Society* (Worcester) 66 (1957): 17–36. For London print runs, see John Brewer, *Party Ideology and Popular Politics at the Accession of George III* (Cambridge, Eng., 1976), 146.

[13] For discussion of the construction of social reality, see Peter L. Berger and Thomas Luckman, *The Social Construction of Reality: A Treatise in the Sociology of Knowledge* (New York, 1966).

[14] Gillies, *Works of Whitefield*, 1:105.

deliver spiritual and material aid.[15] In Whitefield's case, that meant preaching the gospel to the "uttermost parts of the earth," including the wilderness of Georgia. Drawing upon the world of trade Whitefield prepared remote auditors to receive the spoken word through advance publicity, especially that of newspaper advertising. And he employed a commercial vocabulary as well as theological language to convey the necessity of the new birth to his listeners, who themselves increasingly thought in categories of market exchange.

[handwritten: ○Whitefield "Born Again" → wrote books about his rebirth]
[handwritten: ○Consumer Revolution w/ printing press.]

WHITEFIELD'S NEW BIRTH

Throughout Whitefield's thirty-three-year ministry, from 1737 to 1770, the necessity of a conversion experience was central to his message. He asserted that only God's actions were efficacious in redemption, effecting salvation through nothing less than a "union of the soul with God" resulting in the "one thing needful," the new birth.[16] God's grace alone saved men and women; human merit played no role whatever. As early as 1740, Whitefield split with his mentor, John Wesley, over the doctrine of "universal redemption," the idea that salvation was available to all who would but accept it.[17] Whitefield clung to a strict predestination whereby the sovereign God elected whom he wished to save. Whitefield declared that "God chose us from eternity, he called us in time, and I am persuaded will keep us from falling." No one deserved God's mercy or merited his grace through good works. Rather God "will have mercy on whom he will have mercy."[18]

Whitefield's own spiritual new birth shaped his experiential understanding of conversion as the threshold to Christian faith. Experimental religion was not for the fainthearted; it was a vigorous expression of piety extending to the countinghouse during weekdays as well as the meetinghouse on Sundays. He held that only those who had undergone the "indwelling of Christ" were worthy of calling themselves the "Elect." Whitefield claimed that most members of the church were "destitute of a true living faith in Jesus Christ," relying only on a "head-

---

[15] For the market's effects on intellectual categories and perceptions, see Thomas L. Haskell, "Capitalism and the Origins of the Humanitarian Sensibility, Part 1," *American Historical Review* 90 (April 1985): 339–361, "Capitalism and the Origins of the Humanitarian Sensibility, Part 2," ibid. (June 1985): 547–566.

[16] Whitefield, *Sermons on Important Subjects*, 312.

[17] Whitefield discusses his theological dispute with Wesley in a lengthy letter reprinted in *Whitefield's Journals*, 563–588.

[18] Gillies, *Works of Whitefield*, 1:90.

knowledge" without that of the heart.[19] He lamented the flaccid quality of Anglican religion, which practiced a monotonous round of "good works" as if those empty deeds could lead to justification. Whitefield admonished his followers to engage in rigorous spiritual exercises, "watch[ing] against all temptations to sloth . . . liv[ing] every day as holily as [possible], be[ing] frequent in self-examination morning and evening, and wrestl[ing] with God, beg[ging] him to hasten the new birth." Though salvation came only through divine election, the seeker should "never leave off watching, reading, praying, striving, till [he or she] experimentally find[s] Christ Jesus formed within."[20]

To understand Whitefield's idea of the new birth and experimental religion, it is necessary to first examine his religious experience before conversion. Like the vast majority of English men and women, White-field had entered the Church of England as an infant. On Christmas Day 1714 Rector Matthew Yates baptized George at the parish church of St. Mary de Crypt in Gloucester. The Whitefields were active and prominent members of the Anglican congregation situated less than a hundred yards away and on the same side of Southgate Street as the Bell Inn—the family business and residence. His father, Thomas, had served in all the major lay offices—overseer, vestryman, and church-warden. And, as a wine merchant, he had supplied the church with wine for communion. After Thomas's death in 1716, George's older brother Richard followed his father both as proprietor at the Bell and as leader at St. Mary's.[21]

George's early religious experience remains hidden except for scat-tered entries in his published autobiography, an exercise in self-promotion intended to publicize his revivals. Presenting himself in that document as the worst of sinners, Whitefield wrote, "Whatever fore-seen fitness for salvation others may talk of and glory in, I disclaim any such thing. If I trace myself from my cradle to my manhood, I can see nothing in me but a fitness to be damned." Whitefield listed among his boyhood transgressions idleness and prodigality, as evidenced by his attending plays and spending money on sweets and other frivolous things.[22] His point was that even though he had been a member of the established church, he had not experienced the new birth of the vital religion he himself later preached. Parish records reveal nothing of the itinerant's internal struggles with temptations and sins, indicating only

[19] Ibid., 175.

[20] Ibid., 14.

[21] For Whitefield's baptism and his family's officeholding in St. Mary de Crypt, see Parish Records of Gloucester, St. Mary de Crypt, Baptisms, 1694–1763, and Church-warden Accounts, 1707–1763, Gloucestershire Records Office.

[22] *Whitefield's Journals*, 37–38.

that he became a communicant on Christmas Day 1731 at age seven-teen, and that he preached his first sermon at St. Mary de Crypt on June 29, 1736.[23] The Anglican church remained important to White-field, and he never renounced his membership although he became a most severe critic.

Whitefield's conversion narrative provides important clues for dis-covering the nature of his spiritual new birth. First, his salvation came through his reading of evangelical works from seventeenth-century England and eighteenth-century Europe. The central role of reading in Whitefield's conversion is noteworthy because of the scant attention historians have given to print in the evangelical revivals. The focus has been on the orality of the evangelist's ministry, suggesting that the religious awakening represented a face-to-face world in retreat before the oncoming tide of rationalism and print.[24] From the outset, the printed word had a profound influence on Whitefield both in inform-ing his own understanding of experimental faith and in conveying the gospel to a transatlantic audience.

After joining the Holy Club at Oxford—a society of evangelical students—Whitefield began a systematic reading of Puritan and Pietist devotional works under the supervision of John Wesley, who insisted that the members follow a prescribed "method" centered on a careful, close reading of Holy Scripture. Whitefield testified that he "began to read the Holy Scriptures upon [his] knees, laying aside all other books, and praying over . . . every line and word." Wesley also believed that reading should be persistent, subscribing to the notion that if "we read once, twice, or thrice, and understand not, let us not cease so, but still continue reading, praying [and] asking of others." Whitefield's mentor taught his followers to be selective, restricting their study to the Bible, the church's Book of Homilies, and works of Reformers. And reading should be a spiritual as well as an intellectual pursuit, combining regu-lar periods of praying and meditating with reading itself.[25]

The texts Whitefield explored reinforced the importance of reading in personal salvation. Indeed many of the Puritan authors who influ-enced Whitefield wrote for the stated purpose of converting men and women. In the preface to *A Call to the Unconverted*, Richard Baxter exhorted readers to "read this or some other book of this subject to [their families] that they might be a means of winning of souls." Along

---

[23] See n. 21 above.

[24] For orality and the evangelical revivals, see, for example, Harry S. Stout, *The New England Soul: Preaching and Religious Culture in Colonial New England* (New York, 1986); and Rhys Isaac, *The Transformation of Virginia, 1740–1790* (New York, 1982).

[25] See *Whitefield's Journals*, 60. See also, Albert Outler, *John Wesley* (New York, 1964), 107, 124.

with urging people to read his work, Baxter suggested a method of studying the book. "When you have read over this book," he wrote, "I would entreat you to go alone, and ponder a little what you have read." As a result of reading and meditating, Baxter, like Wesley, believed that readers would become acquainted with their "sin and misery," the necessary recognition before they could "turn to God and obey his call." Commenting on the impact of *A Call to the Unconverted*, one contemporary claimed that Baxter's "book of practical divinity has been effectual for more conversions of sinners to GOD, than any printed in our time."[26] Whitefield bore testimony that Baxter's work continued to influence people generations after its publication.

Whitefield was a willing student, subscribing to Wesley's reading method with enthusiasm. Shortly after meeting the leader of "the despised Methodists" at Oxford, Whitefield began a reading program that led to his conversion and shaped his sense of calling. One of the first books he purchased as a student was the *Serious Call to a Devout Life*, by the Dissenter William Law. Noting its impact Whitefield wrote, "God worked powerfully upon my soul, as He has since upon many others by that and his other excellent treatise upon Christian perfection." Then Wesley "put into [Whitefield's] hands [the German Pietist August Hermann] Francke's treatise *Against the Fear of Man*, and a book entitled, *The Country Parson's Advice to His Parishioners*, the last of which was wonderfully blessed to my soul." Then while reading Scougal's *The Life of God in the Soul of Man*, Whitefield realized that conversion was nothing less than a spiritual new birth.[27]

After his conversion, Whitefield's reading changed. "I now resolved to read only such [books]," Whitefield noted, "as entered into the heart of religion and which led me directly into an experimental knowledge of Jesus Christ." The Bible was the centerpiece of his study. "The book of the divine Laws was seldom out of my hands," Whitefield observed in his autobiography, "I meditated therein day and night; and ever since that, God has made my way signally prosperous, and given me abundant success."[28] Thus, one of the ironies revealed in an examination of Whitefield's conversion narrative is that a man who became best known as a great orator before mass audiences found his salvation through not the preached but the printed word.

Whitefield's search for salvation on the printed page reflects his understanding that the new birth was at least in part a rational experience, rooted in Scripture and tradition. In defending himself against

[26] Baxter, *A Call to the Unconverted*, 6, 20.
[27] *Whitefield's Journals*, 46.
[28] Ibid., 48.

charges of enthusiasm, a term suggesting that he claimed direct divine inspiration, Whitefield insisted that his teachings were "based on scripture." He invited his followers and detractors to compare his sermons with those of Protestant founders, contending that "the doctrines you daily hear are no new doctrines, but the very same which were preached two hundred years ago."[29] In 1739 Whitefield admonished John Wesley for appealing too much to the emotions of his audience. To his former preceptor Whitefield wrote, "I cannot think it right in you Honoured Sir to give so much encouragement to those convulsions which people have been thrown into under your ministry." Whitefield warned that such preaching would "take people from the written word and make them depend on visions, convulsions, etc. more than on the promises and precepts of the Gospel."[30] In all cases, Holy Writ must be the ground of authentic faith.

Yet the new birth was more than reading and reasoning. Whitefield opposed expressions of rational Christianity that reduced salvation to intellectual affirmation of prescribed moral precepts. His own conversion had culminated in an experimental knowledge of Christ, a life-changing personal transformation validating the New Testament's great promises of redemption. After his new birth, Whitefield defined true religion in experiential terms. Men and women should seek only those clergymen who themselves had attained "a new nature and an experimental knowledge of, or vital faith in his dear son." To Whitefield, "learning without Piety will only render [ministers] more capable of promoting the Kingdom of the Devil." He warned that "a dead ministry will always make a dead people."[31] The revivalist accused parish priests of replacing the Bible with their own rational powers as the supreme authority in matters of faith. "Our modern pretenders to reason," Whitefield wrote, "indeed set up another principle to act from; they talk . . . of doing moral and civil duties of life from the moral fitness and unfitness of things."[32] To Whitefield, rationalists were in danger of avoiding the Scylla of enthusiasm only to crash into the Charybdis of infidelity.

Whitefield's conversion shaped his views of the nature of the new

---

[29] [John Foxe], *A Sermon of Christ Crucified . . . with a Recommendatory Preface by the Reverend Mr. Whitefield* (1570; reprint, London, 1759), ii–iii.

[30] George Whitefield to John Wesley, June 26, 1739, in the Wesley Collection of Manuscript Letters, John Rylands University Library, Manchester.

[31] Gillies, *Works of Whitefield*, 1:296; See George Whitefield, *Letter from the Reverend Mr. Whitefield to the Students of Harvard College in Cambridge, and Yale College in New-Haven* (London, 1741).

[32] George Whitefield, *The Knowledge of Jesus Christ the Best Knowledge* (London, 1739), 12.

birth, the state of the Anglican church, and the definition of his evangelical mission. Whitefield preached a derivative theology, patterned along lines suggested by the Puritan writers he had encountered. In formulating his interpretation of conversion, Whitefield employed language borrowed from Puritan sermons, diaries, and devotional works. Drawing upon the "biblical pattern of bondage and redemption, wilderness and promised land, death and resurrection," Richard Baxter, William Perkins, John Bunyan, and others depicted salvation as a "two-part cycle of emptying and filling." Through mortification and penance the individual became freed from sin, which made possible "the awakening of the soul and advancement toward union with God."[33] Whitefield's conversion followed that pattern. First, he discovered repentance to be an agonizing experience. He had hoped that the fruits of salvation "would be instantaneously infused into [his] soul" but discovered that "strong temptations" preceded grace. The young evangelical was buffeted by the persistence of "self-love, self-will, pride and envy."[34] Whitefield found guidance in Juan de Castaniza's *Spiritual Combat*, a well-known Catholic devotional manual favored by seventeenth-century Puritans. Castaniza compared the sinner's struggle with warfare, noting "that he that is employed in mortifying his will was as well employed as though he were converting Indians." Even when he made progress against sin, Whitefield discovered "pride creeping in at the end of almost every thought, word, and action." Although failing to eradicate his own transgressions, Whitefield realized after weeks of penance that "the blessed Spirit was all this time purifying [his] soul."[35]

After becoming free from the bondage of sin, Whitefield found "the awakening of [his] soul" through reading the Bible. Filling followed emptying. As his "mind [became] more open and enlarged, [he] began to read the Holy Scriptures . . . [which] proved meat indeed, and drink indeed, to [his] soul." Whitefield "daily received fresh life, light, and power from above" as he experienced the grace of God.[36] Relying no longer on his own good works, the evangelist depended on God to "enlighten [his] soul and bring [him] into the knowledge of His free grace, and the necessity of being justified in His sight by *faith alone*." From Francke, Whitefield had learned to depend upon Scripture for "the things of this life as well as that which is to come."[37] Thus when

---

[33] Cited in Charles E. Hambrick-Stowe, *The Practice of Piety: Puritan Devotional Disciplines in Seventeenth-Century New England* (Chapel Hill, 1982), 78.

[34] *Whitefield's Journals*, 51–52.

[35] Ibid., 53–54, 57.

[36] Ibid., 60.

[37] Ibid., 61–62.

Whitefield's brother unexpectedly gave him money to discharge "extraordinary and unavoidable expenses," the recent convert interpreted his good fortune as fulfillment of the divine promise to "seek first the Kingdom of God and His Righteousness, and all these things shall be added unto you." Continuing to seek guidance from others, Whitefield found in the writings of such Puritans as William Burkitt, James Janeway, and Matthew Henry "admirable use to lead [him] into . . . Gospel truths." Describing the infusion of grace, Whitefield wrote of his conversion: "My understanding was enlightened, my will broken, and my affections more and more enlivened with a zeal for Christ."[38]

Although Whitefield derived his conception of the new birth from his spiritual forefathers, he constructed his own meaning of the conversion process. First, he had no interest in the Puritans' concerns regarding church government. To Whitefield, the new birth occurred within the hearts of individuals and had nothing to do with formal religious affiliation. Proclaiming that salvation transcended traditional church boundaries, he believed evangelicals should convey the gospel to a mass audience. One opponent cynically interpreted Whitefield's catholic attitude toward evangelism, claiming that the itinerant was at the same time "a staunch Churchman in Old England! A thorough Independent in New England! An Anabaptist among Anabaptists! A true-blue Kirkman in Scotland! And a Quaker among Quakers! becoming all things to all men, not that he might gain some, but make some gain of all!"[39] Whitefield warned that too many church members "deceived[d] themselves with false Hopes of Salvation . . . flatter[ing] themselves that they [were] really born again" simply because they attended services and performed good works. But he also offered the hope of a spiritual new birth to men and women who professed no church affiliation, to "those who [were] dead in Trespasses and Sins." He warned that instead of "overcoming the World [many were] immersed in it." He urged them to make the attainment of salvation "the one Business of [their] Lives."[40]

Second, Whitefield emphasized the immediacy of the new birth. Seventeenth-century New England Puritans had presented salvation as a process unfolding over a period of months in which sinners moved through successive stages from initial contrition to final conversion.[41] Whitefield compressed the experience, raising the expectation that men and women could undergo conversion in a finite moment. Indeed, he indicated in his sermons that his auditors and readers could

[38] Ibid.
[39] *South Carolina Gazette*, June 18, 1741.
[40] George Whitefield, *Sermons on Various Subjects*, 2 vols. (Philadelphia, 1740), 2:29.
[41] The stages of conversion are described in Hambrick-Stowe, *Practice of Piety*, 54–90.

experience the new birth while reflecting on a sermon. In his frequently preached and widely distributed sermon *The Marks of the New Birth*, Whitefield called on men and women to "Repent therefore and be converted, that your Sins may be blotted out. See that you receive the Holy Ghost before you go hence."[42] Whitefield publicized testimonials of individuals experiencing life-changing transformations within a specific moment. In his *Short Account of God's Dealing with the Reverend Mr. George Whitefield*, the itinerant recounted that his own salvation took place one night in his room at Pembroke College while he read Scougal's treatise on the new birth.[43] A sixty-four-year-old convert, Will Miller, testified to the instantaneous nature of his conversion, reporting that he was "in the 53d year of [his] second birth which was July 13, 1704 about 5 or 6 at night" while reading evening devotions.[44]

Third, Whitefield assured his followers that they could know for certain if they had experienced the new birth. True conversion left clear marks "whereby [people] may easily judge whether [they] have received the Holy Ghost or not." Whitefield listed five indications of the new birth, including "a Spirit of Prayer and Supplication, . . . not committing Sin, . . . Conquest over the World . . . loving one another . . . [and] Loving our Enemies." Whitefield stated that one could have complete assurance of his or her salvation. He affirmed that "whosoever, upon an impartial Examination, can find the aforesaid Marks upon his Soul, may be as certain, as though an Angel was to tell him, that his Pardon is sealed in Heaven."[45] Whitefield taught that the individual, not the church, possessed means of confirming salvation.

Whitefield's conversion triggered a quarrel with the Anglican church that extended throughout his ministry. Once he understood salvation to be a spiritual new birth, Whitefield recognized how far the established church had departed from Reformation doctrine. The new convert denounced clergymen's "letter-learning" approach to Christianity, which, Whitefield charged, made human intellect the active agent in salvation. He deplored the various expressions of rationalism that had crept into the Christian church—Deism, Arminianism, Socianism, and Arianism.[46] Whitefield recognized the importance of reason in seeking religious truth, subscribing to the view that "reason seems to be the faculty given us by God to direct our enquiries in all things." But he

---

[42] Whitefield, *Sermons on Various Subjects*, 2:30.

[43] *Whitefield's Journals*, 47.

[44] Letter from Will Miller to George Whitefield, September 21, 1756, in Whitefield Manuscript Letters, Evangelical Library, London.

[45] Whitefield, *Sermons on Various Subjects*, 2:20–29.

[46] See Whitefield's letter to John Wesley attacking rationalist Christianity in *Whitefield's Journals*, 584–585.

held that the human mind was unreliable, insisting that it must be "the revelation of God which is to be our judge." Drawing upon a faculty psychology shared with the American revivalist and theologian Jonathan Edwards, Whitefield believed that only those "joined with God in spirit" could perceive nature clearly and enjoy its beauty because the "sensation of pleasure . . . is immediately owing to a principle of perception embedded in nature of which man is basically unconscious."[47] Whitefield warned his auditors that they should "try the suggestions or impressions that [they] may at any time feel, by the unerring rule of God's most holy word: and if they are not found to be agreeable to that, reject them as diabolical and delusive."[48]

Whitefield further charged the clergy with de-emphasizing conversion because they themselves had become immersed in the pleasures of the world. He claimed that rather than maintaining a healthy tension between "God and mammon," settled ministers had embraced earthly pleasures and could no longer be detached judges. The young evangelist deplored clerical attendance at "plays, balls, and assemblies" when those diversions detracted from their propagating the gospel. He believed God was ushering in a second Reformation, aimed not only at the heathen but at pastors who "preach [but] . . . do not experimentally know Christ."[49]

In constructing his view of the Anglican church and its clergy, Whitefield was more interested in promoting evangelicalism than in presenting a balanced evaluation of the state of the church. In fact, the Church of England was far more diverse than Whitefield depicted. Many, including Archbishop Thomas Secker, engaged in considerable self-criticism, leading to reforms aimed at ensuring a better-educated, more disciplined clergy.[50]

To Whitefield, Dissenters had also apostatized. Formalism and worldliness threatened to stifle experimental Christianity in evangeli-

---

[47] Norman Fiering, *Jonathan Edwards's Moral Thought and Its British Context* (Chapel Hill, 1981), 117.

[48] Gillies, *Works of Whitefield*, 5:30.

[49] Ibid., 1:113, 292; *Whitefield's Journals*, 482.

[50] The best primary evidence documenting official church concern for improving the clergy is located in the Society for the Propagation of the Gospel Papers at Lambeth Palace. Throughout correspondence between American missionaries and the archbishop and other church officials resounds the call for greater discipline among clergymen. Secondary sources also present a more balanced view of the Anglican church in the eighteenth century. Of particular applicability for this essay are those assessing the church's performance in America and concluding that the church was not in a state of decline. See Jon Butler, *Awash in a Sea of Faith: Christianizing the American People* (Cambridge, Mass., 1990); and Patricia Bonomi, *Under the Cope of Heaven: Religion, Society, and Politics in Colonial America* (New York, 1986).

cal churches, including those founded by fervent seventeenth-century emigrants to America. Whitefield's view of the new birth drew more upon that of the first New World Puritans than upon the prevailing New England perspective in 1740. For many of the Massachusetts immigrants in the early 1600s, conversion was an intensely personal matter between a man or woman and God. Perry Miller noted that an early Puritan "assumed that an individual encounters the crisis of conversion alone, in the closet or in the fields; after wrestling with the Lord he reports to the congregation, and out of his hard-won liberty swears to the church covenant." But on the eve of the Great Awakening the New England Way had been overturned. Declining church rolls had led to halfway membership in which "owning the covenant" substituted for a personal declaration of conversion. Gradually "the ritual confession became a community affair."[51] Whitefield redefined the new birth in terms of individual regeneration, thus restoring the interpretation favored by New England's first Puritan divines. After reading some printed sermons Whitefield had sent him, one leading Boston evangelical proclaimed that the itinerant preached "the doctrines of the martyrs and other reformers, which were the same our forefathers brought over hither."[52]

For Whitefield and the Puritans who inspired him, conversion was the first step in a lifelong evangelical mission. After undergoing the new birth, the convert experienced a divine calling to a vocation "followed by stages of continued growth in grace toward full union with [God]."[53] Influenced by other members of the Holy Club, Whitefield began to prepare to receive Holy Orders, the Anglican sacrament of ordaining men to the priesthood. After his ordination, John Wesley had accepted the challenge in 1735 of traveling to America and establishing a parish church in Savannah in the new colony of Georgia. Thomas Broughton had been appointed as chaplain to the Tower of London. Charles Kinchin had been elected dean of Corpus Christi College at Oxford. And James Hervey had begun to serve the cure of Dummer. Even prior to appearing before the bishop of Gloucester for ordination, Whitefield seemed destined to serve a parish in Oxford. Sir John Philips of Picton Castle, Pembrokeshire, a member of Parliament and "encourager of the Oxford Methodists," sent word to Whitefield that he would "allow [Whitefield] 30 pounds a year" if the young evangelical would continue as a minister in Oxford. After pronouncing himself satisfied with Whitefield's preparation for the priesthood,

[51] Miller, *Jonathan Edwards*, 134–135.
[52] Cited in *The Christian History, Containing Accounts of the Revival and Propagation of Religion in Great Britain and America . . . 1743 and 1744*, October 29, 1743.
[53] Hambrick-Stowe, *Practice of Piety*, 81ff.

Bishop Martin Benson of Gloucester blessed the young minister's decision to remain in Oxford. "I had myself," the bishop told Whitefield, "made provision for you of two little parishes; but since you choose to be at Oxford, I am well pleased."[54]

Having graduated from Pembroke College in 1736 and taken Holy Orders the same year, Whitefield with sober satisfaction reflected on the transformation he had undergone. He recorded in his diary, "These changes from a servitor to a Bachelor of Arts—from a common drawer to a clergyman—were no doubt temptations to think more highly of myself than I ought to think." After relating the account of his ordination in his autobiography, Whitefield added, "Thus did God, by a variety of unforeseen acts of providence and grace, train me up for, and at length introduce me into, the service of His Church." Four years later, however, Whitefield had left his Oxford parish and had established himself as the Church of England's most vocal critic. The evangelical had proclaimed himself a "presbyter at large" in a worldwide parish.[55] He had sparked an evangelical revival that extended throughout England to Scotland and even Ireland, and across the Atlantic to all thirteen American colonies. He was well known to men and women everywhere in the Atlantic world, for the name "Whitefield" was as well publicized in newspapers as the new consumer goods that merchants advertised to buyers from London to the American frontier. Indeed the commercial transformation of the mid-eighteenth century enabled Whitefield to redefine his own calling and give fuller expression to the Great Commission's dictate of spreading the gospel in "all the world."

[handwritten annotations: • Went about preaching about his new birth • Criticized those who were sinners + told them to become saved • Preached at full congregation @ Oxford.]

THE RISE OF A CONSUMER SOCIETY

Commerce flourished in the Atlantic world during the first half of the eighteenth century. Historians who focus on the so-called takeoff of the Industrial Revolution in the late 1700s tend to ignore the long period of steady growth in English agriculture and manufacturing earlier in the century. Yet not only did more people manufacture goods in farmhouses and workshops between 1700 and 1740; output per worker increased as well. Explanations for economic expansion have focused on supply, concentrating on the factors of production. According to the familiar argument, a larger population increased the labor force; even with no advances in productivity, this meant more aggregate out-

[54] *Whitefield's Journals*, 67, 69, 76–80.
[55] Ibid., 70; Gillies, *Works of Whitefield*, 1:262.

put. Through reclamation of swamps and clearing of forests, more land underwent cultivation, further adding to the potential for higher yields. And although there was no massive rise in the rate of capital investment, technically "simple" innovations in agriculture enabled farmers to produce at a faster pace than that of population growth. While accounting for greater aggregates of input, this interpretation fails to explain why men and women would work harder and why they would seek innovations to increase output. According to one view, the economic culture of early America valued the competency "to procure enough land and productive equipment" to guarantee long-term independence for one's family. But men and women also sought more immediate pleasures that could be satisfied by consumption of manufactured goods.[56]

Fueled by rising population, falling agricultural prices, and changing fashions, consumer demand was the engine that drove expansion in England's domestic and overseas trade. More people meant not only a larger work force but also more customers for the goods pouring out of manufacturers' workshops and merchants' warehouses. As greater productivity on farms led to lower prices by midcentury, families spent less on food, with more money available for manufactured and imported merchandise. Tastes changed as well, as imports of such desirable foodstuffs as tea, chocolate, and coffee found ready buyers first among the wealthy and then, through imitation, those of lesser means. As merchants scrambled to satisfy this growing demand, they drove down their own prices, stimulating demand even further. People wanted things, whether a few pins made in Gloucester or a bottle of Madeira imported from the Wine Islands, and they were willing to work harder to earn the means to participate in the consumer revolution taking place in the mid-eighteenth-century Atlantic world. The effect of such purchases was supplemented by the English government, which primed the economic pump with its extraordinary expenditures during the imperial wars it waged for much of the century. Private and public demand combined to serve as midwives to the birth of a consumer society.[57]

The consumer revolution increased the prospects of more goods and greater profits, motivations that spurred the industry of workers and manufacturers. Visiting Birmingham in 1740, Rev. Samuel Say sent his daughter an eyewitness account of the frenetic activity in that

[56] Roderick Floud and Donald McCloskey, *The Economic History of Britain since 1700*, 2 vols. (London, 1980), 1:1–16. See Daniel Vickers, "Competency and Competition: Economic Culture in Early America," *William and Mary Quarterly* 37 (January 1990): 3–29.

[57] L. A. Clarkson, *The Pre-Industrial Economy in England, 1500–1750* (London, 1971), 127; Floud and McCloskey, *Economic History of Britain*, 13.

growing industrial center. He noted that the people were "all imploy'd and busy in some manufacturing or other almost from infancy." He was impressed by the pace, observing that "when you go into the house of a manufacturer you see swarms of people crowding every room and glass or metal running from hand to hand and formed into buttons and buckles in such an instant of time that it looks like the power of creation." He described the production of nails from the arrival of bars of cold iron at the shop to their extrusion under "prodigious heat" to their being cut into a "great number of small sticks of iron." He was particularly fascinated with a process that took blanks of plain metal out of a fire and shaped them into "all their beautiful forms by one blow of an engine that descended with the weight of more than a 100 pounds." Say concluded his almost breathless account by informing his daughter that he was bringing home samples of buttons and buckles representative of the huge quantity and variety of manufactured goods being produced in the Midlands.[58]

As goods poured from English workshops, manufacturers faced the challenge of improving the transportation system to facilitate distribution of wares throughout the country and to the ports for overseas shipment. Daniel Defoe testified to both the deplorable state of roads in the 1720s and the enormous volume of traffic they carried. Citing the "deep clays" that were "so surprisingly soft" as the major problem with roadbeds in the Midlands, he observed that, nevertheless, those ways had been made "practicable" because they represented the region's economic lifeline, connecting its products with the great London market.[59] Primarily through private as opposed to governmental initiative, a network of turnpikes and canals did emerge to speed the flow of goods at lower costs. Parliament passed acts establishing turnpike companies and giving them power to "levy tolls and borrow capital for road improvements." By 1724, new turnpikes appeared at a rate of eight a year. A burst of activity in river improvements occurred from 1719 to 1721, probably because of the "cheapness of interest rates in those years." Again, the impetus came from individuals, local entrepreneurs interested in both direct returns on their capital and the external economies of cheap transport. They succeeded in lowering shipping costs as, for example, "a horse pulling a barge could move perhaps twelve times as much freight as a packhorse at less than half the cost of land carriage."[60] Hence, manufacturers improved the links by which they conveyed their merchandise to their unseen customers.

[58] Letter from Samuel Say to his daughter, July 21, 1740, Say Manuscript Collection, Dr. Williams's Library, London.
[59] Cited in Clarkson, *Pre-Industrial Economy*, 152.
[60] Ibid., 152–154.

Road improvements translated into reduced traveling times by the mid-1700s, which encouraged more traffic. From 1700 to 1750, travel times fell by 20 percent between Norwich and London and by over 40 percent from Edinburgh to the metropolis. Public passenger service made the trips more reliable. By 1759 a thrice-weekly coach transported travelers between Leicester and London, expanding a decade later into a daily service. Transportation improvements "sped turnover and the pace of life and sucked more remote areas into the hectic economy of consumption and emulation." Reactions to the spread of London goods and ideas to the provinces were mixed. The agriculturist and writer Arthur Young applauded the increased "circulation [of] new people—new ideas—new exertions—fresh activity to every branch of industry . . . which flow with full tide . . . between the capital and the provinces." The country gentleman John Byng lamented the change, wishing that "half the turnpike roads of the kingdom were ploughed up which have imported London manners and depopulated the country."[61] However viewed, better transportation helped create a national market for the new consumer goods streaming from thousands of small shops.

Improvements in transportation and communication extended to overseas trade, encouraging English merchants to hawk their wares in a transatlantic market. Efficiencies, not innovations, account for the changes. Advances in ship design were "minimal between 1675 and 1740 and had little effect on the speed, frequency, or safety of Atlantic crossings." Rather, trade benefited from alterations in the "pace, pattern, and change in the spread of news . . . [made] possible because of more efficient shipping, more numerous newspapers, and more efficient, extensive postal service." By midcentury, more than twice as many ships cleared colonial ports as in 1700, and they sailed on more regular schedules. Increased shipping sped the news of London's latest fashions as more sailors, travelers, and migrants carried information orally and as letters and newspapers reached the colonies more frequently. As a result the "English Atlantic was being shrunk." London-datelined news in colonial newspapers fell in average age from 162 days in the first decade of the eighteenth century to 83 by 1739. For English merchants and their American customers, a shrinking Atlantic undermined local biases and favored "perspectives and preoccupations that connected the broader English Atlantic community."[62]

Manufacturers sold their wares, both domestic and imported goods, through a thickening network of merchants that sped products not

[61] Roy Porter, *English Society*, 207–208.
[62] Steele, *The English Atlantic*, 113, 158–159, 213.

only to London and the provinces but throughout the Atlantic world. Scottish merchants, for example, extended retailing to the sparsely populated Virginia backcountry. In 1743, Francis Jerdone, a merchant in Hanover County, observed, "There are 25 stores within 18 miles round me . . . and 4 or 5 more expected next year from some of the [British] outports." Middlemen became more important links in the lengthening distribution chain, as their warehouses and credit smoothed the flow of goods from workshops to final consumers. A new breed of wholesalers, traveling merchants, carried with them goods worth upwards of a thousand pounds sterling, supplying country shops with "whole pieces" and giving "large credit" to shopkeepers.[63]

What impressed most visitors to England was the number and variety of manufactured goods available for purchase. One midcentury observer described his impressions upon first encountering London's shopping districts. The newcomer was "generally first struck by the multiplicity of cries . . . in the streets, and the variety of merchandise and manufactures which the shopkeepers expose on every hand." He beheld "a thousand shops crowded with goods"; of some the commentator could "scarcely tell the use." Yet he concluded that "the endless variety of tastes and circumstances that diversify mankind" meant that "nothing [was] so superfluous but that some one desire[d] it."[64] As English entrepreneurs sought to satisfy this diverse demand, the composition of Britain's imports changed during the first half of the century. While manufactures constituted about a third of imported goods in 1700, by 1750 they amounted to approximately one-fifth. About 80 percent of the commodities shipped to England at midcentury was either food, drink, and tobacco, or raw materials for manufacturing. English manufacturers turned those commodities into a variety of goods such as "metalwares, clothing, leather and textiles."[65]

As the number and variety of goods expanded, shops and shopping played a larger role in the exchange between buyers and sellers. People continued to purchase items at fairs and markets or from itinerant peddlers, but stores were more numerous and important in the retail chain connecting manufacturers and consumers. For instance, in the northern market town of Kendal, about ten miles from Westmoreland County's only port, twenty-nine shops served its more than six thousand residents by 1784. While most shopkeepers called themselves simply "grocers or mercers or ironmongers or linen drapers," they sold a wider range of goods than those descriptions imply. A second-

---

[63] Porter, *English Society*, 206; Breen, "An Empire of Goods," 492; Ernest Rhys, ed., *A Tour through England and Wales* by Daniel Defoe (London, 1927), 207–208.

[64] *Adventurer* (London), June 26, 1753.

[65] Clarkson, *Pre-Industrial Economy*, 127–128.

generation shopkeeper, Abraham Dent, was usually described as a mercer, but in addition to selling silks and other costly fabrics, cloaks, caps, gloves, garters, and handkerchiefs, he also stocked such grocer's staples as sugar, tea, flour, tobacco, peas, lemons, and dried fruit, and stationer's wares including paper, quills, ink, slates, playing cards, almanacs, magazines, and books.[66] Stationary, well-stocked shops offered consumers daily selections from wide assortments as opposed to weekly, monthly, or quarterly opportunities afforded by fairs, markets, and itinerants.

Shopkeepers in the first third of the eighteenth century began paying as much attention to the display of merchandise as they did to the assortments they sold. In 1726, Daniel Defoe noted that "it is a modern custom, and wholly unknown to our ancestors . . . to have tradesmen lay out two thirds of their fortune in fitting up their shops." By "fitting up" Defoe meant "painting and gilding, [and investing] in fine shelves, shutters, boxes, glass-doors, sashes and the like." Reluctant to accept the innovations in merchandising, Defoe contended that "well-fill'd . . . shelves and the great choice of rich and fashionable goods" attracted and retained customers, arguing that "fools only are most taken with shews and outsides." The latter reference no doubt included the bow windows that began to adorn London shops, protruding onto the sidewalks and forcing passersby to gaze in upon the merchant's wares. Overcoming his initial skepticism, Defoe reluctantly acknowledged that "it is true that a fine shew of goods will bring in customers."[67]

Architecture of retail shops reflected the eighteenth-century commercial transformation. London shops in the mid-1600s amounted to "no more than a front room with an enlarged window opening." By the early 1700s, the new "aggressive attitude toward business" produced a distinctive architectural form. At midcentury, many shops featured two projecting bow windows on either side of an entrance flanked by "richer external details, such as pilasters on either side . . . and a garland frieze above . . . designed to attract customers." Retailers experimented with exteriors throughout the century in their competition for the business of shoppers. By the 1770s, storefronts became less ornamental, giving way to what one scholar has labeled "narrative architecture, which was expected to tell both the purpose and the character of the building." In an emerging consumer society, retailers employed architecture along with advertising and store layout to compete for what a growing number of merchants considered to be an elastic de-

---

[66] T. S. Willan, *An Eighteenth-Century Shopkeeper: Abraham Dent of Kirkby Stephen* (New York, 1970), 8–27.

[67] Daniel Defoe, *The Complete English Tradesman in Familiar Letters Directing him in all the several Parts and Progressions of Trade*, 2 vols. (London, 1726), 1:257–258, 261.

mand, expanded by their making goods available to people of all classes and circumstances.[68]

Like the British, Americans purchased English manufactures in great quantities, making the colonies one of Britain's best markets by the mid-eighteenth century. One observer, critical of the colonists' appetite for consumption, minutely described imports into South Carolina. He noted that "in general, the quantity seems to be too great, and the quality of [manufactured items] too fine, and ill calculated for the circumstances of an infant colony." Listing the goods registered at Charleston's docks, the author recorded them by category. Metallic manufactures included "iron, cast and wrought into all sorts of household utensils and cutlery-wares, guns, pistols, swords, nails of all sorts, lead in sheets, bullets, and shot, tin-wares, pewter in household utensils, brass wrought of all sorts, . . . watches, gold and silver." British woolens included "druggets and drabs, duffils and duroys, serges and shalloons, cloths of all sorts from the finest broad cloth down to Negroe cloth, cloaths—ready made, blankets, hats, stockings, shrouds, and carpets." Under his "Miscellaneous Manufactures" heading, he listed "books, cables and cordage, china and other earthen-wares, chairs and beds, glass-wares—looking-glasses, drinking glasses, and bottles, leather-shoes, boots, saddles, bridles, gloves of all sorts, paper of all sorts, pictures and prints, stationery-wares, and tiles."[69] The writer's lengthy catalog continues for several pages, providing a window into the prodigious quantity and variety of goods arriving at colonial ports, expanding shoppers' choices for shaping their material and cultural existence.

The latest English goods rapidly found their way onto the shelves of American shops. One visitor to Maryland observed that "the quick importation of fashions from the mother country is really astonishing. I am almost inclined to believe that a new fashion is adopted earlier by the polished and affluent American than by many opulent persons in the great metropolis." Rev. Alexander Hewat, just arrived in South Carolina from Scotland in the early 1750s, disapproved of consumption in British America. He commented that Americans' "intercourse and communication with Britain being easy and frequent, all novelties in fashion, dress and ornament are quickly introduced; and even the spirit of luxury and extravagance, too common in England, is beginning to creep into Carolina." By the 1730s, "middling families got into

---

[68] H. Kalman, "The Architecture of Mercantilism: Commercial Buildings by George Dance the Younger," in *The Triumph of Culture: Eighteenth-Century Perspectives*, ed. Paul Fritz and David Williams (Toronto, 1972), 71–85.

[69] *A Description of South Carolina; containing many curious and interesting particulars relating to the civil, natural and commercial history of that colony* (London, 1751), 1–15.

the act [of consuming] and by the 1750s, even the poorer sorts were finding a wide variety of non-essentials increasingly desirable." According to one estimate, by 1774, "the average American spent over one quarter of his or her budget on imports from outside his or her colony of residence."[70]

Colonial expenditures for English imports began a sharp rise in 1740 and continued until the recession following the end of the Seven Years War in the 1760s. In 1720, per capita consumption of British manufactures stood at sixteen shillings, an amount sufficient to purchase fewer than three bottles of choice port wine sold by Whitefield's brother James, or to acquire ten of George's sermons. By 1740, average consumption had increased to slightly more than 1 pound per person. During the decade ending in 1750, consumption grew by almost 35 percent to 1.40 pounds per white man, woman, and child. Then, in the period 1751–1760, per capita expenditures climbed by another 40 percent, rising above 2 pounds per person.[71]

Traveling in the American colonies during 1759 and 1760, Andrew Burnaby, the vicar of Greenwich, noted the widespread trade in "English manufactures," remarking in particular on the "superfluities and luxuries of life." He claimed that "not less than 9,000 waggons" were employed in Pennsylvania's trade. Neighboring New Yorkers also engaged in a vigorous commercial economy, relying on a "circular commerce [to] subsist and grow rich." Burnaby described the process: "With money from Holland [New Yorkers] pay merchants in London; sugars from West Indies [they] carry to Holland; slaves from Africa [they] send to West Indies together with lumber and provisions from neighboring colonies; the rum they distill they export to Africa; and with the dry goods they purchase in London, they traffick in neighboring colonies."[72] In other words, colonists were immersed in a vigorous Atlantic market.

On both sides of the Atlantic, merchants enticed consumers to purchase their goods by persuasive advertising through the expanding

[70] William Eddis, *Letters from America*, ed. Aubrey C. Land (Cambridge, Mass., 1969), 57–58; Lorena Walsh, "Urban Amenities and Rural Sufficiency: Living Standards and Consumer Behavior in the Colonial Chesapeake, 1643–1777," *Journal of Economic History* 43 (March 1983): 111; Carole Shammas, "How Self-Sufficient Was Early America?" *Journal of Interdisciplinary History* 13 (Autumn 1982): 266; Hewat cited in Elmer D. Johnson and Kathleen L. Sloan, eds., *A Documentary Profile of the Palmetto State* (Charleston, 1971), 150.

[71] Per capita expenditures calculated from data in United States Bureau of the Census, *Historical Statistics of the United States, Colonial Times to 1970*, 2 vols. (Washington, D.C., 1975), 2:1168, 1176–1177.

[72] Andrew Burnaby, *Travels Through the Middle Settlements in North America in the Years 1759 and 1760, With Observations upon the State of the Colonies* (London, 1775), 46–50, 70–71.

network of newspapers in the mid-1700s. The communication revolution that both promoted and resulted from the new commercialism is revealed through comparison between the London of Samuel Pepys in the mid-1600s and that of Samuel Johnson in the mid-1700s. Pepys had access to only one daily newspaper, the *London Gazette*, which contained "official matters relating to the Court—proclamations, decrees, promotions and the like, and a little very stale news." For information regarding developments in Europe, Pepys visited the Royal Exchange to converse with foreign merchants. Excursions to Westminster Hall supplemented his knowledge about what was going on at Court or in Parliament. Pepys would then compose a manuscript newsletter for dissemination among a few rich subscribers. The acquisition of books as well as news was confined largely to the wealthy. Printed primarily in large folios or quartos, "books were expensive and so bought mainly by lawyers, clergymen, gentry or prosperous merchants." Only during times of social upheaval did cheaper printed materials of an ephemeral nature—handbills and pamphlets—reach anything "approaching a large audience in London." Distribution of reading material remained backward in the mid-seventeenth century. There were no circulating libraries, book clubs, or magazines. Few specialized publishers provided books for targeted audiences such as children. In summary, "the bulk of publishing . . . was still theological or classical and was still enshrined in massive and expensive" editions.[73]

By the 1750s the nature and distribution of printed materials had totally changed, with a greater choice of publications reaching a wider audience. Spurred by increased freedom of the press made possible by the expiration of the Licensing Act in 1695, newspapers proliferated. London's first two nonofficial newspapers—the *Post Boy* and the *Post Man*—provided readers with a choice. By 1740, London boasted of "three dailies, five weeklies, seven thrice a week, and three thrice a week halfpenny posts, or fifty-three issues of various papers per week."[74] And the number of provincial and colonial newspapers mushroomed as well. In 1700 there were no papers coming off American presses; eleven were available to Whitefield when he arrived in Philadelphia in 1739 to begin the revivals that would become known as the Great Awakening.[75] As the number of papers in London and the provinces expanded rapidly, a distribution network knit the country into one

---

[73] Plumb, *Commercialisation of Leisure*, 5–8.

[74] Louis Moffitt, *England on the Eve of the Industrial Revolution: A Study of Economic and Social Conditions from 1740 to 1760 with Special Reference to Lancashire* (1925; reprint, London, 1963), 246–247.

[75] For growth in number of colonial newspapers, see Isaiah Thomas, *The History of Printing in America, with a Biography of Printers and an Account of Newspapers*, 2 vols. (Albany, N.Y., 1874), vol. 1.

communications system. Coffeehouses and public houses made newspapers available to their patrons, including those from the lower and middling ranks of society. Improved postal service ensured ready access to newspapers in every corner of England. Moreover, a number of magazines emerged aimed at "the new and growing middle-class audience." Joseph Addison and Richard Steele in the *Spectator* produced a daily magazine that opened the world of fashion and the great to all who could read. Just as merchants publicized textiles and other wares as "the latest" or "most fashionable," magazine editors sold their periodicals on the basis of current ideas and fresh thought.[76]

The nature as well as the scope of advertising changed. While generic descriptions such as cloth, paper, and ceramics characterized advertisements in the 1720s, by the 1750s greater specificity reflected merchants' desires to exploit broader markets. For example, a New York advertiser heralded a new shipment of gloves by boasting of "purple gloves, rough gloves, chamois gloves, buff gloves, Maid's Black Silk gloves, Maid's Lamb Gloves," and even "Men's Dog Skin Gloves."[77]

Writing in the mid-eighteenth century, Samuel Johnson traced the development of advertisement, which had "grown up by slow degrees to its present state." The proliferation of newspapers offered merchants greater opportunity to publicize their wares but also demanded more imagination in capturing the attention of those perusing newspapers. The "best puffs" were those advertisements which gained attention "by magnificence of promises and by eloquence sometimes sublime and sometimes pathetic." Johnson noted that "promise, large promise [was] the soul of an advertisement." To illustrate, he cited one draper's claims for duvets. "There are now to be sold," the advertisement read, "for ready money only, some duvets for bed coverings, of down, beyond comparison, superior to what is called otter-down, and indeed such, that its many excellences cannot be here set forth." The merchant, however, could not resist acquainting his readers with just one excellence—"it is warmer than four or five blankets, and lighter than one." Johnson observed that "the trade of advertising is now so near to perfection, that it is not easy to propose any improvement." He added that "every man now knows a ready method of informing the public of all that he desires to buy or sell, whether his wares be material or intellectual."[78] Whitefield would distinguish himself as an advertiser of divinity.

A transformation in print altered the pattern of reading in the

---

[76] Plumb, *Commercialisation of Leisure*, 6.
[77] Cited in Breen, " 'Baubles of Britain,' " 80.
[78] *Idler*, January 20, 1759.

American colonies between the mid-1600s and mid-1700s. In early New England, didactic works predominated. According to one survey, "school books like the primer were among the most widely owned and distributed kinds of books, rivaled only by catechisms, psalmbooks, and the Bible." A religion of the book, Puritanism promoted daily study of Scripture and devotional works. During the 1660s and 1670s, steady sellers included "*Old Mr. Dod's Sayings*; William Dyer's *Christ's Famous Titles*; Thomas Vincent's *God's Terrible Voice*; and Thomas Wilcox's *A Choice Drop of Honey*." Although most books were imported from England, New Englanders established their own presses as early as 1638. However, "press runs were small, prices high, and distribution a matter of catch-as-catch-can."[79] One historian's survey of seventeenth-century Virginia culture indicates that books were important symbols of the emerging elite planter society of the late 1600s. Literacy as well as economics restricted book ownership in the Chesapeake, as less than half of white adult males could read in the 1640s.[80]

By the time Whitefield arrived in America in 1739 to begin his first preaching tour, the scope and nature of the colonial print trade had undergone a remarkable change. Although colonists continued to import the latest titles from London, local presses produced more works by native authors and of local interest. While no reliable statistics are available regarding book ownership, local presses made printed material less expensive and thus within the reach of more people. Colonial printers did not have to recover the shipping and insurance costs embedded in the prices of imported volumes. Printing flourished in the seaports of Boston, New York, Philadelphia, and Charleston. In Boston, the number of printers doubled from ten to twenty between 1700 and 1740. The biggest change was the widespread appearance of colonial newspapers in the eighteenth century. Inexpensive and available to a wide audience including patrons of coffeehouses and taverns, eleven newspapers throughout the colonies not only informed readers of local and overseas affairs but contributed to an intercolonial reading community by making remote colonists known to each other.[81] Increasing literacy also contributed to the growth in demand for inexpensive printed materials. Between the end of the 1600s and 1740, literacy among white adult male Virginians had grown by 35 percent. And the social patterns of reading also changed. According to one study, af-

[79] William Joyce et al., eds., *Printing and Society in Early America* (Worcester, Mass., 1983), 31.

[80] Ibid., 230–231.

[81] Growth in colonial printing determined from Charles Evans, ed., *American Bibliography: A Chronological Dictionary of All Books, Pamphlets and Periodicals Printed in the United States of America from the Genesis in 1639 down to and including the Year 1820* (Chicago, 1904).

fordable newspapers and pamphlets more and more frequently involved "the vulgar in affairs formerly the preserve of the learned."[82]

[handwritten: Boom of transportation, machinery, making items, etc. England experienced time of mass hushing. You could find anything there.]

CHILDHOOD IN GLOUCESTER'S CONSUMER SOCIETY

Had Thomas Whitefield followed his ancestors' vocational calling, the commercial transformation might not have been the shaping influence it was for George. By pursuing trade instead of theology, however, George's father had departed from his family's tradition of ecclesiastical callings. Thomas's great-grandfather, William, had been the vicar of Mayfield, Sussex, in the late sixteenth and early seventeenth centuries. His grandfather, Thomas, like William educated at Magdalen College, Oxford, became rector of Halstead, Kent, in 1639. And his father, Samuel, a graduate of Hart College, Oxford, was the curate at Rockhampton in the final quarter of the 1600s. Why Thomas did not follow his forefathers into the ministry is unclear. Perhaps the family's fortune had declined, and Samuel did not have the means to send Thomas to Oxford. Or Thomas could have been influenced by his wife's father. After marrying Elizabeth Edwards, the daughter of a cutlery manufacturer, Thomas became first a wine merchant in Bristol and then proprietor of the Bell Inn in Gloucester.[83]

Whitefield's brothers and sister all followed their father into the world of commerce, most attempting to establish businesses of their own. The eldest, Andrew, was apprenticed to a Bristol upholsterer but died before entering the trade. Thomas was a merchant, but he failed, declaring bankruptcy to protect himself against creditors. Richard succeeded his father as the proprietor of the Bell and became the highest-rated taxpayer in St. Mary de Crypt parish until his death in the 1760s. James entered the transatlantic trade first as a sea captain and then as a merchant trading in his own name. He developed a flourishing business exporting wines from the Madeiras to the West Indies and southern British American colonies, importing sugar and rice in return. Elizabeth married a Bristol grocer, James Grevile, and ran the business herself after her husband's death. Until his decision to enter the ministry, George, the youngest child, set his eyes on a career in trade.[84] Although diverted from his original plan, he retained his mercantile perspective, applying commercial vocabulary and techniques to his transatlantic revivals.

[82] Joyce et al., *Printing and Society in Early America*, 249.
[83] See C. Roy Huddleston, "George Whitefield's Ancestry," *Transactions of the Bristol and Gloucestershire Archaeological Society for 1937* 59 (1938): 221–242.
[84] Ibid.; *Whitefield's Journals*, 40.

Whitefield participated in the commercial transformation as an employee at the Bell. When Thomas Whitefield died in 1716, his widow Elizabeth struggled to operate the inn while raising a family of six sons and a daughter. After marrying Capel Longden, a Gloucester ironmonger, in 1722, Elizabeth continued to manage the inn. "I from time to time began to assist her occasionally in the public-house," Whitefield recalled in his autobiography, "till at length I put on my blue apron and my [candle] snuffers, washed mops, cleaned rooms, and, in one word, became a professed and common drawer for a year and a half." Upon occasion George had "the care of the whole house upon [his] hands," invaluable experience for an aspiring tradesman. His responsibilities increased when his mother relinquished managerial control to George's brother Richard, "who had been bred up for the business." Because of George's experience, "it was agreed that [he] should continue there as an assistant."[85]

Employment at the Bell exposed George to a wide range of retail activities. In addition to "the main inn, outhouses, [and] stables," the Bell consisted of "several shops." In one of these, George and Richard sold wine, continuing the trade established by their father. Traveling merchants displayed their inventories in the other shops. Having given public notice of their arrival with a new assortment of merchandise, peddlers hawked their goods at the tavern.[86] In July 1736, for instance, one Dr. Taylor advertised himself in the *Gloucester Journal* as "oculist to his Majesty" and announced that he would fit and sell eyeglasses at the Bell.[87]

Whitefield also experienced the commercial transformation as a consumer. He observed the relocation of retail trade from open-air markets to "a good selection of specialist retail shops on the London model, the most fashionable [situated] nearby in Westgate and upper Northgate streets."[88] In his autobiography Whitefield related how he had had "no scruple of taking money out of [his mother's] pocket before she was up . . . and [had] more than once spent money [he] took in the house in buying fruits, tarts, etc., to satisfy [his] sensual appetite." Besides sweetmeats, books and periodicals were Whitefield's passion. In particular he enjoyed romances, "plays, *Spectators*, Pope's *Homer*, and such-like trifling books."[89] And Whitefield learned about the wider Atlantic world by reading the *Gloucester Journal*, the town's newspaper

[85] *Whitefield's Journals*, 40.

[86] N. M. Herbert, ed., *The City of Gloucester*, vol. 4 of *The Victorian History of the Counties of England*, ed. C. R. Elrington (London, 1988), 102–106.

[87] *Gloucester Journal*, July 20, 1736.

[88] Herbert, *City of Gloucester*, 104.

[89] *Whitefield's Journals*, 37–38, 60.

begun by Robert Raikes in 1722 in a shop located across the street from the Bell.

In addition to viewing newspapers as a consumer item offering diversion, Whitefield at an early age learned about their advertising potential. Richard sought to attract customers to the inn by staging a variety of entertainment. Indeed Richard's advertisements in the *Gloucester Journal* represent a catalog of worldly pursuits against which George later preached. During Gloucester's horse-racing season each August, Richard announced as part of the festivities that "there will be Balls and Assemblies every night at Mr. Whitefield's Great-Room at the Bell." Another advertisement trumpeted: "At the Bell Great Room, a Concert of Vocal and Instrumental Musick, plus several of Mr. Handel's concertoes will be performed on the harpsichord. After the concert, there will be a Ball for the ladies." Publicizing a less polite form of entertainment, the newspaper referred to a "great Cock-Match" to be fought at the Bell Inn.[90] When George returned to Gloucester in 1739 to preach, he turned newspaper advertising to his own ends. On April 24, the *Gloucester Journal* reported the Bell's latest attraction, noting that the young evangelist had preached to "some thousands in a Field belonging to the Bell Inn."[91]

In addition to his direct experience in running the affairs of a local business, Whitefield learned about overseas trade from his brother James. He spent several months in Bristol with James, who was building a flourishing trade in the American and West Indies markets. Direct evidence points to James's financial support of the young minister, but his more important contribution may have been the fund of knowledge he imparted regarding the world of commerce, especially the needs and opportunities in America. As a merchant exploiting colonial demand for British merchandise, James was the first Whitefield who made himself known to colonists.[92]

The February 2, 1739, issue of the *South Carolina Gazette* informed its readers that one James Whitefield had opened a store at the head of Mr. Burford's Wharf in Charleston. The Bristol merchant advertised his goods: "a choice parcel of bottled Port wine at 4 pounds per dozen, Beer and Cyder, by the quantity, at 50 shillings. Also Barbados Rum, Muscovado sugar and sundry sorts of dry goods at reasonable rates, for ready money only."[93] Subsequent advertisements over the next twenty-five years indicated that James maintained a steady trade between England, the Wine Islands, the West Indies, and the British-American

---

[90] *Gloucester Journal*, August 31, 1742, May 10, 1743, and July 3, 1744.
[91] Ibid., April 24, 1739.
[92] See, for example, *South Carolina Gazette*, February 15, 1739.
[93] Ibid., February 2, 1739.

mainland colonies. By 1764, his son had assumed management of the retail business and relocated in Savannah, Georgia, advertising in the *Georgia Gazette* "sundry sorts of European and East-Indian articles . . . assortment of jewelry . . . [and] rich gold and silver laces."[94]

One of George Whitefield's first advertisements in a colonial newspaper points to James's influence on his brother's transatlantic mission. Shortly after arriving in Philadelphia on October 30, 1739, George— by then a much-publicized evangelist—placed an advertisement in the *Pennsylvania Gazette* paralleling James's notices in South Carolina. He informed Philadelphia readers that he was conducting an auction to sell a shipload of manufactured goods he had brought with him from England. Any profits from the sale would go toward building an orphan house in Georgia. Whitefield listed the goods, which a merchant— perhaps his brother James—had assured him were in great demand by the colonists. The items included "Brass Candlesticks, Snuffers and snuff-Dishes, four, six, eight, ten and twenty-penny Nails, Pidgeon, Duck and Goose Shot, bar Lead, Pistol Powder, . . . English Cordage, Ratling, Worming, Marline and Spun-yarn Ruggs and Blankets, Duffils strip'd . . . Scotch Cloth, cotton Romalls, Seirsuckers, white Dimities, Carradaries, Cherconees, long Romalls, colour'd Ginghams, . . . broad Cloth, Shalloons, long Ells, Buttons, Buckrams, and sewing-Silk."[95] In addition to illustrating a direct tie between transatlantic commerce and the evangelical revivals, the sale was a success. Whitefield reported that the proceeds more than covered the transportation costs of moving his orphanage staff from England to Georgia.

The influence of George and James Whitefield in their respective transatlantic undertakings was reciprocal. George's growing fame and connections in British North America opened new opportunities for James. The shift from Charleston to Savannah suggests that James's son may have moved to Georgia, where George had excellent political and commercial ties. He also benefited from connections with the evangelist's orphan house superintendent, James Habersham, who had become one of the province's wealthiest and most influential citizens, presiding over the provincial council in the 1760s. Through Habersham's contacts, young James Whitefield flourished in the coastal and West Indian routes that had enriched Habersham. With his growing prosperity, James maintained a home in Savannah and acquired at least five hundred acres, adjacent to George's orphan house lands, located "about twelve miles west from town."[96] Thus the paths of

[94] *Georgia Gazette*, January 5, 1764.
[95] *Pennsylvania Gazette*, November 8, 1739.
[96] *Georgia Gazette*, January 5, 1764.

2. Philadelphia, ca. 1754, a thriving British Atlantic port. Courtesy of the Library Company of Philadelphia.

the two brothers intertwined as they plied the trade of their goods and ideas in an Atlantic market bursting with new possibilities.

Beyond his family's enterprises, the town of Gloucester afforded Whitefield a firsthand view of the consumer revolution. Exploiting the rich iron deposits in the nearby Forest of Dean, enterprising merchants transformed Gloucester into a "city of smiths." By 1735, pin making was the city's "chief manufacture," followed by the production of such related products as nails and wire. The industry continued to prosper throughout the 1700s. By century's end, after the introduction of steam-driven machines, Gloucester boasted "nine [pin] factories, employing at least 1,500 persons, and supplying a large market in Spain and America." This meant that about one in every four persons worked in the industry.[97]

Some of Whitefield's childhood friends were instrumental in introducing him to the world of print, especially bookselling and newspaper publishing. Gabriel Harris, whose father owned Gloucester's most prominent bookstore, remained a faithful supporter throughout Whitefield's ministry. As a boy, Whitefield spent considerable time in the Harris home, gaining the approbation of the elder Harris, who provided both books and money toward George's studies at Pembroke College. Then, he helped promote the young minister by sending one of Whitefield's early sermon manuscripts to an older clergyman, who not only liked the discourse but paid Whitefield a guinea for the document—a sum sufficient to cover almost two weeks of the student's expenses. When Whitefield published his first sermons in 1737, his bookselling friends, "Mssrs. Harris, Sen. & Jun.," promoted the works to their Gloucester customers.[98]

Whitefield also captured the fancy of Robert Raikes, the founder of the *Gloucester Journal*. To potential advertisers, Raikes boasted of the newspaper's circulation, claiming that it "extended the farthest of any Country News-Paper in England, by Special Messenger." As Whitefield began his public ministry, the young evangelist and the publisher discovered a mutuality of interests. After attending Whitefield's first sermon, Raikes provided favorable publicity for the evangelist in his hometown. In one early account of Whitefield's preaching, Raikes referred to the itinerant as one "who is much followed and whose preaching is so deservedly approved of." At Whitefield's urging, Raikes published in six successive issues during 1737 extracts from William Law's treatises on practical piety. Whitefield noted that "God was pleased to give [the reprints] His Blessing."[99] But Whitefield was not awed by the

---

[97] Herbert, *City of Gloucester*, 102–104.

[98] See for example, *Gloucester Journal*, August 9, 1737.

[99] Ibid., March 29, 1737. *Whitefield's Journals*, 63.

favorable publicity. The commercialization of his ministry was an extension of a familiar landscape, cultivated in a town where he had spent his youth among family and friends pursuing expanded markets with the new means at hand.

[handwritten annotation: • Helped his mom run family inn • Used Ga. newspaper to publicize his ministry.]

THE LANGUAGE OF GOODS

The expanding consumer market produced a lexicon of goods that Whitefield employed to condemn overconsumption and its attendant worldliness. In particular, he denounced sins of self-fashioning promoted by the growing array of choices in consumer goods—sins such as selfishness, pride, envy, and vanity. Consumer goods served as props for presenting self to others—markers of social identification. The landed elite on both sides of the Atlantic underscored their place at the top of society with their suits and gowns, fancy china, and fine furniture. They also attended plays, concerts, and balls, which became showcases for self-presentation. For the poor, emulation had spawned envy, discontent, insolence, and insubordination.[100] By the mid-1700s, it also produced an appetite for participating in the spreading market.

Authors such as Henry Fielding, Tobias Smollett, and Daniel Defoe criticized the effects of mass consumption on social relations, fearing such evils as lower productivity and political leveling. Defoe admonished young tradesmen to be wary of the "general inclination among all sorts of people to an expensive way of living." Defoe warned that costly housekeeping, dressing, and equipages represented "a slow fever [eating] into the two most essential branches of . . . trade, namely, . . . credit and cash."[101] In 1751, Fielding lamented that the "introduction of trade . . . hath indeed given a new Face to the whole Nation, hath in great measure subverted the former State of Affairs, and hath almost totally changed the Manners, Customs, and Habits of the People, more especially the lower sort."[102]

More than any other consumer good, clothes enabled men and women of the mid-1700s to make social statements. Merchants supplied the finest silks and linens in a wide assortment of colors. Tailors created dresses and suits by which their wearers could attract attention at the numerous assemblies—gatherings whose purpose appeared to be primarily for those attending to engage in self-fashioning. Samuel Johnson claimed that "all assemblies of gayety [were] brought to-

---

[100] See *Idler*, April 21, 1759.

[101] Defoe, *The Complete English Tradesman*, 110–111.

[102] Henry Fielding, *Enquiry into the Cause of the Late Increase in Robbers* (London, 1751), xi.

gether" by vain motives. He observed that the theater or ballroom served as venues of display where a woman had "the pleasure of wearing fine clothes, and of showing them, of outshining those whom she suspects to envy her." Further, she had the satisfaction of "escaping for two hours the superiority of a sister, or the control of a husband."[103] Men, too, succumbed to the temptation to speak through their possessions. Johnson noted that advertisements of auctions were "a signal which at once puts a thousand hearts in motion, and brings contenders from every part to the scene of distribution. Seduced by example, and aflamed by competition," the bidders shifted their eyes from the goods on sale to those who threatened to deny them their pleasure.[104] Although men and women had long employed goods to fashion their social identities, the consumer revolution afforded an unprecedented explosion of choices.

Self-fashioning was not confined to the affluent. When Voltaire arrived in London in 1726, he landed near Greenwich where the banks were crowded with people enjoying a festival. He observed that even the watermen "showed by [their] looks, [and] dress" that they lived in a land of plenty. He noted that the young girls, "mostly dressed in calicoes" exuded an uncommon "neatness, vivacity, and pleased contentedness." In the evening, Voltaire discovered from his hosts, a group of merchants, that all those "good-looking persons, in their calico dresses, were maidservants or country girls; [and] that all [those] resplendent young men so well mounted and caracoling round the race-course were students or apprentices." He soon learned how to differentiate between the wealthy and those of lesser means, observing dress and demeanor of the well-bred at tea where the women "made a great noise with their fans."[105]

The American colonist had long realized the social significance of fashion. From the earliest days of settlement in the New World, British Americans had communicated social status through fashions. Under John Winthrop's leadership, the Massachusetts General Court passed sumptuary laws prescribing dress appropriate for one's standing in society. However, by the 1740s, a flood of standardized, affordable consumer goods often made appearances deceptive. When a Maryland physician, Andrew Hamilton, traveled through the colonies, he witnessed an encounter between two strangers who dealt with each other strictly on the basis of appearance. While stopping at an inn in New Castle, Delaware, with a companion, one William Morison, Hamilton

[103] *Idler*, August 12, 1758.
[104] Ibid.
[105] Francesca M. Wilson, ed., *Strange Island: Britain through Foreign Eyes, 1395–1940* (London, 1955), 71–72.

noted that the landlady looked disapprovingly at Morison's "greasy jacket and breeches and a dirty worsted cap." Taking him for a plowman, the lady gave him "cold veal scraps for his breakfast." Indignant, Morison ripped off his cap and replaced it with a linen one from his pocket. Moreover, he indicated that he "had good linnen in his bags, a pair of silver buckles, silver clasps, and good sleeve buttons, two Holland shirts, and some neat night caps; and that his little woman att home drank tea twice a day."[106] Boorish in his behavior, Morison rested his claims of being a gentleman solely on his possessions. In a consumer society where fashion communicated standing, he was, to a large extent, correct.

Whitefield added his voice to the chorus condemning the evils of consumption. His sermonic pronouncements against luxuries echoed those of Puritan divines a century earlier. He was unsparing in his criticism of those who placed the pursuit of earthly gain above concern for eternal salvation. More than the churches that preached what he considered false doctrine, the consumer market represented Whitefield's greatest competitor for the time, money, and affection of his audiences. Soliciting funds for the Georgia orphan house, Whitefield wrote, "let that money, which you might expend to pamper your own bodies, be given to feed the poor." And he thundered against the "misspending [of] precious time [in] play-houses, horse-racing, balls and assemblies."[107]

Whitefield admonished his audiences against the insidious effects of consumption on men and women. The flood of goods, especially clothing, expanded the means of self-fashioning, which, for Whitefield, indicated misplaced values. For the evangelist, the more socially prominent had made a bad bargain in choosing vanity over charity. "Our great men had much rather spend their money in a playhouse, at a ball, an assembly, or a masquerade, than relieve a poor distressed servant of Jesus Christ," Whitefield warned. Continuing his condemnation of selfish expenditures, he added, "They had rather spend their estates on their hawks and hounds, on their whores, and earthly, sensual, devilish pleasures, than comfort, nourish, or relieve one of their distressed fellow-creatures."[108]

Whitefield's own experiences in the consumer market unsettled him. After his conversion at Oxford, Whitefield remembered his childhood expenditures as self-indulgence. He recalled his youthful penchant for

---

[106] Cited in Richard Bushman, "American High-Style and Vernacular Cultures," in *Colonial British America: Essays in the New History of the Early Modern Era*, ed. Jack Greene and J. R. Pole (Baltimore, 1984), 375.

[107] Whitefield, *Sermons on Important Subjects*, 87, 176, 478–486.

[108] Ibid., 479.

reading and attending plays, a diversion that extended to his days at Oxford. From an early age, Whitefield enjoyed books and spent freely for them: first, romances, which were his "heart's delight," and later, in college, theological and devotional works. Although he had limited funds, Whitefield preferred spending his earnings as a drawer at the Bell or a servitor at Pembroke College rather than saving them. In his diary, Whitefield recorded that monetary gifts from his brother James or from such admirers as Sir John Philips quickly were translated into expenditures, usually for more books.[109]

During the weeks preceding his conversion, while in his second year at Oxford, Whitefield expressed his altered inward state through his outward appearance and behavior. If possessions represented self-indulgence, then denying oneself the things of this world symbolized self-denial, a prerequisite for the new birth. He believed that by giving in to his "sensual appetite," he had allowed his possessions to fill him with pride. To prepare himself for the indwelling of the Holy Spirit, he therefore "began to leave off eating fruits and such like." Rather than spend on himself, he "gave the money [he] usually spent in that way to the poor." He selected for himself the "worst sort of food" although his circumstances "furnished [him] with variety." Having formerly dressed as a gentleman, Whitefield now "thought it unbecoming a penitent to have his hair powdered." Putting aside his best clothes, which he had kept in immaculate condition, Whitefield "wore woolen gloves, a patched gown and dirty shoes."[110] In other words, Whitefield employed consumer goods to fashion the image he desired. Whether he wanted to be viewed as an Oxford gentleman or as a pious seeker, he presented himself accordingly with the appropriate accessories.

As he began his public ministry, Whitefield discovered that the consumer transformation provided both the diversions that he believed led Christians astray and the means for him to rail against those temptations. In 1735, on a visit to his home in Gloucester, George learned that a band of itinerant "Strollers" were to perform. Having decided that plays had consumed too much of his own time and money and had taken his attention away from loftier ideas, Whitefield decided to wage a public crusade against the troupe. He therefore prepared a series of extracts from *The Absolute Unlawfulness of the Stage Entertainment*, by the Dissenter William Law, and convinced Robert Raikes to print portions in the *Gloucester Journal*. Whitefield observed that "God was pleased to give [the newspaper releases] His blessing."[111] More important for his

---

[109] *Whitefield's Journals*, 37–38. See accounts also throughout his unpublished diary, Miscellaneous Manuscripts, British Library, London.

[110] *Whitefield's Journals*, 53.

[111] Ibid., 63.

future ministry, he discovered that the same instruments entertainers employed to lure people to their plays could advance his own ends. Whitefield's ambivalence toward the commercial transformation continued throughout his ministry as he turned market devices against its own excesses.

However, the language of goods was also available to Whitefield's opponents, allowing them to fashion a very different image of the evangelist. They too employed consumer products—books, paintings, plays—to expose the revivalist as a fraud. His opposers flooded the market with anti-Methodist publications, issuing more than four hundred during his lifetime with about one-fourth appearing in his first two years of ministry. The accusations centered on two charges: preaching enthusiastic notions and fleecing people of their money. Alexander Pope sneered at Whitefield's preaching, comparing the itinerant's "harmonic twang" with an ass's braying. The playwright Samuel Foote parodied Whitefield's fund-raising through the character Mr. Squintum, a "blockhead deal[ing] in scripture as a trade."[112]

• Whitefield against commercialization.
↳ thought it led people astray from Christ
↳ wore simple clothes, dirty shoes.

PROCLAIMING THE NEW BIRTH IN THE LANGUAGE OF GOODS

Although Whitefield condemned the consumer market and the worldliness it promoted, he discovered within it a fresh language for delivering his message of the new birth and a vocabulary for explaining his evangelical mission to himself and the world. While commercial discourse was only one of several languages Whitefield employed, in a rapidly expanding consumer society it increasingly communicated images drawn from daily experiences of men and women. He always preached in biblical terms and frequently used tropes from such arenas as agriculture and the military, but his sermons reflect a particular familiarity with commercial discourse. Perhaps his boyhood experiences in retail trade and his early ministry in the commercial capital of London influenced his conception of the gospel in market terms. Whatever the path, Whitefield found within the consumption he deplored a means of communicating his faith.

Whitefield conceived of his mission in commercial terms. Reflecting on the beginning of his ministry, Whitefield pictured himself as a merchant for the Lord. "I intended to make an hundred and fifty ser-

[112] For polemical writings against Whitefield, see Richard Green, *Anti-Methodist Publications Issued during the Eighteenth Century* (London, 1902). Pope's quotation found in John Butt, ed., *The Poems of Alexander Pope*, 10 vols. (New Haven, Conn., 1963), 5:307–308. Foote called Whitefield "Dr. Squintum" in *The Minor: A Comedy in Three Acts*, in *The Dramatic Works of Samuel Foote, Esq.*, 2 vols. (New York, 1809), 1:30.

mons," he wrote, "and thought I would set up with a good stock in trade."[113] Just like a trader, he too would accumulate an inventory of wide assortment to sell in the marketplace. Throughout his ministry he urged lay followers to see themselves engaged in Christian commerce. While on a preaching circuit, Whitefield wrote a merchant, "I am travelling, and you are trading, for Jesus Christ."[114] To another he admonished: "go, dear Sir, and trade for God. Let merchants see by your example that Jesus Christ can make many saints in a store."[115] As he embarked on one of his seven American journeys, Whitefield lamented losing "the sale of some gospel goods at Gravesend market-place" and urged his fellow laborers to "meet with thousands of moneyless customers" to "sell" the gospel. Then, referring to his own mission to the colonies, the evangelist voiced his desire for a fruitful "trading voyage [wherein he would] sail into harbour with a well full and choice cargo of heavenly wares."[116] A final example of the commercial metaphor warrants full quotation. To a lay follower, Whitefield wrote: "Blessed be God for making you a Christian merchant, and teaching you the art of trafficking for the Lord. You trade on a safe bottom. Your all is insured, and you shall receive your own with good usury at the great day. Go on, my dear man, spend and be spent for Christ's people; it is glorious employ. I would not but be thus engaged for millions of worlds."[117]

Upon occasion Whitefield consciously became what one Bostonian derisively called him, a "Pedlar in Divinity." While preaching in Philadelphia, Whitefield exclaimed that he was going "to turn merchant" to communicate the gospel. He declared that he had "valuable commodities to offer for sale." However, unlike the vendors of ordinary merchandise, the evangelist indicated that he would sell his goods to his auditors not if they would "come *up* to [his] price . . . [but] if [they would] come *down* to [his] price." He urged his listeners to "*buy* the truth," adding that the "milk and wine" of a spiritual new birth could be purchased "without money and without price."[118]

Although Whitefield found much in the marketplace to criticize, he also discovered a framework for restating the gospel in a vocabulary familiar to his audiences. He often cast his theology in mercantile terms—shopping, spending, insuring, banking, selling. One publisher claimed the itinerant "preached in what [was] called MARKET-

---

[113] [The Banner of Truth Trust], *Select Sermons of George Whitefield* (Edinburgh, 1985), 195.

[114] Gillies, *Works of Whitefield*, 2:361–362.

[115] Ibid., 137.

[116] Ibid., 3:397.

[117] Ibid., 2:134.

[118] Cited in Joseph B. Wakeley, *Anecdotes of the Rev. George Whitefield, with a Biographical Sketch* (London, 1875), 133–134.

LANGUAGE," adding that Whitefield thought such discourse was "most likely to be understood and remembered by the common people." In one of his sermons delivered in commercial discourse, the revivalist recast the biblical account of Jesus' preaching to the publicans and sinners. Whitefield noted that Matthew, a tax collector, became a disciple, leaving "a profitable employ under the government, that perhaps brought him in some four hundred pounds a year." He observed that Matthew joined Jesus immediately without asking "leave to settle [his] accounts." While Whitefield's illustration and language reflected the rational calculation of commerce, his theological point was quite different: that "man must have no use of his common reason." Indeed, Matthew is presented as coming out of the world—the marketplace— and joining Jesus in a great public feast, a public display "to let the world see that he did not repent of his bargain."[119]

Although the idea of a salvific economy did not originate with Whitefield, his language in representing salvation as a market transaction is striking. Christ "purchased [at] . . . an expense of blood" the redemption of sinners. "It was a hard bargain," Whitefield exclaimed, "but Christ was willing to strike the bargain that you and I might not be damned forever."[120] Once he secured salvation, Christ offered the treasure to sinners. Whitefield expressed the offer in consumer terms: "I counsel you to come and buy of Jesus Christ gold, white raiment, and eye-salve." Those who chose to "buy without money" profited. Again, in the calculus of the marketplace, believers are always compared to something that is "good and profitable," and unbelievers are always described in terms of that which is "bad, and good for little or nothing."[121] In other words, believers make good deals.

In addition to viewing salvation as buying and selling, Whitefield saw it as investing. For the evangelist, God represented a safe investment and man an insecure one. "God trusted man once," Whitefield explained, "he set Adam up, gave him a blessed stock, placed him in a paradise of love, and he soon became a bankrupt, some think in twenty-four hours, however, all agree it was in six or seven days." Salvation is the story of an investment shifted from the hands of frail humans to those of omnipotent God. "Now, blessed be God, we are under a better dispensation," the evangelist exulted, "our stock is put into Christ's hands, [and] he knows how to keep it."[122] Whitefield exhorted his

[119] George Whitefield, *Christ the Physician of the Soul: A Sermon by the Reverend Mr. George Whitefield Taken by a Master of Short-Hand Word for Word as he Preached it* (n.d.), 5. Located in the Wesley College Library, Bristol, England.

[120] *Select Sermons of Whitefield*, 190.

[121] Ibid., 91, 113, 187–188.

[122] Whitefield, *Sermons on Important Subjects*, 573–574.

followers to be "laudably ambitious, and get as rich as [they could] towards God." He declared the "bank of heaven . . . a sure bank" on which he had "drawn thousands of bills . . . and never had one sent back protested."[123]

Whitefield employed the language of self-fashioning as a way to describe the new birth, an act of putting aside the old person and putting on the new. In a sermon on the dangers of self-pride, Whitefield told his audience that the problem began with Adam and Eve. Before their Fall in the Garden of Eden, man and woman were whole and perfect beings. Their sin resulted, however, in corruption that could only be reversed by divine redemption, a process Whitefield described in terms familiar to his eighteenth-century audience. The revivalist wrote, "If you look upon man sanctified by the spirit of Christ, you look upon him as drest in his resurrection cloaths, with his body fashioned like Christ's glorious body and presented blameless before the Father."[124]

Whitefield's auditors also expressed their spiritual conversions through alterations in dress. The *Gentlemen's Magazine* reported that "several of fine ladies, who us'd to wear French Silks, French Hoops of four yards wide, . . . Bob Wigs and white Satin Smock Petticoats," became Methodists and switched to "plain Stuff-Gowns, no Hoops, common Night Mobs, and plain Bays."[125] When Whitefield first met the American revivalist Jonathan Edwards, he noted with pleasure that Edwards's family expressed piety through clothes. He recorded in his journal that the "children were not dressed in silks and satins, but plain, as become the children of those who, in all things, ought to be examples of Christian simplicity."[126]

For Whitefield, dress signified more than a changed heart; it represented orthodoxy. Charged with being a fanatic who claimed he received special revelations from God, Whitefield sought to establish his theological soundness through a closer identification with the Anglican church. In addition to frequent declarations of his allegiance to the Thirty-Nine Articles, the revivalist always preached in traditional vestments, including a gown and wig. Scrupulous about his appearance, Whitefield went to great lengths each night to prepare his attire for the next day's services.[127] In all the portraits he commissioned, he appears in clerical garb. Thus, in part, the evangelist attempted to fashion his

[123] Gillies, *Works of Whitefield*, 3:66.

[124] Whitefield, *Christ the Physician*, 9.

[125] Cited in *New York Gazette*, July 30, 1739.

[126] *Whitefield's Journals*, 477.

[127] William Jay, ed., *Memoirs of the Life and Character of the late Reverend Cornelius Winter* (Bath, 1808), 81–82.

place in society and his mission to the world out of the language of goods.

Whitefield's familiarity with a shopkeeper's daybook provided another metaphor for his faith. He urged his followers to take an accounting of their spiritual lives. "I think a good tradesman whether he deals largely or not, will take care to keep his day-book well," Whitefield explained, adding, "if a man will not keep his day-book well it is ten to one but he loses a good deal when he comes to count up his things at Christmas." Then applying the lesson to converts, the evangelist continued, "now I take it for granted, a good spiritual tradesman will keep his spiritual day-book well." A good Christian will be able to look at his accounts at the end of a day and proclaim, "I have died a little more to the world than yesterday, [and] this day I hope that I have been a little more alive to God than I was yesterday."[128]

From his association with the Holy Club, Whitefield had learned a method of accounting for his spiritual thoughts and actions which paralleled that employed by merchants. Samuel Wesley, John's and Charles's father, had inspired his sons to keep a "Christian diary," viewing this as a tool for advancing "true Piety." Beginning in 1735, Whitefield adhered to the Wesleyan model, which by that time had evolved from paragraph to columnar style for a "more exact" rendering of how each hour was lived. The several columns resembled a businessman's daybook in which precise amounts indicate funds received for merchandise sold and those dispersed for new inventory or other expenses. Separate columns of Whitefield's diary indicated the hour, the activities of that hour, the number of minutes spent in devotion, his attitudes and feelings, the resolutions kept and broken, and special blessings received. A series of symbols and abbreviations enabled him to record such finer points as "degrees of attention" in prayers, indicating whether he was zealous and fervent in praying, or cold and indifferent. He also recorded receipts and expenditures of money each day. Periodically, he "cast up" his accounts, rendering a summary of readings, compositions, letters, and acquaintances.[129] Such a methodical approach to his spiritual life carried over into the way he planned and organized his public ministry.

Thus Whitefield borrowed from the commercial world a language for preaching his message throughout his thirty-three-year ministry to strangers seen and unseen. The spreading consumer culture had repelled and attracted him. He denounced its misplaced priorities of

128 Whitefield, *Sermons on Important Subjects*, 685.

129 Richard P. Heitzenrater, "The Oxford Diaries and the First Rise of Methodism," *Methodist History*, July 1974, 110–135.

satisfying selfish indulgence with luxuries and diversions while ignoring the basic needs of poor people. He lamented the growing reliance on rational institutions such as the marketplace while faith in God languished. Yet he discovered within the new commercialism techniques, categories, perceptions, and language to convey the gospel more efficiently to a transatlantic audience.

Ministers such as Cotton Mather and Benjamin Colman had used commercial language in their preaching a generation before the Great Awakening.[130] What was new about Whitefield was not just his appropriation of the language of the market but his adaptation of marketing strategies. Yet Whitefield's commercialization of religion need not suggest a secular orientation. Rather it indicates the assimilative powers of Christianity to re-present itself through transformations, including that of the marketplace. Hence, Whitefield intuitively and self-consciously, albeit at first tentatively, appropriated merchandising techniques for igniting the transatlantic revivals.

[130] See for example, Benjamin Colman, *The Merchandise of a People: Holiness to the Lord* (Boston, 1736).

○ Used commercialism as a way to preach + "sell" the word of God.

CHAPTER 2

Whitefield's Adaptation of
Commercial Strategies

IN 1739, the first year of his ministry, press coverage helped ensure Whitefield and his revival widespread popular acceptance. While Whitefield was not yet ordained as an Anglican minister and was little known outside Gloucester and Oxford, he became the best-known evangelist in the Atlantic world, in large part because of newspaper advertising that interpreted his preaching as a second Reformation.[1] The London evangelical bookseller James Hutton witnessed Whitefield's emergence as the dominant figure in the early stirrings of the revival. In 1737, Whitefield came from Oxford to London "amongst other young awakened preachers," not yet distinguished from the zealous band of aspirants to the ministry. Meanwhile, Whitefield's mentor John Wesley, who had traveled as a missionary to the new colony of Georgia, had written requesting his assistance in Savannah, and Whitefield had accepted, forgoing "some advantageous proposals, which were designed to hold him back in England." Hutton reported that "notice of this was given in the papers, with some prominence . . . which brought together great numbers."[2]

A recent convert, William Seward, first recognized newspaper publicity as a powerful instrument for presenting Whitefield to the English public. In managing Whitefield's newspaper publicity, Seward applied the same promotional strategy that had made him a successful stockjobber. Converted under the preaching of Wesley and Whitefield, Seward became, in his own words, a "Fool for Christ's sake." He brought to Whitefield's revivals the same penchant for hype that had enabled him to become treasurer of the South Sea Company, the trading firm that in the 1720s had whipped English investors into a speculative frenzy with hyperbolic claims of profit potential. The bitter memory of the South Sea Bubble, the 1721 crash of the grossly overpriced stock, lingered

---

[1] My analysis of Whitefield's adaptation of commercial techniques and tropes was first developed in article form. See Frank Lambert, " 'Pedlar in Divinity': George Whitefield and the Great Awakening, 1737–1745," *Journal of American History* 77 (December 1990): 812–837.

[2] [James Hutton], "The Beginning of the Lord's Work in England to 1746," *Proceedings of the Wesley Historical Society* 15 (1926): 183–184.

even into the mid-1750s. In defining stockjobber in his dictionary, Samuel Johnson revealed his own low opinion: "a low wretch who gets money by buying and selling shares in the funds." Seward explained his change of professions to his brother, Thomas, in a letter that he arranged to have reprinted on the front page of the London *Daily Advertiser*. He assured his brother that he was not following Whitefield "out of a blind zeal," promising that he would "follow him no farther than he follows Christ." Whatever his motivation, Seward found the *Daily Advertiser* and other public papers as useful in promoting religion as in selling investments. His daily reports on Whitefield's growing popularity, as measured by crowd size and donation amounts, paralleled the daily stock quotations. Those who had followed Whitefield's admonition to "lay up treasures in heaven" could exult in visible signs that their spiritual investment was appreciating in value.[3]

Seward's initial newspaper advertisements presented Whitefield as a selfless young evangelist who, forgoing lucrative opportunities in England, was undertaking a missionary journey to Georgia. The September 19, 1737, advertisement in the *Daily Advertiser* announced that the "Rev. Mr. Whitefield, a young Gentleman of distinguish'd piety, very eminent in his Profession, and a considerable fortune, will go voluntarily to preach the Gospel in Georgia."[4] Hutton noted that thereafter "everybody ran after him." Hutton further observed that Seward "also had the result [of Whitefield's performance] put in, viz. that much money was collected at the preaching" for charity schools. For Hutton, it was the "novelty of the thing"—the bold advertising of Whitefield and his success—that attracted "many hundred people . . . curious to hear this Whitefield." The bookseller noted that the other young revivalists also "preached in a more than ordinarily earnest way," but Whitefield, benefiting from the prominent publicity, "was everywhere made known" and emerged as the leading evangelical preacher.[5]

Although the London clergy had long employed newspapers to publicize charity sermons, under Seward's guidance Whitefield transformed mere notices into advertisements rivaling those promoting the latest consumer goods. Typical ecclesiastical entries in the *Daily Advertiser* announced sermons by presenting the bare essentials: who was to preach, for what charity, in which church, and at what time.[6] Rarely did the ministers provide the press with a report of the services, such as the

[3] Porter, *English Society*, 220; Samuel Johnson, *A Dictionary of the English Language in Which The Words are deduced from their Originals* (London 1755); *Daily Advertiser*, July 27, 1739.

[4] *Daily Advertiser*, September 19, 1737.

[5] Hutton, "Beginning of the Lord's Work," 183–184.

[6] See, for example, *Daily Advertiser*, September 19, 1737.

number attending and the amount collected. Whitefield's extensive application of the new merchandising techniques also set him apart from his evangelical predecessors and contemporaries. While the revivalist exploited the power of newspaper publicity to "spread his fame" abroad, even his early colleagues in English Pietism, John and Charles Wesley, rejected advertising as a means of promoting their religious enterprises, viewing it as a tasteless "sounding [of] a trumpet."[7]

By contrast, Seward sold Whitefield to the readers, complete with advertising puffs, those appealing details designed to pique interest. Seward's paid advertisements appeared on the front page in the form of news articles written by a third party, just the kind of publicity the innovative merchandiser Josiah Wedgwood considered the most powerful form of advertising.[8] The format recounted recent successes and announced upcoming events. In describing Whitefield's performance at St. Swithin in September 1737, Seward reported that the evangelist preached an "*excellent*" charity sermon before a "*crowded*" congregation whose contributions were "*remarkable.*" He noted that Whitefield's sermon on the "*greatness* of the charity of the poor widow's mites" inspired the auditors to contribute more than five pounds including "no less than 800 halfpence," an indication that even poor auditors added their coins to the offering. He concluded by announcing Whitefield's next sermon as a continuation of the evangelist's "*truly pious*" undertaking to promote the "*good effects* [charity schools] have on the lower ranks of the people."[9] Seward employed similar language in promoting Whitefield's revivals and his own stockjobbing business. His advertisement of November 11, 1739, for instance, announced that he offered for sale shares "in a *new method*, much *more advantageous* to the purchaser than they can *possibly* be bought *any other way*" (emphasis mine).[10] Whether publicizing sermons or securities, London's daily newspapers provided a powerful means of self-presentation, a lesson Whitefield learned and applied even after Seward's death in October 1740.

Reflecting on his reaction to reading the first newspaper account of his ministry, Whitefield wrote in 1740 that the "advertisement chagrined me." He requested that "the printer . . . would put me in his paper no more." The publisher replied that "he was paid for doing it, and that he would not lose two shillings for anybody." Whitefield over-

[7] Charles Wesley, *The Journal of the Reverend Charles Wesley*, 2 vols. (London, 1849), 1:159.

[8] Seeking to "puff" his pottery wares, Wedgwood wrote his partner, Thomas Bentley, on February 11, 1771, exhorting him, "pray get another [unsolicited] article in the next paper." See McKendrick, Brewer, and Plumb, *Birth of a Consumer Society*, 125.

[9] *Daily Advertiser*, September 28, 1737.

[10] Ibid., November 11, 1737.

came his opposition to newspaper publicity when he observed its efficacy in attracting crowds to his charity sermons. In a letter to his Gloucester friend Gabriel Harris, Whitefield surmised that Harris had read of his "mighty deeds" in the newspapers. Although initially opposed, the young revivalist quickly learned that a newspaper notice reached thousands of people, informing distant readers of local events.[11]

Noting the increase in attendance following the press coverage, Whitefield overcame his reservations and developed a sustained advertising campaign to promote his charity sermons in London prior to departing on his second American trip. While collecting for the Georgia orphan house early in 1739, Seward placed two or three notices per week in the *Daily Advertiser*, relying also on verbal communication at the services to publicize upcoming meetings. However, because of an embarrassing episode, Whitefield's "press agent" announced in the May 3 edition that "daily notices [would] be given in [the] paper." Although Whitefield had announced at a Sunday sermon when and where he would preach over the next few days, many people, including several "persons of distinction," awaited the evangelist at the wrong site.[12] Thenceforward, daily newspaper advertising became a standard feature of Whitefield's publicity until his embarkation for America almost three months later.

By using commercialism to his advantage, Whitefield surpassed all other preachers.

NEWSPAPERS AND THE NEW BIRTH

Although newsletters circulated in England during the seventeenth century, their high cost limited readership. Only a select few could afford the subscription prices of the manuscript news-sheets containing foreign news, domestic affairs, parliamentary news, and political gossip. Written on three sides of two leaves, the letters usually reached their readers through the post, at an additional cost. By making newsletters available at coffeehouses, publishers widened the readership. Indeed, one publisher, John Dyer, discovered that his newsletter was a good drawing card for his coffeehouse. However, for the vast majority of Englishmen the manuscript papers' subscription price was prohibitive. In 1689 one thrice-weekly publication cost subscribers £4 sterling per year plus postage, which raised the total to about £5 12s. At a time when carters and diggers earned about eight or nine shillings a week, the newsletter represented almost one-fourth of a laborer's annual

---

[11] *Whitefield's Journals*, 87–88. Gillies, *Works of Whitefield*, 1:29.
[12] *Daily Advertiser*, May 3, 1739.

income. As late as 1710, no more than three hundred people subscribed to Dyer's newsletter.[13]

When the Licensing Act expired in 1695, intense competition produced a flood of printed newspapers that poured from London and provincial presses. By 1731, one observer noted that "no less than 200 Half-sheets per month are thrown from the Press only in London, and about as many printed elsewhere in the Three Kingdoms." The *Gentleman's Magazine* extracted articles from nineteen London newspapers and from twenty-two in the provinces. Competition lowered subscription prices. By the 1730s, the price of most London papers was 2½*d.* per copy or £1 12*s.* a year for a thrice-weekly subscription. At that rate, newspapers cost about one-third the price of newsletters. From 1695 to 1735, the price of a single issue dropped from almost twice the cost of a loaf of bread to little more than one-half, making newspapers affordable for a much larger proportion of the reading public.[14]

Along with the proliferation of newspapers in the eighteenth century came an expansion of the reading public, encompassing even the poor. In 1758, Samuel Johnson observed that "not many years ago the nation was content with one gazette; but now we have not only in the metropolis papers for every morning and every evening, but almost every large town has its weekly historian who regularly circulates his periodical intelligence." Johnson expressed skepticism concerning the contribution of many newspapers to the enlightenment of the general population. Reflecting his own class bias, he chastised journalists who pandered to "the common people of England" whose minds lack the "skill for full comprehension." "One of the amusements of idleness is reading without the fatigue of close attention," Johnson wrote, "and the world therefore swarms with writers whose wish is not to be studied, but to be read." To Johnson the expansion of newspaper readership required journalists to acquaint themselves with "the lower orders of mankind." The successful newspaper publisher "is to consider himself not as writing to students or statesmen alone, but to women, shopkeepers, and artisans, who have little time to bestow upon mental attainments, but desire, upon daily terms, to know how the world goes; who rises, and who falls; who triumphs, and who is defeated."[15] In other words, newspapers satisfied a growing demand for news at all social levels.

[13] Donovan H. Bond and W. Reynolds McLeod, eds., *Newsletters to Newspapers: Eighteenth-Century Journalism* (Morgantown, W.Va., 1977), 7–11; Porter, *English Society*, 108.

[14] *Gentleman's Magazine and Historical Chronicle* 1(1731); Bond and McLeod, *Newsletters to Newspapers*, 184; Porter, *English Society*, 13.

[15] *Idler*, May 27 and November 11, 1758; Samuel Johnson, "Of the Duty of a Journalist," *Universal Chronicle*, April 8, 1758.

Journalistic practices of the mid-eighteenth century gave Seward and Whitefield the opportunity to write their own copy. Without a staff of reporters, newspaper publishers solicited contributions of "news," sometimes delivering reports "of which [they] know not the authors." Johnson feared that the pressure of deadlines prevented the publisher from ensuring the accuracy of reports submitted by volunteer reporters. In order to "transmit the earliest intelligence," Johnson lamented, the editor "relates transactions yet fluctuating in uncertainty," before he can verify reports and check sources. The pressure to attract readers by providing entertaining accounts of events compromised accuracy. Although admonishing journalists to maintain high standards of impartiality and honesty, Johnson also acknowledged the competitive nature of the print trade. He therefore excused newspaper editors for occasionally hurrying "down the current of a popular clamour."[16]

During the first two years of Whitefield's ministry, Seward acted as the evangelist's chief reporter and press agent. While traveling with the itinerant, Seward provided newspaper publishers in Britain and America with a steady stream of material. He forwarded copies of Whitefield's sermons, journals, and letters to newspaper and magazine publishers, booksellers, and leading evangelical ministers. He sent newspaper articles to printers in other towns on Whitefield's itinerary. And he wrote firsthand accounts of Whitefield's successes. In his own journal, published in 1740 in England and the colonies, the zealous Seward portrayed his role in newspaper reporting and press relations. Successive entries during 1740 reveal the nature and extent of his activities in Philadelphia: "April 27. Wrote paragraph for the News of our Brother's preaching, etc., particularly . . . [an account] to be published in New York. April 29. Wrote and examined sundry things for the Press; Particularly Mr. Whitefield's Letter. . . . May 2. Call'd at Mr. [Benjamin] Franklin's the Printer."[17] Seward was an effective advance man, flooding printers with publicity weeks before Whitefield's arrival to begin preaching.

While Seward and others performed the role of press agents, Whitefield himself exercised direct control over press coverage. After he dispatched Seward to England in April 1740 on a fund-raising mission, the itinerant reported his own performances and successes, producing third-person accounts of his latest preaching tour in the Middle Colonies. He opened a typical report with a statistical account of his activ-

---

[16] Johnson, "Of the Duty of a Journalist."

[17] William Seward, *Journal of a Voyage From Savannah to Philadelphia, and from Philadelphia to England, in 1740* (Boston, 1740), 16–22.

ities, indicating he was onshore thirty-three days, traveled "hundreds" of miles, preached fifty-eight sermons, attracted crowds up to twenty thousand, and collected "near 500 pounds sterling." Then, assessing the power of the revival, he wrote, "Great and visible effects followed his preaching. There was never such a general awakening, and concern for the things of God known in America before." He closed by announcing his intentions to visit New England in the fall and return to Philadelphia afterwards.[18] Thus, Whitefield produced advertisements for his revivals under the guise of journalism—just the kind of "objective" third-party report Wedgwood instructed his associates to insert in newspapers to promote pottery sales.[19]

Almost from the beginning, Whitefield's ministry became entwined in the spreading Atlantic market. While in Georgia in 1738—in response to Wesley's call for assistance—Whitefield made a decision that placed him squarely at the intersection of commerce and religion, and resulted in new opportunities and tensions. Upon arriving in the colony the young evangelist "found so many objects of charity, . . . [including] orphans [and] . . . poor people's children," that he determined to establish the orphanage outside Savannah he would later name Bethesda. His motivation was evangelical: he intended to "preach chiefly to the children's hearts . . . [and] instruct them by the Church of England's Articles." He aimed to structure the charity as a voluntary enterprise, financing it through contributions. Making his first plea in his published *Journals*, Whitefield expressed confidence in the orphan house's success if "some of those who are rich in this world's goods contribute towards it." He returned to England in late 1738 to raise funds for the charity that would continue as a primary focus of his transatlantic ministry until his death in 1770.[20]

Bethesda was more than an act of faith. The orphanage plunged Whitefield deep into the Atlantic commercial world, requiring him to develop many of the entrepreneurial skills demanded of merchants engaged in far-flung trade. Insisting on operating the orphanage as an independent charity, Whitefield organized it outside the control of the Anglican church and the Georgia trustees. Without their financial backing, however, he faced the enormous undertaking of raising funds to establish and maintain the orphan house. Whitefield's ministry, therefore, of necessity occurred as much in the marketplace as in the pulpit. He faced all the problems merchants encountered: raising funds to engage in transatlantic trade, discovering in Georgia an ex-

---

[18] Gillies, *Works of Whitefield*, 1:179.

[19] McKendrick, Brewer, and Plumb, *Birth of a Consumer Society*, 9–33.

[20] Gillies, *Works of Whitefield*, 3:432–433; *Whitefield's Journals*, 156.

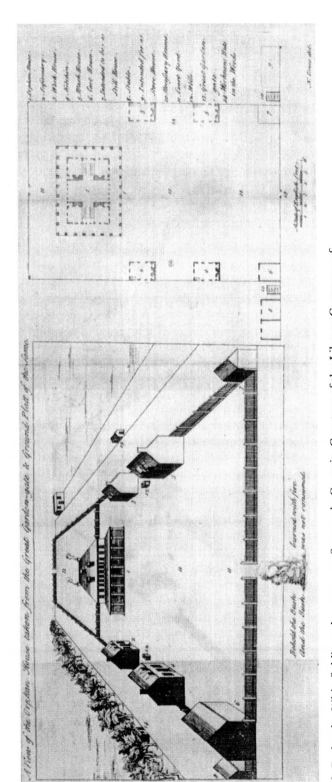

3. Bethesda, Whitefield's orphanage near Savannah, Georgia. Courtesy of the Library Company of Philadelphia.

portable commodity, establishing lines of credit with London and colonial merchants, juggling bills of exchange to maintain creditworthiness, and advertising his charity amid numerous claims competing for public attention.

One example will suffice to illustrate the complexities Whitefield faced in operating his transatlantic charity. After securing in 1739 a grant of five hundred acres twelve miles west of Savannah, Whitefield and James Habersham, his associate who acted as business manager, established a cotton manufactory at Bethesda, "a thing not known before in Georgia," or indeed, anywhere else in the colonies. Whitefield delighted in its early success, reporting nearly four hundred yards of woven cloth with an equal amount in process.[21] However, Whitefield's entrepreneurial spirit offended the imperial sensibilities of the Georgia trustees, who indicted Whitefield's enterprise as a direct violation of the Navigation Acts. "As the Trustees are sensible that the setting up of looms in Georgia will be highly disagreeable to the Parliament and the Publick," the trustees recorded in their minutes of June 11, 1740, "they are determined that no looms should be set up at the orphan-house or in any part of the colonies." The experience demonstrates Whitefield's employment of market means to serve spiritual ends and his frustration in attaining economic independence for Bethesda.[22] It also meant that Whitefield's ministry would be closely interrelated with the Atlantic market.

When Whitefield began touring England in early 1739 preaching charity sermons for Bethesda, he increasingly held services outside churches and literally in marketplaces. Having worked at a public house, the itinerant knew that inns opened their doors to all sorts of traveling salesmen and performers. Thus when he arrived at a public house in Windsor, he insisted on conducting a religious service. "Others sing songs in public houses," he argued, "why should not we sing psalms?" Having raised the question, Whitefield put the proposition to the test at his next stop, Basingstoke. Acting very much like a peddler arriving in town with merchandise, Whitefield "gave notice" that he would preach in a "large dining room in the public house." After preaching to "above a hundred very attentive hearers," Whitefield expressed the hope that he would "learn more and more every day that no place is amiss for preaching the Gospel."[23] Encouraged by his success at Basingstoke, the revivalist preached in market squares, guildhalls, trade fairs, and workshops.

[21] Gillies, *Works of Whitefield*, 3:432.

[22] Allen D. Candler, *The Colonial Records of the State of Georgia*, 32 vols. (Atlanta, 1904), 30:143.

[23] *Whitefield's Journals*, 209.

Whitefield's marketplace religion encountered stiff opposition from clergymen and magistrates who desired rigid boundaries between the sacred and the secular. When Whitefield returned to Basingstoke in July 1739, he again attempted to preach at the inn. However, the magistrate forbade the evangelist to preach there, maintaining that the worship of God was to be confined to "places consecrated and set apart for His service and not in brothels and places where all manner of debauchery may have been committed." Whitefield insisted that his ministry was being placed at a competitive disadvantage, a view strengthened by a "stage built [nearby] for . . . cudgellers and wrestlers." Why should revelers have greater access to audiences than preachers? At Broad-Oaks in Essex, the competition was religion itself, "a decent, genteel and fashionable religion" that catered to the "lovers of pleasure more than lovers of God." Whitefield felt compelled to offer experimental religion to all, even if the bishops claimed itinerancy to be "not regular." To the evangelical, sinners were everywhere and required his "going out into the highways and hedges and compelling poor sinners to come in."[24] Like the new merchants, Whitefield envisioned a much greater demand for his "product" than did the clergy.

The nature of Whitefield's newspaper publicity changed between his first two American trips, reflecting a growing commercialization of religion. In the three months prior to his embarking for Georgia in December 1737 on the first journey, Whitefield and Seward developed the theme of a selfless young preacher, tireless in preaching on behalf of English charity schools and sacrificial in traveling to Georgia as pastor of poor settlers. Seward provided publishers with a steady stream of articles setting Whitefield apart from the many other ministers who preached charity sermons. Seward publicized what he characterized as extraordinary results of Whitefield's preaching. In a typical account, Seward noted that at one church the collection, which "usually amount[ed] to about ten shillings," under Whitefield's pleading reached the "remarkable" sum of £5 18s.—a tenfold increase. On another occasion Seward reported that Whitefield preached four sermons in four different churches on the same day with "every church so crowded that numbers were obliged to withdraw for want of room." The reports indicated that Whitefield attracted all sorts of people but mainly commoners. At a service in St. Andrew Holborn, the revivalist managed to secure a large collection "considering the audience, which consisted of common people, who filled the church as soon as the doors were open'd, so that the better sorts could not get to their pews." Throughout the publicity campaign, Seward reminded readers that

---

[24] Ibid., 291, 293, 309–310.

Whitefield was "going voluntary to Georgia," despite invitations to stay in England. An article in the October 25 *Daily Advertiser* noted one such opportunity, reporting that the parishioners at St. Mary at Hill would offer the rectory to Whitefield upon the resignation of the presiding clergyman.[25]

After Whitefield returned from Georgia in December 1738, his publicity reflected a shift in strategy. During his absence, Whitefield's popularity had increased, in large part because of a print war between rival booksellers seeking exclusive rights to publish the evangelist's *Journals*. The result was enormous sales. Priced at sixpence, the *Journals* were within reach of common men and women whose purchases resulted in six editions within nine months.[26] In the publication, Whitefield announced that he was returning to England to raise money to establish the orphanage in Georgia. As the revivalist began preaching in London, increasingly his sermons criticized Anglican clergymen, accusing them of no longer teaching Reformation principles, especially the doctrine of justification. Now Whitefield was preaching a new message, one in open competition with those of the settled ministry. Consequently, the clergy denied him access to their pulpits. Resorting to preaching in open fields, Whitefield found himself outside the church confronted with the challenge of raising funds without institutional support.[27] Hence the preacher appealed directly to a mass audience through both the printed and the spoken word and thereby transformed his local charity appeals into an international revival.

Whitefield attracted huge crowds during spring 1739 and reported even larger ones. Whitefield and Seward forwarded unprecedented crowd estimates to newspaper publishers, who were eager to print any news about the increasingly popular revivals. Relying on newsmakers to report their own events, newspaper editors published crowd figures without criticism or comment. Prior to May, Seward and Whitefield described audiences as "large" or "numerous" without offering numerical estimates. Then on May 1, they reported that twenty thousand people attended services at Kennington Common and thirty thousand at Moorfields. The May 7 *Daily Advertiser* indicated that on the previous day twenty thousand men and women had heard Whitefield preach at Moorfields and fifty thousand at Kennington Common. One week later the numbers reported swelled to fifty thousand at Moorfields and sixty thousand at Kennington Common.[28]

[25] See *Daily Advertiser*, September 28, October 3, October 25, and December 5, 1737.
[26] For the battle over publication rights for Whitefield's *Journals*, see ibid. August 3 through August 8, 1738.
[27] For clergymen's denying Whitefield the pulpit, see, for example, ibid., April 28, 1739.
[28] Ibid., May 1, 7, and 14, 1739.

Whitefield and Seward fabricated crowd estimates, reporting huge crowds as a means of demonstrating that the revival was indeed a second Reformation. From the outset, opponents questioned the accuracy of the prorevivalists' numbers. One skeptic claimed that crowd reporting was a "misrepresentation in favour of Mr. Whitefield's success; for in all those articles of news which give an account of the vast crowds who compose his audience, their numbers are always exaggerated, being often doubled and sometimes trebled."[29] Suspicious about reported audience sizes, Benjamin Franklin conducted his own experiment to see how many people could hear the preacher in an open-air service, concluding that at least twenty-five thousand people could hear the evangelist.[30] An outspoken critic of the revivals, Timothy Cutler, an Anglican priest in Boston, verified Whitefield's claim that twenty thousand men and women gathered on Boston Common for his farewell sermon on Sunday, October 12, 1740.[31] However, when the itinerant revised his *Journals* in 1756, he removed what he considered "justly exceptionable" passages, including references to crowds of "more than twenty thousand." Whitefield changed estimates of fifty and sixty thousand to "so many thousand that many went away because they could not hear."[32] But in 1739, the exaggerated figures aroused the curiosity of people on both sides of the Atlantic awaiting the evangelical's arrival in their communities.

Whitefield limited his statistical assessments of success to the size of crowds and amount of donations. He did not estimate numbers converted because the new birth was primarily a matter known only to individuals and God. While Whitefield encouraged converts to affiliate with congregations headed by evangelical ministers, he developed no follow-up machinery to gather information regarding spiritual maturation. His mission was "to plant" the gospel seed, and others were called "to water" the tender plants. Or, in market language, Whitefield proclaimed that his "business seems to be to evangelize."[33] Nevertheless, newspaper accounts of the revivalist's services usually included some judgment concerning audience reaction. Seward wrote in a typical report that in a crowd of twenty thousand at Kennington Common "an awful silence was kept during the whole time of Singing, Prayers, and Sermon."[34]

[29] *Pennsylvania Gazette*, May 8, 1740.

[30] Ibid., November 15, 1739.

[31] *New York Gazette*, November 19, 1740. For Cutler's crowd estimate, see William S. Perry, ed., *Historical Collections Relating to the American Colonial Church* 5 vols. (Hartford, 1871) 3:347.

[32] *Whitefield's Journals*, 31, 265.

[33] Gillies, *Works of Whitefield*, 1:262–263.

[34] *Daily Advertiser*, May 3, 1739.

Seward and Whitefield did more than report news; they created it, staging events to attract crowds and then publicizing them through newspaper accounts. The revivalist had borrowed the idea of preaching out-of-doors in open fields from a Welsh evangelical, Griffith Jones. What Whitefield added to the practice was extensive newspaper publicity. In May 1739, Whitefield began preaching in the coalfields around Bristol, proclaiming the necessity of the new birth to grimy colliers emerging from the pits. In newspaper reports that circulated throughout Britain and America, Seward estimated the initial crowd to be five or six thousand, and subsequent gatherings in the district to comprise as many as twenty thousand miners and their families. While addressing spiritual needs, Whitefield also expressed concern for the colliers' temporal circumstances. The May 3 edition of the *Daily Advertiser* announced that the evangelist was soliciting subscriptions for a school for miners' children. Having met with success among colliers, Whitefield preached open-air sermons in other parts of Bristol's manufacturing district, exhorting, for example, workers in the "Brick-Yard near the Glass House." In all cases Whitefield and Seward forwarded accounts of the services to London newspapers. After Whitefield left Bristol, he proclaimed in the papers that "there is a great Reformation among the colliers since Mr. Whitefield's preaching there, and many of them have earnestly invited him . . . to come again to them."[35]

When Whitefield returned to London from his triumphant preaching tour near Bristol, he continued to deploy his successful formula for staging and publicizing events. He provoked confrontations with parish clergymen over access to their pulpits. Having made anticlerical charges a commonplace in his sermons, Whitefield nonetheless announced that he was holding services in particular parish churches. When denied, the evangelist would lead his followers to the churchyard and deliver his sermon there. The April 28 *Daily Advertiser* noted that "being denied the pulpit by the Churchwardens, [Whitefield] preach'd from a tombstone in Islington Church-Yard." He scheduled preaching regularly on weekend afternoons in London's great public parks such as Hyde Park, Moorfields, and Kennington Common. He also preached at tracks on days of horse races, delivering one sermon from "the weighing-chair on the horse-course." London's crowded shopping districts provided opportunities to address large numbers of people. Upon one occasion, "finding 2-or-3 thousand people in the street, he preach'd to them from the Shop-Window." Just as consumer goods were displayed and advertised for sale, Whitefield transformed himself and his message into commodities and offered them to a mass audience.[36]

[35] Ibid., March 27, April 3, and May 16, 1739.
[36] Ibid., April 28, May 3, and May 26, 1739.

In addition to being effective means of publicizing Whitefield's revivals, newspapers were well suited for conveying his message to those
who did not hear him preach. Presenting himself as an instrument of a
new dispensation of God's grace in the Atlantic world, Whitefield discovered in newspapers a vehicle for communicating a sense of immediacy and urgency. Like Pentecost or the Reformation, the mid-
eighteenth-century evangelical revivals represented a special act of
Providence—a present moment full of undeniable manifestations of
divine presence. Newspapers reported events as they unfolded, enabling readers to follow the course of actions almost as they occurred.
Newspapers did not demand readers' reflection on timeless truths but
confronted them with the latest happenings in the world of nature and
the march of time.

Samuel Johnson believed that accounts of the novel and unusual
explained why common readers favored newspapers over more enduring forms of print. He contended that the "Ephemerae of learning
have uses more adequate to the purposes of common life than more
pompous and durable volumes." Refusing to "allow much merit to
Whitefield's oratory," Johnson claimed that the evangelist's "popularity
. . . [was] chiefly owing to the peculiarity of his manner." Alluding to
Whitefield's bizarre antics in attracting crowds, Johnson added that he
too "would be followed by crowds were he to wear a nightcap in the
pulpit, or were he to preach from a tree." Indeed newspaper accounts
of Whitefield's services frequently focused on unusual circumstances
rather than sermon content. Newspaper publishers readily printed the
revivalist's colorful descriptions because they were just what printers
desired: entertaining accounts "seldom intended to remain in the
world longer than a week."[37]

Colonists in British North America were also attracted to "fresh
occurrences," foreign and domestic. Readers eagerly followed news
accounts, whether in reports of recent political or military developments in remote lands, or of the latest fashions displayed by London's
aristocrats, or of current commodity prices quoted on European markets. One eighteenth-century Connecticut letter-writer pondered the
appeal of printed news. "This inquisitive disposition for novelty," he
explained, "is almost universal and peculiarly gratified with utility in
the vehicle of a news-paper." From daily or weekly news supplies, "the
plebeian furnishes himself with matter for a week's conversation."[38]

Thus newspapers were ideally suited to convey Whitefield's message
of the new birth. Just as newspapers announced the availability of the
"latest fashions" in wearing apparel, they proclaimed what Whitefield

[37] [Samuel Johnson], *Rambler*, August 6, 1751.
[38] *New London Gazette*, October 2, 1772.

heralded as the most recent and greatest outpouring of God's spirit since the Protestant Reformation. Implicit in his pronouncements was the transitory nature of this special dispensation. Hence there was a sense of urgency in his plea: "Now is the acceptable time of salvation." Having claimed that a revival was occurring and that he was an instrument in its propagation, Whitefield filled newspapers with its progress. Each day his followers could read about swelling crowds and dramatic conversions, and thereby ride the movement's current. Seward claimed that "the blessing that attends his ministry is amazing! Captive souls are loosed from the bonds of death, and flock to Christ, as Doves into their windows!" Whitefield sent regular reports of his American itinerancy to London newspapers, informing readers that "never [had America seen] such a general awakening." The *Daily Advertiser* represented Whitefield's latest installment of his *Journals* as a report of "that great work which is now daily carrying on by the ministry of Mr. Whitefield." Subscribers were able to follow the "progress of true religion in the world." True religion was an event occurring in the present, not received tradition from the past. And daily press releases reinforced the notion of a fresh outpouring of the Holy Spirit in the Atlantic world.[39]

Newspapers did more for Whitefield than convey his message; they also helped him forge an evangelical community spanning the British Atlantic. Through frequent reports circulated throughout Britain and America, Whitefield enlarged the vision of thousands of men and women, lifting their gaze beyond parish boundaries to a much more expansive body of believers. While books had helped sixteenth-century Protestants transcend national perspectives, newspapers connected like-minded evangelicals in the mid-1700s. According to Benedict Anderson, in his assessment of the cultural effects surrounding the rise of newspapers, inexpensive, daily newspapers wrought "fundamental changes in modes of apprehending the world." In the sixteenth century books had emerged as "the first modern-style mass-produced industrial commodity" as thousands of exact copies circulated throughout Reformation Germany and other European countries. The newspaper was "an extreme form of the book, a book sold on a colossal scale . . . of ephemeral popularity, . . . one-day best sellers." The newspaper that becomes obsolete "on the morrow of its printing . . . creates . . . [an] extraordinary mass ceremony: the almost precisely simultaneous consumption" of the same printed material by thousands of readers. Although men and women read in silence and alone, they are aware of others—an "imagined community"— . . . [of] whose identity

[39] See *Daily Advertiser*, August 16, 1740; *A Collection of Papers Lately Printed in the Daily Advertiser* (London, 1740).

he [or she] has not the slightest notion." As the newspaper reader observes exact replicas of his own paper being read in coffeehouses and taverns, he or she "is continually reassured that the imagined world is visibly rooted in everyday life." Anderson links newspapers to the rise of nationalism. For Whitefield, by contrast, newspapers made possible another kind of community, a transatlantic community of faith whose members, often unknown to each other, exulted in the proliferating evidence pointing to an awakening of experimental religion in Britain and America.[40]

To this point it appears that Whitefield exercised a free hand in shaping and reporting revival news. Though an enterprising publicist, Whitefield operated within the constraints of a print trade whose members pursued profits as aggressively as the evangelist sought souls. Newspaper and magazine editors were far from passive agents for Whitefield to exploit; they mediated his revival message. Sometimes the mediation had theological overtones as publishers interpreted Whitefield in accordance with their own or their readers' religious preferences. Always the mediation was commercial as publishers competed for increased market share. For instance, the Tory newspaper *Fog's Weekly Journal* opposed the Oxford group known as the Holy Club as early as December 1732, viewing it as a threat to the Anglican church.[41] The *Gentleman's Magazine* and other publications maintained a more balanced editorial position, printing articles defending and attacking Whitefield.

Just as publishers printed Whitefield's own accounts of his ministry, they also published reports from antirevivalists. Sometimes hostile interpretations appeared in newspapers that had previously included only favorable renditions. For instance, Caleb D'Anvers, publisher of the *Craftsman*, faithfully and exclusively reprinted Whitefield's versions until Anglican clergymen began to attack the revivalist. In 1737, D'Anvers followed the *Daily Advertiser*'s lead in promoting the young evangelist's charity sermons. But after Whitefield returned from Georgia in 1739, praise turned to ridicule. The April 7 edition gleefully recounted "some Arch Wags [had] advertis'd" a sermon by the itinerant at an appointed time; a large crowd assembled to hear him preach, only to wait in vain for his arrival. The reporter concluded that the episode revealed Whitefield's ineptitude and proved that the preacher's following included "many Fools."[42] Why D'Anvers switched from supporting to attacking Whitefield is unknown. Whatever the reason, the pub-

[40] Benedict Anderson, *The Imagined Community: Reflections on the Origins and Spread of Nationalism* (London, 1983), 28, 38–39.

[41] *Fog's Weekly Journal*, December 1732.

[42] *Craftsman* (London), April 7, 1739.

lisher, D'Anvers, not the preacher, Whitefield, determined what interpretation the *Craftsman's* readers would see.

Even editors who supported Whitefield could not resist promoting
anti- as well as prorevivalist works. Of the London newspapers, none
expressed approval of Whitefield more than did the *Daily Advertiser*.
Yet the *Daily Advertiser* followed a neutral advertising policy, with the
result that works for and against Whitefield could be displayed on
the same page. The June 5, 1739, edition advertised a polemic by the
Anglican clergyman Rev. Dr. Joseph Trapp. The copy suggested that
the work was "very proper to be read by all persons, especially at this
time, as a preservative against the dangerous principles and practices
of Mr. Whitefield and his followers." In the same issue, James Hutton
announced publication of Whitefield's latest *Journal*. Although the
Daily Advertiser printed few articles against Whitefield, advertisements
themselves sometimes resembled reports in their lengthy texts. One
notice for an anti-Whitefield publication represented the pamphlet as
exposing "Mr. Whitefield's extraordinary manner of preaching the
gospel, his criminal presumptions, and enthusiastick doctrine."[43]
Readers perusing advertising pages could follow the major debates
surrounding the revivals.

Publishers could influence interpretation through composition and
layout. Where in a publication an article appeared could shape how
readers regarded it. The April 1739 edition of the *Gentleman's Magazine*
lifted a report on Whitefield's revival services from the *Daily Advertiser*
and placed it on the same page as stock quotations. Whether inten-
tional or not, the juxtaposition could only have strengthened the suspicion voiced by many that Whitefield was reaping enormous profits in
the name of religion. The first security listed was that of the South Sea
Company, whose stock manipulation had sullied the reputation of
stockjobbers, including, perhaps, that of William Seward.[44] Following
the name of each company was the latest stock price. For instance,
South Sea 100⅝; Royal African 102; India Bonds 61 11*s*. Immediately
following the securities quotations was a report on Whitefield's trip to
the West Country. The article presented a statistical account of the
revivalist's success in attracting auditors and collecting funds for his
Georgia orphanage. According to the report, written by either Whitefield or Seward, "5 to 6,000" people heard the evangelist on Hannum
Mount near Bristol. A subsequent service at the same location attracted

[43] *Daily Advertiser*, June 5, 1739.

[44] Although *stockjobber* was a pejorative term to many in the eighteenth century, including Samuel Johnson, as the century advanced the term carried a less negative conno-
tation and for many became interchangeable with the more positive word *broker*.

"20,000." Donations amounted to "141 10s."[45] The printer's placing Whitefield's report on the financial page suggests that the evangelist reckoned souls just as securities brokers evaluated stocks.

[handwritten annotations:]
- Whitefield using newspapers and articles to get the word out
- Newspapers helped him gain popularity
- papers published writing by those against Whitefield as well.

REVIVALIST MAGAZINES

Rather than place himself at the mercy of printers whose objectives differed from his, Whitefield sought a vehicle that would give him control over his portrayal in print. His opportunity came in 1741 when he injected new life into a moribund evangelical magazine established by London printer John Lewis. Like newspapers, magazines triumphed in the first quarter of the eighteenth century as publishers defined new markets and exploited them with innovative publications tailored to market demand. With the *Spectator*, Addison and Steele cultivated "the new and growing middle-class audience," providing a periodical of essays on "manners, social morality and self-improvement" that enabled readers "to participate in the world of the great yet be free from its anxieties." The most successful magazine in the 1700s, the *Gentleman's Magazine*, with a national circulation of ten thousand copies, was a compendium of weekly events culled from England's expanding newspaper network. Following a similar approach but specifically targeting evangelicals, Lewis published in September 1740 the first issue of the *Christian's Amusement containing Letters Concerning the progress of the Gospel both at Home and Abroad etc.* By printing in one place letters and newspaper accounts of the revival's progress, Lewis hoped to satisfy evangelicals' desire for revival news and to make the enterprise profitable.[46]

William Seward, in Wales on a fund-raising trip for Whitefield, applauded Lewis's announced plan to publish an evangelical magazine. Upon hearing of the proposal, Seward wrote Lewis, pledging his support and sending an account of his Welsh travels that the printer included in one of the first issues. Another Whitefield supporter, Welsh itinerant Howell Harris, encouraged Lewis: "Your paper has been sweet and edifying to me and to others and I wish I could know how to promote the work." Despite well-wishers' offers to help, sales of the *Christian's Amusement* languished. Part of the problem was the growing,

[45] *Gentleman's Monthly* 9 (1739): 162.

[46] Plumb, *Commercialisation of Leisure*, 6–8; Susan Durden, "A Study of the First Evangelical Magazines, 1740–1748," *Journal of Ecclesiastical History* 27 (July 1976): 256–257; *The Christian's Amusement containing Letters Concerning the progress of the Gospel both at Home and Abroad etc.*, September 1740.

bitter, and widely publicized theological rift within evangelicalism between Whitefield and Wesley over predestination. In early 1741, Lewis confided to Harris that he was not "sell[ing] enough to pay for the paper and print." Seeking solace in his faith, Lewis wrote, "Know that myself and all my business are in his hands. Therefore if it be of God's will it will stand, if not, it will come to a nought." In that state of mind, Lewis must have viewed as providential Whitefield's expected arrival from America in March 1741. "I am willing to weather till Mr. Whitefield is amongst us," he wrote to a friend, "in hopes that he will both advise and assist me therein."[47]

Welcoming the offer of a printer to fashion a magazine for his own purposes, Whitefield effectively assumed management of the London-based magazine in April 1741, renaming it the *Weekly History*. In taking this initiative Whitefield fulfilled not only his longing to control an independent evangelical periodical but the desire expressed by other evangelicals for a publication dedicated to their cause. One subscriber noted that the "polite world have their Spectators, Tatler's, Guardian's, and Comedies," adding that "the Children of God also [should have] their proper entertainment, their weekly amusement, their divine miscellany, and the historical account of the progress of their Lord's kingdom." Whitefield responded to this demand by supplying editor Lewis with "fresh matter every week," including sermons, journals, and letters. According to many readers, the magazine fulfilled their desire for a periodical dedicated to evangelical news. One *Weekly History* subscriber wrote approvingly: "I have read over all the Weekly Papers, and the more I read, the more is my faith confirmed in the good Work that is going on."[48]

Consisting of four quarto pages, the weekly periodical circulated among several hundred subscribers primarily in England and Wales. While subscription figures are not available, itinerant preachers who aligned themselves with Whitefield delivered at least five hundred copies on their circuits. Interested in making the newsletter available to a wide readership, in 1742 Whitefield convinced Lewis to lower the price of a penny per copy to a halfpenny. Because the *Weekly History* also circulated through Whitefield's letter-writing network, evangelicals in Scotland and America either read it themselves or heard it read at society meetings or church services. Howell Harris illustrates how the

---

[47] Howell Harris to John Lewis, March 19, 1740; John Lewis to Howell Harris, ??1740; John Lewis to Mrs. James, January 31, 1740/41 in the Trevecka Collection at the National Library of Wales, Aberystwyth, Wales. Seward's observations located in William Seward's Diary, July–September, 1740, General Manuscript Collection, Chetham Library, Manchester.

[48] *Weekly History*, July 4, 1741, and February 20, 1742; Gillies, *Works of Whitefield*, 2:90.

magazine's readership expanded as volumes passed from hand to hand. In a letter to another Welsh itinerant, Daniel Rowlands, Harris wrote, "I have hereby sent you some of my *Weekly History* which when you have read I beg you would send them to Longhouse . . . and desire them to let Br. Howell Davies see them all and if he sees fit to take them all and show dear Mr. Griffith Jones." The paper also circulated among Whitefield's followers in the American colonies. Joseph Perriam, a young man Whitefield had taken to Georgia, referred to "look[ing] over the Accounts of the *Weekly History*" as a means of following the revival's progress in Britain and in the other colonies.[49]

By 1741, Lewis had relinquished editorial control to Whitefield, enabling the evangelist to determine content and format. Even while traveling in Scotland and America, Whitefield sent Lewis explicit instructions concerning what to include in the magazine. For instance, during his dispute with Wesley over human agency in salvation, from Savannah Whitefield directed the editor to print his side of the controversy in both the *Daily Advertiser* and the *Weekly History*. The paper became the official organ of the Whitefield Methodists, as the Calvinist branch of the movement became known. In autumn 1743, the paper assumed a new title, describing its purpose and scope: *Christian History or General account of the Progress of the Gospel in England, Scotland, America as far as the Reverend Mr. Whitefield, his fellow-labourers and Assistants are Concerned.*[50]

Whitefield influenced the shaping assumptions underlying the epistolary periodical. Under his leadership the accounts of the evangelical revivals became more optimistic than those compiled by Lewis, emphasizing successes while minimizing setbacks. Letters supportive of Whitefield's ministry appeared as uninterpreted, uncritical, firsthand reports, attesting to the advance of experimental religion. The seventh issue reprinted Rev. Josiah Smith's lengthy postscript published in the January 15, 1741, *South Carolina Gazette* containing "letters from several eminent ministers in Boston on Whitefield's reception in New England." The following issue printed accounts from two of those pastors, William Cooper and Benjamin Colman, testifying to the effectiveness of Whitefield's work among them. Subsequent editions printed testimonies from Gilbert Tennent of New Jersey and Jonathan Edwards of

[49] For circulation figures, see "London Tabernacle Minutes, 1743–47," in *Two Calvinistic Methodist Chapels, 1743–1811*, ed. Edwin Welch (London, 1975), 13. For decision to lower price of the *Weekly History*, see the issue for November 13, 1742. See also Durden, "First Evangelical Magazines," 262; Gomer M. Roberts, *Selected Trevecka Letters* (Caernarvon, 1965), 48; *Christian History*, April 11, 1741.

[50] See letter from George Whitefield to a Friend in London printed in *Weekly History*, May 2, 1741.

Massachusetts, and a conversion account from Hugh Bryan, a wealthy South Carolina planter who experienced the new birth under Whitefield's preaching.[51] The message was clear: Whitefield's revival was bearing fruit.

The *Weekly History* and its successors afforded Whitefield a vehicle for explaining his theology without the challenge of rival interpretations. Lewis dedicated all four pages of each issue exclusively to Whitefield's perspective. For instance, the fifth issue, published early in 1741, contains a long letter from Whitefield to a friend in London summarizing his views on original sin, divine election, and the necessity of the new birth. A letter from an English revivalist, Joseph Humphrey, follows, supporting Whitefield's sentiments against the Wesleyan notions of universal redemption and human perfection. A closing epistle from Whitefield argues that he had preached election before leaving for America in 1739, a response to critics who charged him with having only recently converted to Calvinism.[52]

The *Weekly History* served as a means of advertising evangelical writings endorsed or written by Whitefield. In the fifth issue, Lewis recommended a book entitled *The Perfectionists* primarily because it was prefaced by a letter from Whitefield refuting Wesley's doctrine of perfectionism. The editor, also a bookseller, publicized a new hymnal by John Cennick, another evangelical itinerant in England, emphasizing that the "hymns [were] commonly sung by the Reverend Mr. Whitefield." In advertising Colman's sermon *Souls Flying to Jesus Christ*, Lewis drew attention to an introduction giving a brief account of the "great and remarkable success that has lately attended the labours of the Rev. George Whitefield and Rev. Mr. Gilbert Tennent" in New England. Advertisements for Whitefield's own works appeared frequently, often conveying the promise of fresh material from the Grand Itinerant. In a typical advertisement, Lewis announced a "forthcoming volume of sermons, preached by the Rev. Mr. Whitefield: Never before printed."[53]

The *Weekly History* also provided evangelical shopkeepers and artisans with a new advertising vehicle. Lewis informed subscribers that he would accept advertisements for goods and services, and many enterprising tradesmen eagerly responded with copy. One woman appealed directly to her brothers and sisters in the faith. Her advertisement read: "Sister Betty Angus sells Holland Shirts of all Sorts, that come

[51] *Weekly History*, May 23 and 30, 1741.

[52] Ibid., May 2, 1741.

[53] See, for example, advertisements in ibid., June 6 and September 12, 1741, and June 5, 1742.

from Holland ready made; and Cambricks of all sorts, and Irish Cloth for shirts, and makes them for the Brethren very cheap; and handkerchiefs." Printers, tailors, stationers, and many others placed notices in the *Weekly History*. Whitefield had blurred the boundaries between the meetinghouse and the countinghouse. Selling consumer goods through revivalist periodicals permitted readers to identify themselves as believers while also peddling their merchandise.[54]

Ironically, John Lewis discovered that publishing the revivalist periodical restricted his market access. Some "common hawkers of News," he claimed, had informed their customers that Lewis refused to sell the magazine through peddlers, a charge the publisher vehemently denied. Lewis also indicated that "the printers of News [would] not advertise [the *Weekly History*] even though [he paid] 'em an extraordinary price for the same." They would, however, accept advertising copy from Lewis—a bookseller as well as a printer—for books and pamphlets. In a clever bit of deception, he frequently mentioned his magazine in advertisments for Whitefield's printed sermons and other evangelical works. "If we at any time are obliged to make use of the Wisdom of the Serpent," he wrote, justifying his ruse, "it should be for the glory of God."[55]

Inspired by the *Weekly History*, revivalists in Scotland and America produced weekly evangelical magazines. Rev. William McCullough began the *Glasgow Weekly History* in December 1741, borrowing heavily from material Lewis printed in his periodical. Of the more than 150 items McCullough included in his paper during the first six months of publication, almost 60 percent were "culled from Lewis." Then in November 1743, James Robe, a revivalist minister from Kilsyth, printed the first volume of another Scottish evangelical magazine, the *Christian Monthly History*. Robe intended his periodical "to encourage further conversions and to sustain those already converted." He hoped that "the good news of a great and effectual door being opened up to the Lord's servants . . . will . . . have a Tendency to make serious Impressions and awaken a concern upon Careless and secure sinners." In other words, Robe reprinted letters recounting personal experiences of the new birth to inspire others to examine their own spiritual lives.[56]

On March 5, 1743, Thomas Prince of Boston published the first issue of the *Christian History*, patterned after Lewis's London *Weekly History*. In advertising the new magazine, Prince announced that it would "be wholly confined to Matters of Religion, and no Advertisement inserted

---

[54] Ibid., August 1, 1741.
[55] Ibid., June 6, 1741.
[56] Durden, "First Evangelical Magazines," 266–267, 270.

THE

Chriſtian Hiſtory,

CONTAINING

ACCOUNTS

OF THE

Revival *and* Propagation

OF

RELIGION

IN

GREAT-BRITAIN &c AMERICA.

For the YEAR

I 7 4 3.

❖❖❖❖❖❖❖❖❖❖❖❖❖❖❖❖❖❖❖❖❖❖❖❖❖❖

B O S T O N, N. E.
Printed by S. KNEELAND and T. GREEN,
for T. PRINCE, junr. 1744.

4. *The Christian History*, evangelical magazine of
the Great Awakening. Courtesy of the Library
Company of Philadelphia.

but of Books and Pamphlets or other Things of a religious Importance." He indicated that the periodical would be printed on "large
Page [with] good Paper and Character" and would, at the rate of "2
shillings new Tenor per Quarter, [be] delivr'd at any House in Town
unenclosed; and 6d new Tenor more per Quarter, inclos'd, seal'd, and
directed." Prince filled his magazine with letters from colonial evangelicals as well as reprints from the *Weekly History* and the *Glasgow Weekly
History*.[57]

The revivalist magazines played an important role in promoting a

[57] *Christian History*, March 5, 1743.

transatlantic community among evangelicals. Indeed, forging links between experimental Christians in England, Scotland, and America was a stated purpose of the periodicals. Robe sounded the unitive theme: "to maintain the community of sincere Christians in present times." He contended that his magazine was "a choice Means to promote the Communion of Saints upon the Earth." After reprinting testimonials from Robe's publication, Prince commented on the shared experience of evangelicals throughout the Atlantic world. He observed that "the Method of the Spirit's Operation is alike in all these Congregations; and the Effects of it upon the Bodies of the awakened which have not been so common at other Times, are also much the same." By providing New Englanders with "fresh occurrences" of revivalism in Britain and other colonies, Prince presented the evangelical awakenings as interconnected—both intercolonial and transatlantic. A Scottish evangelical, the Reverend Mr. Willison, echoed Prince's sentiment upon reading about the revival in New England. He wrote of his reassurance upon "seeing the extraordinary Work there at present (tho' several Thousands of Miles distant from Scotland) is of the same Kind with that at Cambuslang, and other Places about [Scotland]." The evangelical magazine network papered over great distances, drawing likeminded men and women into one family of faith. And by including accounts of revivals of past ages, Prince and the other editors tied the current awakenings to a rich Puritan and Protestant tradition.[58]

THE PRINTED WORD

In addition to creating transatlantic revivalism through newspapers and magazines, Whitefield flooded the Atlantic world with his printed sermons and *Journals*. During 1737, the first year of his ministry, he published ten editions, primarily sermons. In 1738, the year of his first American trip, Whitefield saw thirty more works in print including six editions of his first of seven *Journals*. Then in 1739, the year he began his first preaching tour of America, he published almost ninety editions. While it is impossible to determine the size of each print run, records of those that do exist indicate a *minimum* of one thousand copies. That number was often doubled, tripled, or quadrupled when newspapers and magazines reprinted a work in whole or in part through serialization. Adopting what he termed a "print and preach" strategy, Whitefield bracketed his oral sermons with publications that first prepared men and women to hear the gospel and then reinforced

[58] Ibid., March 5 and April 9, 1743, and October 6, 1744.

the spoken word with a more enduring instrument. When he arrived in Philadelphia in October 1739, he found printers in Boston, Philadelphia, and New York publishing reprints of London publications.[59]

Whitefield's published discourses served as a means to attack opponents and encourage followers. Observing that "critics attacked his writing violently," Benjamin Franklin concluded, "I am of the opinion if he had never written anything, he would have left behind him a much more numerous and important sect."[60] Franklin believed that the itinerant's published sermons gave advantage to his enemies because, unlike statements delivered in preaching, "unguarded expressions and erroneous opinions" in print could not be "afterwards explained or qualified." Whitefield viewed his works differently. He intended to replace "bad books"—those written by such rationalists as Archbishop John Tillotson—with "good books": books adhering to Calvinist tenets. Whitefield encouraged his followers to display the badges of their new birth through material goods—the books they carried and the dress they wore. He exhorted them symbolically "to put on [their] cockades" that men and women would know them "to be Christ's."[61] His printed sermons also served as an advertisement for the kind of discourses auditors could expect at his services.

To thousands, the printed sermons had important symbolic significance. They represented the principles of the revival—primacy of the individual in salvation, renunciation of unconverted ministers, and emotional experience as the basis of true religion. Opponents like Charles Chauncy and Timothy Cutler of Boston noted the symbolic nature of the sermons, crediting their ubiquitous presence with perpetuating religious enthusiasm.[62] Printed sermons in Whitefield's revivals were analogous to consumer goods displayed by the followers of the radical English politician John Wilkes. Pro-Wilkes potters sold mugs, punchbowls, and other ceramic articles adorned with the candidate's political slogans. Mercers marketed "Wilkite" clothing such as coats with specially embroidered buttons, cuffs, and handkerchiefs. Other merchandise symbolizing the radical cause included tobacco pipes, candlesticks, and tankards.[63] All of these goods served as visible

[59] Number of publications calculated from Richard Owen Roberts, *Whitefield in Print: A Bibliographic Record of Works by, for, and against George Whitefield* (Wheaton, Ill., 1988).

[60] Lemay and Zall, *Autobiography of Franklin*, 107.

[61] Gillies, *Works of Whitefield*, 1:277, 6:406–407; Whitefield wrote a polemic against Tillotson and other rationalists entitled *A letter from the Reverend Mr. George Whitefield to a Friend in London Shewing the fundamental error of a book entitled The Whole Duty of Man* (Philadelphia, 1740). For Whitefield's view of goods as badges, see *Eighteen Sermons Preached by the Late George Whitefield* (Springfield, Mass., 1808), 249.

[62] See for example, Perry, *Historical Collections*, 2:350.

[63] See McKendrick, Brewer, and Plumb, *Birth of a Consumer Society*, 238–239.

means by which supporters identified with and participated in a movement. Similarly, Whitefield's supporters identified themselves with books, pamphlets, portraits, and wax likenesses of the revivalist.

Whitefield dispersed his sermons in large numbers, with publishers eager to satisfy the demand during the revival's peak years. From the first year of his ministry in 1737, the evangelist's discourses sold well. Of his sermon on the necessity of a new birth, the evangelist noted, "This sermon sold well . . . and was dispersed very much both at home and abroad." As he provided his bookseller, Hutton, with a steady supply of homilies for publication, he observed that they "were everywhere called for."[64] After first landing in Philadelphia, Whitefield authorized Franklin's rival, publisher Andrew Bradford, to print two of his sermons after Bradford forecast sales of one thousand copies, a significant press run for any publication in the mid-1700s.[65] In the spring of 1740, the itinerant reported to a London supporter that "God is pleased to give a great blessing to my printed sermons. They are now in the hands of thousands in these parts."[66]

Whitefield's *Journals* also sold well. In the summer of 1738, competition between publishers for rights to the first volume of Whitefield's *Journals* resulted in a windfall of publicity. The rivals, Thomas Cooper and James Hutton, advertised their editions on the same pages of the *Daily Advertiser* for a full week! They also engaged in a front-page debate over whose edition offered the more faithful rendition of Whitefield's manuscript. Cooper began the controversy in an August 3 advertisement: "This day is publish'd (Price 6d) *A Journal of a Voyage from Gibraltar to Georgia* by George Whitefield, B. A." The next day, Hutton countered by indicating that "whereas a surreptitious copy of the Reverend Mr. Whitefield's journal is advertised by Thomas Cooper without the author's approval, . . . this is to give notice, that in justice to Mr. Whitefield, his journal from London to Savannah in Georgia will speedily be published, (for little more than prime cost) with a preface giving the reasons of the publication by me, James Hutton." Cooper maintained that his edition's authenticity would be substantiated when Hutton's version appeared "unless Hutton and friends alter the original." The matter ended when Cooper accepted Hutton's offer of "a sum of money that [Hutton] might have the impression deliver'd up to him to burn."[67]

While no evidence points to Seward's involvement, someone as shrewd and zealous as he is very likely to have placed copies of White-

---

[64] *Whitefield's Journals*, 86.
[65] Ibid., 360.
[66] Gillies, *Works of Whitefield*, 1:167.
[67] See issues of *Daily Advertiser* from August 3 through August 8, 1738.

field's diary in the hands of two rival printers. The itinerant had mailed the document to Hutton, at the time an ardent supporter. Seward may have forwarded his copy to Cooper. Whatever the case, the competing advertisements heightened interest in the *Journals*, increasing their sales and thus promoting the revivals.

From his first entry on December 28, 1737, Whitefield intended his *Journals* for an audience. After arriving in Savannah in May 1738, the evangelist sent the first edition, fifty-eight octavo pages, to an evangelical religious society in London. In a prefatory note, Whitefield wrote, "According to your request I have herewith sent you an account of what God has done for my soul since I left England." After Cooper and Hutton published his first volume, Whitefield wrote six more *Journals* for publication.[68] In the preface to his second installment the itinerant explained his views on printing subsequent volumes: "Though the Journals already published were printed without my knowledge, yet as God has been pleased to let me see, by letters sent to me, that He has greatly blessed them, I now, upon the importunity of friends, consent to the publishing a Continuation of them, that those pious persons who have interceded in my behalf, may see what God, in answer to their prayers, has done for my soul."[69] No doubt Whitefield was also heartened by brisk sales.

Whitefield's *Journals* were made available in a variety of sizes and at different prices. All seven volumes appeared in octavo, and most in pocket versions, either duodecimo or sextodecimo. The *Journals* contained a total of 485 pages spanning the period December 1737 to March 1741, with individual volumes ranging from the 38-page second installment to the 115-page third volume. As Whitefield became more popular and demand for his works increased, publishers raised the prices of the *Journals*. In 1738, James Hutton charged subscribers sixpence for the first volume. The seventh volume, released in 1741, commanded a shilling in London, a 100 percent increase. In America, Benjamin Franklin sold Whitefield's *Journals* for eightpence, or threepence more than he charged for his popular almanac.[70]

A comparison of Whitefield's *Journals* with that written by the Quaker leader George Fox serves to illustrate the special character of the evangelist's work. While Fox dictated his journal at the age of fifty when he was a prisoner in Worcester near his ministry's end, Whitefield recorded his activities and thoughts daily during the beginning of his

[68] *Whitefield's Journals*, 97.

[69] Ibid., 154.

[70] See Austin, "Bibliography of Works of Whitefield," 169–181. For information concerning Franklin's editions of Whitefield's journals, see Leonard W. Labaree, ed., *The Papers of Benjamin Franklin*, 29 vols. (New Haven, 1960–1992), 2:248.

itinerancy in his early twenties. The young revivalist provided much greater detail, devoting almost five hundred pages to a period of three years, compared to Fox's nearly eight hundred pages spanning twenty-four years. And the accounts differ in tone. Before publication, a Friends' editorial committee "removed some of the vigorous touches" in Fox's journal in order to render "the whole . . . quieter" and to avoid offense. Whitefield's work reflects the raw quality of a hastily written document, usually recorded at the end of the day. It reflects the exuberance of youth and the censoriousness of a partisan. Whitefield's *Journals* were self-promotional, intended to generate support for his revivals by revealing the young evangelist as leader of a second Reformation.[71]

Whitefield's *Journals* publicized the evangelist and his mission. While viewing God as the sole dispenser of grace, Whitefield perceived himself to be a divine instrument. Shortly after arriving in Pennsylvania in 1739, Whitefield compared his wandering through America to the travels of the biblical patriarchs. On November 3, Whitefield wrote, "Methinks going thus from place to place with my friends, somewhat resembles the patriarch Abraham's frequent removes, when called to leave his kindred and his native country." Noting that word of his disembarkation had preceded him, the itinerant added, "[God] hath sent His angel before us to prepare our way."[72] Whitefield's descriptions of his effects on colonial society were intended to confirm his divine commissioning. His entry for July 19, 1740, depicted in some detail the transformation in Charleston, South Carolina, since his arrival:

> At my first coming, the people of Charleston seemed to be wholly devoted to pleasure. One, well acquainted with their manners and circumstances, told me that they spent more on their polite entertainments than the amount raised by their rates for the poor. But, now the jewellers and dancing-masters begin to cry out that their craft is in danger. A vast alteration is discernible in ladies' dresses; and some, while I have been speaking, have been so convinced of the sin of wearing jewels, that I have seen them, with blushes, put their hands to their ears, and cover them with their fans.[73]

One notes that Whitefield's assessment was couched largely in the language of goods; his ministry had altered consumption patterns. And his mission had competed successfully with that of parish clergymen.

[71] Norman Penney, ed., *The Journal of George Fox*, 2 vols. (Cambridge, Eng., 1911), 1:xv.

[72] *Whitefield's Journals*, 341.

[73] Ibid., 444.

Whitefield's *Journals* were polemical as well as promotional. He drew sharp distinctions between his message of the new birth and the rationalism he charged clergymen with preaching. As he departed New England on October 29, 1740, he wrote about the region's ministers: "Many, nay most that preach, I fear, do not experimentally know Christ." Attacking institutions as well as people, Whitefield railed against Harvard. Again casting his message in market terms, he charged that "bad books are become fashionable among the tutors and students." He lamented that rationalists such as Samuel Clark and Archbishop Tillotson had replaced evangelical writers like Thomas Shepherd and Solomon Stoddard.[74] When he revised his *Journals* in 1756, Whitefield conceded that he had written "too rashly of the colleges and ministers of New England." He determined to "own and publickly confess my public mistakes."[75] Many of his followers, however, approved the author's original version, which seemed to breathe the fire of the old Puritan divines.

When publishing his magazine, sermons, or *Journals*, Whitefield considered the reader as a consumer. He wrote for a mass audience including the poor. In a letter to his fellow evangelist James Hervey, Whitefield disclosed his plans to sell four sermons for sixpence, noting that he wrote "for the poor, you for the polite and noble." While Hervey selected for one of his works "a very neat paper, with an elegant type," Whitefield instructed his printer to reduce paper costs for a sermon "designed for the poor . . . [because] the poor must have them cheap."[76]

Whitefield employed a number of innovative merchandising techniques to reach a larger audience. One of the marketing strategies he favored was serial publication of his sermons and *Journals*. Introduced by imaginative publishers earlier in the eighteenth century, "this method of weekly publication allure[d] multitudes to peruse books, into which they would otherwise never have looked."[77] To exploit the potential for selling "big, expensive books," publishers began to offer the reader a volume in affordable portions, so many pages per week or month "at a cash price so low that he cannot possibly resist."[78]

By serializing his *Journals*, Whitefield not only made purchasing eas-

[74] Ibid., 462.

[75] Gillies, *Works of Whitefield*, 2:248.

[76] Ibid., 141, 479; Luke Tyerman, *The Oxford Methodists: Memoirs of the Rev. Messrs. Clayton, Ingham, Gambold, Hervey, and Broughton, with Biographical Notices of Others* (New York, 1873), 250.

[77] *Grub-Street Journal*, October 26, 1732.

[78] See R. M. Wiles, *Serial Publication in England before 1750* (Cambridge, Eng., 1957), 133–194.

ier but created a heightened sense of anticipation as readers followed the evangelist's progress toward their own communities. From 1737 through 1741, the formative years of his transatlantic revivals when promotion was most needed, he wrote and published the seven volumes of his *Journals*. At the end of the first, describing events from his departure from England to his arrival at Savannah, he wrote, "I . . . close this part of my Journal," setting the stage for an ongoing account. He also serialized his spiritual autobiography. In 1740, during his second passage to America, he wrote for publication the first part of his life, designed to inform readers of important events and influences up to the time of those described in the first installment of his *Journals*. At the close of the first of two volumes, he wrote, "I shall hereafter relate God's further dealings with my soul, and how He led me into my present way of acting." Advertisements for subsequent volumes of both the *Journals* and the autobiography emphasized the "latest edition" or "most recent account."[79] About every six months, the itinerant sent new editions to his publishers on both sides of the Atlantic.

Whitefield also published sermons in serialized form. In 1739 he agreed to the fourteen-week serial publication of *The Christian's Companion: or, Sermons on Several Subjects*. Each week subscribers received one sermon of approximately twenty-four pages for twopence. Although each sermon had a separate fascicule signature, pagination was continuous through the 336 pages.[80] By offering the discourses for a low price per unit, booksellers and hawkers could augment subscription sales by selling individual volumes.

Whitefield stimulated publication sales through creative pricing schemes. Recognizing that merchants like Thomas Noble of New York bought hundreds of books and sermons for distribution, Whitefield offered quantity discounts. The sermon on the new birth sold for "six pence; or two guineas per hundred for those who give them away," the latter terms representing a 16 percent discount.[81] Through John Lewis, Whitefield offered a cash discount to encourage early payment for subscription sales.[82] Through flexible pricing Whitefield expanded the market for his publications and simultaneously extended the scope of his publicity.

Whitefield best displayed his merchandising acumen in efforts to increase the *Weekly History's* sagging circulation and bolster its anemic revenue. At Whitefield's insistence, late in 1742 John Lewis announced

---

[79] *Whitefield's Journals*, 70, 152.

[80] Wiles, *Serial Publication*, 315, 320.

[81] See title page of George Whitefield, *Nature and Necessity of Our New Birth in Christ Jesus, in order to Salvation* (London, 1737).

[82] *Weekly History*, September 18, 1742.

his intention "to begin next in a more commodious manner as we are likely to be furnished with more materials," no doubt from the evangelist himself. The editor pledged "to let our readers have more reading for their money"; by changing the layout and removing the large title, they liberated "much [more] room for useful reading." And for consumer convenience, the magazine would be made available in pocket-size, perhaps an innovation Whitefield borrowed from Benjamin Franklin, who produced a pocket-size version of his almanac. Lewis also promised home delivery, dispensing the magazine at "people's houses, at the price of one penny." Through such imaginative merchandising, Whitefield and his associates reversed the fortunes of the publication, which survived past the revival's decline.[83]

Whitefield's promoters also recognized the value of consumer goods bearing the preacher's name or image for publicizing and funding the revivals. After William Seward returned to London from America in 1740, he employed the evangelist's latest printed works as premiums to solicit contributions for Whitefield's humanitarian work in the colonies. In the July 3 edition of the *Daily Advertiser* Seward advertised preaching services to be held at Moorfields and Kennington Common "for the Benefit of the Negro-School in the Province of Pennsylvania." As an incentive to attend and contribute, Seward announced that donors would receive copies of either Whitefield's report on the progress of the orphan house or his attack on the rationalist work *The Whole Duty of Man*.[84] Others attempted to profit from consumer goods related to the popular revivalist. One entrepreneur advertised in the *Weekly History* a picture of Whitefield along with a "parallel between him and the renowned Wickliff" available for sale at threepence.[85] The itinerant was not the only person to benefit from his popularity.

Whitefield was more an astute borrower than an innovator in advertising. Merchants who viewed markets as restricted to a fixed number of clients did not advertise to create consumer demand. Instead, they merely provided information about the availability of their goods and the terms of sale. However, English capitalists in the eighteenth century expanded both domestic and foreign markets and advertised in order to exploit what they considered to be an elastic consumer demand.[86] With a similar view, Whitefield sought to generate interest in his revivals through aggressive advertising. Opponents protested "the various methods taken up by Mr. Whitefield and his adherents, for

---

[83] Ibid., November 13, 1742.

[84] *Daily Advertiser*, July 3, 1740.

[85] *Weekly History*, June 27, 1742.

[86] See Daniel Boorstin, "Advertising and American Civilization," in *Advertising and Society*, ed. Yale Brozen (New York, 1974), 11–23.

trumpeting abroad his fame, and magnifying his person and performance."[87]

Whitefield recognized that negative as well as positive publicity could generate interest in his revivals. Especially during his first three American trips, the evangelist engaged in polemics to differentiate his message of the new birth from what he considered the "stirrings of dry bones," rattling from unconverted ministers. In a published letter to the students at Harvard and Yale, he charged both colleges with allowing their "light [to] become darkness." That incendiary tract attacking cherished institutions sparked a heated exchange of supporting and opposing publications. Whitefield wrote of the debate: "A few mistaken, misinformed good old men are publishing halfpenny testimonials against me." However, he agreed with Benjamin Colman that his opponents had done him a "real service" by giving the evangelist's friends an opportunity to "publish testimonials in [his] favour."[88]

Whitefield recorded in his *Journals* an example of how opponents' published charges served in the end to benefit him and the revival because they kept readers' attention focused on him. Upon arriving in a small community in North Carolina in December 1739, the evangelist met an old man whose curiosity regarding the revival had been raised through newspaper reports attacking the itinerant. Whitefield noted that "this was not the first time, by many, that I have found the advantage of the things my adversaries have inserted in the public papers: they do but excite people's curiosity, and serve to raise their attention." He was unworried about printed attacks because people of "seriousness and candour naturally infer that some good must be doing where such stories and falsities are invented."[89]

Testimonials and endorsements were key elements in Whitefield's publicity. They introduced and recommended him to a local community. For instance, when he first arrived in Boston in 1740, he brought with him a strong testimonial from Josiah Smith, a Harvard-educated preacher in Charleston, South Carolina. A friend of Benjamin Colman, Smith testified to the positive changes Whitefield's preaching had wrought in Charleston. He extolled the itinerant's oratorical prowess and pronounced his theology orthodox. Whitefield delivered the document to Colman and another leading clergyman, William Cooper. Both Colman and Cooper wrote their own endorsements of the evangelist as a preface to Smith's testimony and published the whole as a pamphlet promoting the revival. Whitefield continued to benefit from

[87] *South Carolina Gazette*, June 18, 1741.
[88] Gillies, *Works of Whitefield*, 2:76.
[89] *Whitefield's Journals*, 373.

the testimony by reprinting it in the *Christian Weekly* and circulating it throughout the letter-writing network.[90]

[handwritten: Used ALOT of publication to get the word out. Knew how to keep his name in papers. Any publicty = Good publicty]

THE PRINT TRADE AND REVIVALISM

[handwritten: Was endorsed, name became tridemark.]

Printers and booksellers supported Whitefield, in part because he was good business, but throughout his ministry the evangelist maintained an ambivalence toward the print trade. Whitefield's description of his first encounter with a printer seeking to publish one of his works illustrates the booksellers' competitive world and the young preacher's conflicting perceptions of publishing. In his diary entry for May 9, 1736, along with the usual notations concerning his religious devotions for the day, the Oxford student mentioned that he had received a letter from Charles Rivington, a London printer best remembered as publisher of Samuel Richardson's epistolary novels *Pamela* and *Clarissa*. Always looking for new authors, Rivington had been given Whitefield's name by Thomas Broughton, a member of the Holy Club and an official in the Society for the Promotion of Christian Knowledge (SPCK), a voluntary organization that published religious works at low costs. Although Whitefield was not ordained, Rivington sought to preempt rival printers by securing the promising evangelical's future printing business.[91]

Although elated, Whitefield was wary of Rivington's overtures, for he read in the print trade's potential two disparate messages. Anticipating a means of disseminating the message of the new birth to a wide audience, Whitefield recorded in his diary his conviction that "surely God has some design in bringing on me this new acquaintance." Subsequent events proved the relationship to be mutually fruitful. A year later, Rivington published Whitefield's first printed sermon, *The Nature and Necessity of a new Birth in Christ*. The sermon "sold well to persons of all denominations, and was dispersed very much both at home and abroad, [resulting in a] second impression . . . soon called for."[92] Yet Whitefield feared that the publicity and popularity accompanying the publication could lead to the sin of pride. Seeking divine protection from the alluring world, he penned a prayer, "Lord, keep me from climbing." As evangelicals eagerly purchased his early writings, Whitefield implored a friend, "Entreat the God of all grace to give me humility so shall success not prove my ruin."[93]

[90] *Christian History*, January 12 and 19, 1744/45.
[91] See Whitefield's manuscript diary, British Library.
[92] Ibid.; *Whitefield's Journal*, 86.
[93] See Whitefield's diary.

Whitefield sought to resolve his dilemma by relying on evangelical booksellers to publish his works. Through his participation in London religious societies, Whitefield made the acquaintance of two book-sellers, James Hutton and John Syms. While Syms acted as Whitefield's business agent, distributing books through other itinerants and ac-counting for revenues, Hutton became the revivalist's primary pub-lisher from 1738 through 1740. The son of a bookseller and a fervent evangelical, Hutton sold early Methodist hymnals, catechisms, and de-votional books for use in revival services. Whitefield and Wesley relied upon Hutton to keep them supplied with an adequate inventory for worship. While preaching for a fortnight in Bristol during 1739, John Wesley wrote Hutton an urgent message requesting "50 more Hymns [by] next Friday." Seward maintained an account with Hutton and authorized the bookseller to ship large quantities of sermons to both Wesley and Whitefield to distribute among their audiences. Located near Temple Bar, Hutton's shop served as the London postal drop for evangelicals, in particular that small band of supporters known as the Fetter Lane Society.[94] Hutton's major role was that of Whitefield's pub-lisher. Having forced Thomas Cooper to cease printing the rival ver-sion of Whitefield's *Journals* in 1738, Hutton sought exclusive publica-tion rights to the revivalist's works. Concerned about others' releasing pirated versions of the evangelical's writings, Hutton placed an adver-tisement in the *Daily Advertiser*: "the publick is desir'd to take notice that the Reverend Mr. Whitefield has frequently advertised under his own hand that no sermons or other works, said to be his, are genuine unless they are printed for James Hutton." Indeed Whitefield had expressed concern over unauthorized, and in some cases inaccurate, versions of his works. However, Hutton's motive may have been more mercenary. According to Whitefield, Hutton made "hundreds" from publishing the popular itinerant's books and pamphlets.[95]

In publishing Whitefield's works, Hutton relied on one of England's foremost printers, William Strahan. The relationship between Strahan and Whitefield continued beyond 1741 when Hutton embraced Mora-vianism and refused to publish Whitefield's writings. Indeed, Strahan and Whitefield maintained a mutually beneficial association lasting most of the evangelist's ministry. It was in Strahan's financial interest to print the preacher's huge output of sermons, *Journals*, and letters, and Whitefield gained a savvy business adviser and generous creditor. By 1739 Strahan had already established himself as one of England's lead-

[94] George Eayrs, ed., *Letters of John Wesley: A Selection of Important and New Letters* (London, 1915), 93, 99.

[95] *Daily Advertiser*, July 18, 1739. For Whitefield's comments on Hutton's profiting from printing the evangelist's works, see Gillies, *Works of Whitefield*, 1:256.

ing printers, building a reputation that would attract such authors as Edward Gibbons, David Hume, Adam Smith, and Samuel Johnson. In addition to printing Whitefield's books and pamphlets, Strahan became a banker for the evangelical, extending large amounts of credit. Printing costs constituted Whitefield's single greatest expense, and Strahan enabled the revivalist to flood the Atlantic world with print even when he had insufficient cash.[96]

Whitefield had overlapping but not coextensive interests with members of London's print trade. Insofar as printers and booksellers promoted and distributed his works to a wide audience, their hopes for large sales converged with Whitefield's concern for disseminating the gospel beyond the reach of his voice. Publishers promoted the revivalist's ministry through extensive advertising of his printed works. Booksellers recognized Whitefield as an author who had "made sermons, once a drug, a vendible commodity."[97] Consequently, enterprising publishers vied with each other to exploit the lucrative demand for the evangelist's writings. In one issue of the *Daily Advertiser*, for instance, a print-seller advertised a portrait of Whitefield, "neatly engrav'd from a drawing taken by an excellent painter," and on the same page, a bookseller advertised two of the evangelist's sermons plus a collection of prayers "recommended by George Whitefield."[98] In the mid-eighteenth-century Anglo-American world, the name "Whitefield" sold, and those in the print trade competed vigorously to capitalize on it.

In addition to publicizing Whitefield by advertising his works, publishers distributed his sermons and *Journals* through bookselling networks. One example will suffice to demonstrate how books published in London circulated through a provincial distribution chain. In 1738, a London bookseller, J. Hodges, published a collection of Whitefield sermons, *Several Discourses Upon Practical Subjects*. On the title page Hodges listed booksellers in seven other towns where readers could purchase copies. Following a crescent-shaped distribution pattern, the consortium of booksellers extended from London to the north through Oxford, west through Gloucester, into southern Wales, and southward to Bristol, ending at Bath.[99] Spanning the heart of White-

[96] See J. A. Cochrane, *Dr. Johnson's Printer: The Life of William Strahan* (London, 1964), 69. See also Robert D. Harlan, "William Strahan's American Book Trade, 1744–76," *The Library Quarterly* 31 (July 1961): 235–244.

[97] See Josiah Smith, *The Character, Preaching, etc., of the Reverend Mr. George Whitefield, Impartially Represented and Supported, in a Sermon, Preach'd in Charlestown, South-Carolina, March 26th 1740* (Boston, 1740).

[98] *Daily Advertiser*, December 25, 1737.

[99] See title page of George Whitefield, *Several Discourses Upon Practical Subjects, The*

field's greatest support during the first year of his ministry, Hodges's network represented the bookseller's best hopes for sales and the evangelist's desires for reinforcing the spoken word.

Booksellers did not always act in Whitefield's best interest. Sometimes they published unauthorized versions of his sermons, misrepresenting the evangelist to his readers. Throughout his ministry Whitefield warned against pirated editions of his works. After one of his first preaching journeys to Scotland, a Scot, Joseph Gurney, published a collection of the itinerant's sermons reconstructed from Gurney's shorthand notes. Whitefield charged Gurney with numerous editorial mistakes resulting in an adulterated text. A London bookseller, S. Bladen, published Whitefield's last sermon without the revivalist's permission. Protesting to a supporter, Whitefield encouraged his correspondent to "advertize against the publisher . . . [because] he makes me to speak false concord, and even nonsense." Whitefield concluded that "the sense and connection are destroyed, [and] the whole is entirely unfit for the public review." Despite the mediation of a print trade that permitted pirated and erroneous publications, Whitefield continued to hope his printed works would spread the gospel. "If one sentence is blessed to the conviction and edification of any single individual," he wrote, "I care not what becomes of my character," even through poorly edited publications.[100]

Printers also influenced the reception of evangelical works by publishing critical reviews. Whitefield's friend and fellow member of the Oxford Holy Club, James Hervey, expressed his anxiety as he awaited a forthcoming assessment of his book *Theron and Aspasia*, published in 1754. Hervey had asked Whitefield to read his manuscript and offer criticisms for revision. After Whitefield played "critic [and] . . . mark[ed] a few places," he returned the work to Hervey, who expressed his appreciation for Whitefield's "revising my poor compositions, which, I am afraid, you have not treated with becoming severity." In his letter to Whitefield, Hervey reported on critiques that were beginning to appear in periodicals. Hervey wrote, "the author of the *London Magazine* has taken notice of *Theron and Aspasia* and, really, in a very respectful and honourable manner." Sensing that other reviewers would be less charitable, Hervey informed Whitefield, "I will hear my sentence from the *Gentleman's Magazine* next month." When it appeared in February 1755, the review justified Hervey's fears. Dismissing the book as a "compendium and a defence of Calvinistic divinity," the reviewer chas-

---

Arguments of Which may be Collected from the Contents. To Which is added, The Oxford Methodists (London, 1738).

[100] Gillies, *Works of Whitefield*, 3:406.

tised Hervey for ignoring Enlightenment principles of inquiry. The critic charged Hervey with attempting proof, not "by principles of reason, but by quotations from scripture." While no record exists of reader reaction to the review, its very appearance indicates that evangelicals, like other writers, operated within print media outside their control.[101]

Hervey and Whitefield also found themselves at odds with publishers' pricing policies. Whitefield refused to write a recommendation for a two-volume edition of Benjamin Jenk's *Meditations* because he feared it was too expensive.[102] Concerned that Samuel Richardson, Hervey's printer, was preparing a volume of his works that would be too expensive for most evangelicals, Hervey protested, insisting on publishing "two small pocket volumes" as well as the more expensive octavo version. Pursuing "spiritual prosperity." Hervey operated at cross purposes with Richardson and his publisher, Charles Rivington. "I write not for profits," Hervey avowed, "but to serve the cause of God." Advertising a new edition of Hervey's works, Rivington announced that "there will be five thousand volumes ready for sale," to which Hervey responded, "Oh may they be five thousand trumpets to proclaim far and near the glories of Him who died for our sins and rose again for our justification." It was not that Whitefield and Hervey were indifferent to profits—indeed, Whitefield sought profits to fund charities—but that their goal was to distribute as many evangelical works as possible, which often meant publishing less expensive works than printers and publishers desired.[103]

Whitefield turned the print trade more to his purposes by becoming a part of it as publisher, bookseller, and distributor of his own works. After 1741, when Hutton refused to publish Whitefield volumes because of the bookseller's growing Moravian convictions, Whitefield assumed greater control over his publications. He had already established himself in the evangelical marketplace, with many of his sermons and all his *Journals* appearing in multiple editions and reprints. He had easy access to public newspapers on both sides of the Atlantic as well as the *Weekly History* to promote his ministry and his books and pamphlets. And with the establishment of the Tabernacle, a church building near Moorfields in London, Whitefield had a headquarters for publishing and distributing his works.[104]

---

[101] Tyerman, *Oxford Methodists*, 279, 300. *Gentleman's Magazine* 25 (1755): 130.

[102] Gillies, *Works of Whitefield*, 3:194.

[103] Tyerman, *Oxford Methodists*, 240–241, 262.

[104] Whitefield acquired property for his tabernacle in Moorfields on March 16, 1753. See lease for forty-three years in the British Library, Miscellaneous Papers, Add. Ch. 46,346. For operation of Book Room see Welch, *Two Calvinistic Methodist Chapels*.

Over the course of his ministry, Whitefield published more volumes under his own name or that of the Tabernacle than did any other publisher. Even before the split with Hutton, Whitefield frequently published individual sermons in his own name. In 1739, eight sermons were "printed for C. Whitefield" (the initial appears to be a misprint). In 1740, the number increased to nine. One can only wonder at Hutton's reaction to Whitefield's intervention in the print trade. Strahan continued as Whitefield's printer but increasingly printed directly for the revivalist. In 1743, for example, Strahan printed "for the Author" the sixth edition of *A Journal of a Voyage from London to Savannah in Georgia*. But Whitefield published evangelical works other than his own. In 1755, he published *The Believer's Knowledge of a Living Redeemer*, a sermon written by one of his itinerant associates, Thomas Adams. He also republished such Puritan classics as the martyrologist John Foxe's *A Sermon of Christ Crucified*, which originally appeared in 1570. "I chose to publish it," Whitefield wrote in a preface, "that you might have a specimen of that foolishness of preaching which, in the days of our forefathers, was so mighty, through God, to the pulling down . . . of the outward strongholds of popery."[105]

Whitefield edited as well as published evangelical works. In 1755, he published *A Communion Morning's Companion*, a revivalist handbook for use during the Eucharist. To demonstrate his orthodoxy concerning communion, Whitefield "thought it most advisable . . . to extract the Meditations and practical Remarks on the public form of Administration from our own Bishops." He "particularly fix'd on Bishop Ken [of Winchester] . . . because his set Meditations on the Redeemer's Passion were some of the first Things that made a religious Impression on [Whitefield's] own Soul." In 1748, Whitefield published an abridgement of William Law's *Serious Call to a Devout Life*. Explaining his editing, Whitefield said he sought to "render Mr. Law's *Serious Call* more useful to the Children of God, by excluding whatever is not truly Evangelical, and illustrating the subject more fully from the Holy Scripture."[106] As editor, Whitefield could shape others' works to conform with his own objectives.

Whitefield enjoyed tremendous advantages in selling and distributing his printed works. First, he recommended his own publications to

---

[105] See George Whitefield, *A Journal of a Voyage From London to Savannah in Georgia*, 6th ed. (London, 1743). Thomas Adams, *The Believer's Knowledge of a Living Redeemer* (London, 1755). Foxe, *A Sermon of Christ Crucified*, ii.

[106] See preface of George Whitefield, *A Communion Morning's Companion* (London, 1755), 2. Whitefield's abridgement of William Law's *Serious Call* was entitled *Law Gospelized; or, an Address to All Christians Concerning Holiness of Heart and Life* (London, 1748), cited in Gillies, *Works of Whitefield*, 4:375.

his audiences. He frequently lingered after services, autographing and distributing large numbers of his printed sermons. Second, he publicized forthcoming works by placing advertisements in works already in publication. For example, Whitefield announced in one of his *Journals* that he was preparing a sermon for the press entitled "The Indwelling of the Spirit," which he heartily "recommend[ed] to all." Because the sermon was publicized in the *Journals*, which appeared in five editions, it was a huge success, creating sales that resulted in five editions for the sermon as well.[107] Thus Whitefield advertised forthcoming works in best-selling volumes, paving the way for other best-sellers.

Whitefield circulated his writings through a transatlantic letter-writing network. Long before the Great Awakening, evangelicals on both sides of the Atlantic had corresponded with each other, reporting their successes and needs in propagating the gospel.[108] Jonathan Edwards had been a prolific letter-writer, sending accounts of the western Massachusetts revivals in the mid-1730s to English revivalists. Thus, Whitefield borrowed an established mode of communication to publicize his ministry and distribute his books and pamphlets. As he corresponded with like-minded persons, Whitefield frequently enclosed copies of his publications. To a ship's captain sailing to America via Bermuda, Whitefield wrote: "With this I send a box of books to be disposed of among my dear Bermuda acquaintances." He added, "I have sent half a dozen volumes of my volume of twenty-three sermons to be disposed on [along] with the small tracts." To another individual, the itinerant penned, "With this I send you the promised pamphlet with a single eye . . . to promote the Mediator's glory." Recipients of Whitefield's publications often extended circulation by reading and forwarding volumes to others. After acknowledging receipt of "the Continuation of [Whitefield's] Journal," one R. Pearsall wrote in 1739 from Bristol, "I sent your first journal to a friend of mine att a distance." More than fifteen hundred of Whitefield's letters survive, many of them alluding to enclosures to be read and distributed.[109]

Whitefield established a reciprocal relationship with correspondents in the letter-writing network. Ralph Erskine, a Scottish Presbyterian evangelical, asked Whitefield to "send any Print" he could spare, including the revivalist's own publications and any newspaper accounts of the revival. Upon receiving a parcel from Whitefield, Erskine replied, "I received . . . Six of your last Sermons . . . with some of the

---

[107] Gillies, *Works of Whitefield*, 4:303. *Whitefield's Journals*, 303.

[108] For an illuminating description of the evangelical letter-writing network, see O'Brien, "A Transatlantic Community of Saints."

[109] Gillies, *Works of Whitefield*, 2:165, 3:64. R. Pearsall to George Whitefield, March 5, 1739, in Whitefield Manuscript Letters, Evangelical Library, London.

former Sermons [which] I gave to the Brethren." In return, Erskine pledged to "send [Whitefield] the Prints relating to our Publick Affairs in the associate Presbytery." Upon receiving such papers, Whitefield forwarded them to Lewis for publication in the *Weekly History*.[110]

Another effective distribution mechanism was the network of evangelical religious societies. Whitefield communicated to his most faithful followers through societies—small bands of Pietists in Britain and America who met weekly for prayer and exhortation. At least once monthly, at a meeting designated Letter Day, members read letters and printed material from Whitefield and other itinerants describing the success of the gospel. Whitefield's colleague Howell Harris stated the purpose of these special days: "to provide a means to strengthen the people's faith and to stir up them to liberality as well as to gratitude." At the close of each session, the leader took a collection for the evangelists' support. In 1740, writing from America to a London society member, Whitefield sent "one of each sort of the pamphlets [he] had published" in the colonies, requesting that his correspondent send them on to Scotland after reading them.[111]

Whitefield also circulated his works by becoming a bookseller himself. In 1741 Whitefield established a Book Room at the Tabernacle. He appointed John Syms to supervise all operations concerning the publication and distribution of revivalist works. Syms's responsibilities included securing low-cost printing of Whitefield's works as well as those Whitefield published. He corresponded with evangelical itinerants urging them to promote Whitefield's publications in their travels. Indeed, his correspondence closely resembles that of any wholesaler trying to entice retailers to carry more of his merchandise. In a representative letter to Howell Harris in Trevecka, Wales, Syms offered the evangelist "nine bound Journals (which [normally] sell for 4s a piece) . . . binding and lettering being done in the best manner but shall charge you only 1.10.0 for them." By offering a 16 percent discount, Syms hoped to encourage Howell to purchase the volumes. In addition to quoting low prices, Syms relied on Whitefield's endorsement as an inducement to buy. In 1745, Syms accompanied Whitefield to America and sent Herbert Jenkins, a London evangelical minister, several volumes of Thomas Prince's *Christian History*, "well bound in calf and lettered on the backs," emphasizing that "Mr. Whitefield recommended them to his friends here very much." After Syms joined the Moravians in 1745, Thomas Boddington, a merchant, became the book

---

[110] Ralph Erskine, *A Letter from the Reverend Mr. Ralph Erskine to the Reverend Mr. George Whitefield* (Philadelphia, 1741), 4.
[111] Gillies, *Works of Whitefield*, 1:134–135.

steward at the Tabernacle, continuing to urge evangelicals to purchase Whitefield's printed works.[112]

By reprinting a work in different publications, Whitefield widened the readership for his writings. For example, in 1740 while preaching in South Carolina, Whitefield engaged Peter Timothy of Charleston to print a pamphlet entitled *A Letter From the Rev. Mr. Whitefield from Georgia, to a Friend in London, Shewing the Fundamental Error of a Book Entituled The Whole Duty of Man*. Shortly afterwards, upon arriving in Philadelphia, Whitefield gave Benjamin Franklin a copy, and the Pennsylvania printer first reprinted it in his *Pennsylvania Gazette* and then published the document as a pamphlet. In April, Seward took a copy to London where it appeared as a reprint in the *Daily Advertiser*. Then Seward included the letter in *A Collection of Papers Lately Printed in the Daily Advertiser*, which was printed and "sold by the Booksellers in Town and Country" for sixpence. Eager to print anything bearing the popular preacher's name, printers on both sides of the Atlantic accommodated Whitefield's desire to convey his printed message to as many people as possible.[113]

Thus as Whitefield sailed for America in August 1739 to begin his first colonial preaching tour, he departed England with boxes of publications to distribute in the colonies. He also took with him two years' experience in publicizing his ministry through the print trade. He would arrive in Philadelphia to find Pennsylvanians well prepared for his visit after months of newspaper coverage. Indeed, Philadelphia's *American Weekly Mercury* reprinted Seward's initial report of Whitefield's success at St. Swithin, complete with superlatives describing the evangelist's preaching and fund-raising.[114] Even in Virginia with a dispersed population and an Anglican establishment, Whitefield's name was well known. Writing in 1738, the prominent Tidewater planter William Byrd revealed his knowledge of the famous preacher, describing an outdoor religious service on the Virginia-Carolina border as "Devotion being perform'd in the Open Field, like that of Mr. Whitefield's Flocks." Perhaps Byrd had read of Whitefield in London newspapers or in the *Virginia Gazette*, which had reported the evangel-

[112] John Syms to Howell Harris, November 5, 1743; John Syms to Herbert Jenkins, November 30, 1745. Both letters are in the Trevecka Collection at the National Library of Wales, Aberystwyth.

[113] Whitefield's polemic appeared first as George Whitefield, *A Letter From the Rev. Mr. Whitefield from Georgia, to a Friend in London, Shewing the Fundamental Error of a Book, Entituled The Whole Duty of Man* (Charles-Town, S.C., 1740). Editions of the same title were reprinted in 1740 in Philadelphia and London. Reprints also found in the *Pennsylvania Gazette*, April 10, 1740, and *Daily Advertiser*, July 2, 1740.

[114] *American Weekly Mercury*, January 24, 1738.

ist's services as unparalleled in preaching to "so great a concourse of people."[115] At any rate, Whitefield arrived in America well equipped to implement his "print and preach" strategy.

[handwritten margin notes: - Some printers against him. & Printed criticisms of his sermons, etc. - Went to America in 1733 for evangelical tour - Sold books himself - worked w/ evangelical printers.]

THE "PEDLAR IN DIVINITY"

Whitefield shared with the new merchants of the consumer revolution not only similar strategies but a common view of elastic market demand. Improvements in communications and marketing enabled traders to escape the "cosseted constraints" of local markets and sell their goods to strangers at great distances. And increased disposable income resulting from falling agricultural prices in the first half of the eighteenth century prompted merchants to consider means of selling consumer goods to the middling and poorer people, not just the wealthy.[116] In a similar way, Whitefield discovered in the new merchandising techniques vehicles for conveying the new birth's necessity to people far beyond the confines of a single local parish, or the entire Anglican church, or even the very boundaries of Britain itself. Although subscribing to the Calvinist doctrine of election, Whitefield believed that God used the "meanest instruments" to awaken sinners to his grace. Hence, the evangelist felt compelled to employ every means—even those "the world" used to merchandise its baubles—to deliver the gospel to all people.

As Whitefield succeeded in generating unprecedented crowds, he raised the ire of those who opposed his violation of traditional ecclesiastical boundaries and clerical conduct. The Boston rationalist Charles Chauncy protested the way Whitefield hawked religion like a traveling salesman peddling his wares, objecting especially to the itinerant's weekly advertisements of his preaching schedules and results. An anonymous writer to the *Boston Weekly News-Letter* proposed a remedy for the evangelist's blatant commercial activities in the name of religion. The correspondent wrote that as there was "a very wholesome law in the province to discourage Pedlars in Trade," the time had arrived "to enact something for the discouragement of Pedlars in Divinity also."[117] These outcries point to one of the greatest ironies of the

[115] *Virginia Gazette*, December 30 to January 6, 1937/38.

[116] McKendrick, Brewer, and Plumb, *Birth of a Consumer Society*, 198.

[117] Chauncy's attitude toward Whitefield's publicity found in Charles Chauncy, *A Letter from a Gentleman in Boston to Mr. George Wishart, concerning the state of religion in New England* (Edinburgh, 1742). Comment on "Pedlars in Divinity" in *Boston Weekly News-Letter*, April 22, 1742.

Great Awakening: the Calvinist Whitefield embracing mass marketing. While Chauncy and other proto-Unitarians rejected Whitefield's Calvinism as narrow and decidedly un-enlightened, they also denounced his innovative, rational adaptations of the latest commercial means to propagate his message to vast audiences.

- Some didn't like the way Whitefield "sold" religion like a hustler on the street.

CHAPTER 3

Creating an Intercolonial
Revival

THROUGHOUT the 1720s and 1730s evangelical preachers sparked revivals from New England to New Jersey. In his long pastorate at Northampton, Massachusetts, Solomon Stoddard reported five "harvests" of souls in the Connecticut Valley between 1679 and 1718. In the late 1720s, the Pietist minister Jacob Frelinghuysen inspired a renewal of piety among the Dutch Reformed in New Jersey. At the same time the Presbyterian evangelists William and Gilbert Tennent led revivals in churches they had established between New Brunswick, New Jersey, and Staten Island, New York.[1] Stoddard's grandson, Jonathan Edwards, succeeded him and led a spiritual awakening in 1734–1735 resulting in the "Conversion of Many Hundred Souls in Northampton and Neighbouring Towns and Villages." While sharing a common message, these evangelical revivals remained local, private affairs, contained within specific geographic and denominational boundaries. Although each proclaimed the necessity of a spiritual new birth and the primacy of divine grace in salvation, the awakenings did not expand and fuse into a larger, united movement.[2]

George Whitefield's arrival in October 1739 changed the scope and character of colonial evangelical revivals. The itinerant, whose English successes had inspired American evangelicals, connected the local awakenings, fashioning them into an intercolonial movement—crafting a national event before the existence of a nation. He proclaimed the message of the new birth in every colony through the spoken and printed word. And he lifted the revivals out of narrow denominational constraints by helping to create a "religious public sphere," in which supporters and opponents of revivalism debated the Great Awakening before a literate, rational, and independent audience.[3] Whitefield's transformation of revivals into a national, public

---

[1] For discussion of colonial revivals prior to Whitefield's arrival in 1739, see John Gillies, *Historical Collections Relating to Remarkable Periods of the Success of the Gospel, and Eminent Instruments Employed in Promoting it* (Glasgow, 1754), 282–297.

[2] This chapter represents a highly revised version of my article "Subscribing for Profits and Piety: The Friendship of Benjamin Franklin and George Whitefield," *William and Mary Quarterly* 50 (July 1993).

[3] The concept of a religious public sphere is developed in T. H. Breen, "Retrieving

event took place largely outside churches and meetinghouses. Continuing the practice developed in England, he preached in marketplaces and employed newspapers to reach a mass audience. The network of colonial newspapers represented a necessary if not sufficient explanation of the Great Awakening.[4]

Whitefield introduced a new model of revivalism to America, a paradigm which contrasted with that employed by Edwards. Edwards embraced a communal approach in which a community's pastor led the entire village or town in a spiritual awakening. Conversion led to reform in this local perspective. Specifically, Northampton's revival resulted in an observable change of behavior among the town's youth. Before the revival, young people had, according to Edwards, roamed the lanes and roads in loud boisterous gangs; afterwards they began to convene for prayer and exhortation. Whitefield, on the other hand, lifted his gaze beyond a community and preached to all who would listen. He delivered his message to a mass audience consisting of disconnected individuals throughout the colonies. In the words of one historian, Whitefield set out "to transform the entire nation."[5] His intercolonial vision demanded a strategy different from that favored by Edwards and others who viewed revivalism in congregational terms. Whitefield found commercial strategies better suited for his mission.

Historians have generally overlooked the press's role in Whitefield's transformation of colonial revivalism. While noting that advance publicity prepared men and women for the itinerant's visits, most scholars have focused on the evangelist's oratory and the large crowds he attracted. A reexamination of his use of the press reveals what was distinctive about Whitefield, separating him from earlier revivalists such as Edwards and Tennent. An inquiry into Whitefield's employment of print need not reduce the story to an McLuhanesque subordination of message to medium. Central to Whitefield's appropriation of print was his conviction that persons everywhere should hear the gospel.

Whitefield's exploitation of the colonial press sharply distinguished him from his evangelical predecessors. While Edwards wrote an ac-

---

Common Sense: Rights, Liberties, and the Religious Public Sphere in Late Eighteenth-Century America," in *Rights in American History*, ed. J. F. Pachesco (forthcoming). The religious public sphere is discussed in chapter 5.

[4] Although Whitefield did not use the term "Great Awakening" in capitalized form, he did refer to revivals as a "general awakening" and a "great awakening." He viewed the awakening of the 1740s as intercolonial, extending from "Georgia, [to] South-Carolina, New-York, Philadelphia, and New-England." Revivalism would not sweep Virginia and North Carolina until the 1750s and 1760s. See [The Banner of Truth Trust], *Letters of George Whitefield; For the Period, 1734–1742* (Edinburgh, 1976), 188, 242.

[5] For different conceptions of revivalism, see Michael Crawford, *Seasons of Grace: New England's Revival Tradition in Its British Context* (New York, 1991), 165.

count of the Connecticut Valley revival of 1734–1735, he did not publish his account until 1736, months after the awakening had subsided, and then only at the urging of the Boston minister Benjamin Colman.[6] And the Tennents failed to promote their revival by exploiting the newspaper rivalry between Philadelphia's leading printers, Andrew Bradford and Benjamin Franklin. Indeed, Gilbert Tennent's name did not appear in the *Pennsylvania Gazette* or the *American Weekly Mercury* until after Whitefield's arrival had woven local spiritual stirrings into an intercolonial event. By contrast, Whitefield publicized his itinerancy through a "print and preach" strategy that inundated the colonies with pamphlets, broadsides, and newspaper articles. He particularly exploited the expanding network of colonial newspapers, inserting third-person accounts of his revival services including reports he wrote himself. Having developed a bold, innovative press campaign in England from 1737 to 1739, the Grand Itinerant arrived in America as a well-publicized success with advance publicity designed to attract large crowds to his services. As a result, Whitefield crafted a new religion out-of-doors, beyond parish boundaries and clerical authority.

EXPLOITING THE INTERCOLONIAL PRINT NETWORK

When Whitefield began his first American preaching tour in 1739, he had access to a thriving colonial print trade operating in British North America. Learned seventeenth-century settlers who could afford to purchase books had depended almost exclusively on English imports. For most, the Bible and perhaps a devotional guide constituted the extent of private libraries. Printed works were expensive, especially when freight and insurance costs increased prices for colonists. Having to import paper, local printers published very few works. In 1677, colonial printers produced only 15 titles, and these came from two presses, Samuel Green's in Cambridge and John Foster's in Boston. By 1700, six printers in three towns—Boston, Philadelphia, and Annapolis, Maryland—published a total of 65 titles. Then in 1739 when Whitefield arrived, sixteen print shops in nine locations ranging from Boston to Charleston, South Carolina, printed 136 works. Through this more extensive print trade Whitefield was able to circulate his books and pamphlets in all the colonies. Because print shops catered primarily to a local clientele, Whitefield frequently had the same piece reprinted in several different cities. For instance, in 1740 he released a theological apology simultaneously in Boston, New York, and Phila-

[6] Miller, *Jonathan Edwards*, 136–137.

5. Benjamin Franklin, Whitefield's friend and and printer.

delphia. Printers also sold books through chapmen and booksellers in remote places. Benjamin Franklin regularly sent Whitefield's works to shops operated by his sister-in-law in Newport, Elizabeth Timothy in Charleston, Jonas Green in Annapolis, and William Parks in Williamsburg. In comparison with colonial evangelicals fifty years earlier, Whitefield enjoyed a far more extensive print trade, enabling him to disseminate large numbers of identical works to colonial readers who could read them at roughly the same time.[7]

The establishment of an intercolonial network of newspapers also

[7] Publication data found in Evans, *American Bibliography*, 1:42–44, 1:139–148, 2:136–151.

enabled Whitefield to publicize his revivals throughout British America. In 1700, there were no colonial newspapers. By 1739, almost a dozen weeklies operated in five cities from Boston to Charleston. For two years before his arrival, Whitefield had appeared as news in colonial papers. Publishers reprinted articles from England describing enormous crowds and large donations as well as mounting opposition to the evangelist. Newspapers not only publicized Whitefield and the revivals but presented them as news—events occurring in the present. When colonial readers followed Whitefield's progress first across Britain and then throughout the colonies, they read about a religious event taking place within an imagined world newspapers made possible. Papers routinely carried stories about current matters that directly influenced readers' lives—wars, disasters, coronations, recessions. Now colonists read about a religious event, heralded as a second Reformation, that was spreading across the Atlantic world. Some took in the news with anticipation, others with skepticism, but no doubt nearly all with curiosity.[8]

Because paper was the major expense in printing, local papermaking represented a breakthrough for colonial printers, enabling them to provide their wares at competitive prices. Thomas Fleet, publisher of the *Boston Evening-Post* claimed that paper "stands us in near as much as all the other charges." By importing English-manufactured paper, which bore shipping and insurance costs, colonial printers paid higher prices than did their London counterparts. In 1730, Daniel Henchman of Boston, "having petitioned for, and received some aid from the legislature of Massachusetts, erected a paper mill, which was the first set up in that colony." Richard Fry, a Boston "Stationer, Bookseller, PaperMaker, and Rag Merchant," advertised for rags to make paper at his Milton mill and reported receiving rags "upward of Seven Thousand Weight." Because Fry made his own paper, he was able to sell printed goods at lower prices. For instance, Fry advertised in the *Weekly Rehearsal* that he would "sell all Sorts of Accompt Books done after the most acute manner, for Twenty per Cent cheaper than they can have them from London." Eager to control his business from papermaking to postal delivery, the enterprising Benjamin Franklin invested in paper mills to ensure a reliable supply of inexpensive paper for the *Pennsylvania Gazette*. By 1775 paper was manufactured "in all parts of the union."[9]

The establishment and improved efficiency of an intercolonial postal

---

[8] For growth of colonial newspapers, see ibid.

[9] Thomas, *History of Printing in America*, 1:211–213. Fleet cited in 2:234. *Weekly Rehearsal*, May 1732.

service helped Whitefield attain his goal of delivering the gospel to every colony. In the seventeenth century, individual colonies ran their own postal services. In 1639, Massachusetts Bay Colony appointed Richard Fairbanks to "take care that [letters] bee delivered, or sent according to their directions, and hee is alowed for every such letter a 1d." Soon thereafter, local merchants initiated a monthly postal service between Boston and New York City. Then in 1692, Whitehall intervened by granting a royal patent to Thomas Neale "to establish and organize postal services in America." In justifying such action, the patent noted that "there never yet hath bin any post established for the conveying of Letters within or between Virginia, Maryland, Delaware, New York, New England, East and West Jersey, Pennsylvania, and Northward as far as our Dominions reach in America." The lack of an intercolonial postal network produced "a great hindrance to the Trade of Those parts." Progress in actually connecting all British North America under a unified postal system proved difficult given the enormous distances and numerous waterways that had to be traversed.[10]

However, by 1739 when Whitefield arrived, reports of progress appeared in the colonial press. William Parks, publisher of the *Virginia Gazette*, announced in the June 22, 1739, issue a new packet service south of Virginia. Parks claimed that for the first time "a communication may be carried on, by Post, all the way from Piscataway and Boston in New England, thro' the principal Towns and Places in New York, Pennsylvania, Maryland, Virginia, North Carolina to Charles-Town in South Carolina, and from thence there are frequent opportunities to Georgia." He concluded that the result would "certainly be a great benefit to the Public, and particularly to the trading part of it."[11] While Parks's report may have been too optimistic, the convergence of its timing with Whitefield's visit points to a significant advantage the revivalist enjoyed over earlier colonial evangelicals in being able to reach an intercolonial audience.

Whitefield took advantage of advances in the colonial print trade to extend his message to all colonies. Although he attracted his largest crowds in the commercial centers of Boston, New York, Philadelphia, and Charleston, his revivals reached the remotest parts of British America. During his 1739–1740 American trip, he traveled to and preached in every colony. After leaving Philadelphia in late November 1739, Whitefield rode horseback through Delaware, Maryland, Vir-

[10] Alex L. ter Braake, ed., *The Posted Letter in Colonial and Revolutionary America* (State College, Pa., 1975), B.1, B.4–5.
[11] *Virginia Gazette*, June 22, 1739.

ginia, North Carolina, and South Carolina, to Georgia. The farther south he traveled, the more dismal prospects appeared for a spiritual awakening. In Virginia and Maryland, irreligion reigned because of "people living at a distance" from the few churches scattered among a dispersed population.[12] He observed that "in North Carolina there is scarcely so much as the form of religion."[13] Yet, despite the obstacles, Whitefield spread the message of the new birth throughout the region in the spoken and printed word. Because of the absence of a concentrated population and a newspaper network, the evangelical awakening unfolded much more slowly in the Chesapeake and Lower South. The seeds Whitefield sowed in 1739–1740 would not bear fruit until the 1750s and 1760s.

Although unable to preach to large crowds or write in widely circulated local newspapers, Whitefield disseminated the gospel even in the backcountry of the Lower South. A decade earlier William Byrd had described the remoteness of North Carolina, measuring its distance from Virginia in cultural as well as spatial terms. His enduring memory of Edenton, North Carolina, was a "Dirty Slash [ditch] run[ning] all along the Back of it, which in the Summer is a foul annoyance, and furnishes abundance of that Carolina plague, musquetas." His description of the town's religious life was no more flattering: "I believe this is the only Metropolis in the Christian or Mahometan World, where there is neither Church, Chappel, Mosque, Synagogue, or any other Place of Publick Worship of any Sect or Religion whatsoever."[14] Yet as Whitefield approached Edenton on December 19, 1739, he discovered that even there men and women knew about him through the press and longed for his visit. One old man informed Whitefield that his son-in-law who lived three miles away had read of the evangelist in the newspaper—a striking testimony to the wide circulation of colonial newspapers and to their importance in publicizing the revivals.[15]

Durham, New Hampshire, was another remote village Whitefield reached through his market strategy. Although pastor Nicholas Gilman resided in a "somewhat remote location in Durham, New Hampshire," he kept abreast of revival news from the Boston press. He reported reading Whitefield's life, *Journals*, *Sermon on Religious Societies*, and *Answer to the Bishop of London's Pastoral Letter*. Moreover, Gilman followed the revival's progress by reading accounts printed in the *Bos-*

---

[12] *Whitefield's Journals*, 388

[13] Ibid., 389.

[14] *William Byrd's Histories of the Dividing Line Betwixt Virginia and North Carolina* (New York, 1967), 96.

[15] *Whitefield's Journals*, 373.

ton Gazette. From the pulpit, Gilman apprised his parishioners of the awakening.[16]

Whitefield widened the revival's scope by exploiting commercial distribution channels that delivered English goods to the remotest parts of British North America. By 1740, Scottish factors crisscrossed the backcountry of the Chesapeake and Carolinas peddling their wares through country stores and chapmen. Their inventories included bundles of Whitefield's sermons and *Journals*. Residents of Hanover County, Virginia, missed Whitefield on his trips through their colony in 1739 and 1740, but they acquired a volume of his printed sermons from a Scottish peddler. It was a "book of his sermons preached in Glasgow and taken from his mouth in short Hand."[17] Until they found a pastor, the layfolk worshiped by reading Whitefield's sermons aloud.

Through reading Whitefield's sermons, the Virginians spread the revival. Acting as a surrogate preacher, a layman, Samuel Morris, began to read the sermons aloud at meetings attended by ten to twelve faithful souls. While the writings of reformers like Martin Luther had introduced the members to "the Way of Justification," the "Concern was not very extensive." But when Morris read Whitefield's works, "many were convinced to seek deliverance with the greatest solicitude." As the readings continued, the group grew too large to meet in homes and built its first meetinghouse. Unable to find a suitable pastor—that is, one who was evangelical and Calvinist—these dissenting evangelicals continued to rely on Whitefield's printed sermons. "When the report of these Sermons and the effects occasioned by reading them was spread Abroad," Morris reported, he was invited to several places to read them, and "by this Means the concern was propagated." Centering their worship on Whitefield's printed sermons, the group survived and evolved into the first Presbyterian church in Virginia.[18]

To convey his message to native Americans living west of English settlements, Whitefield relied upon Indian traders. His greatest opportunities came from peddlers who themselves had experienced the new birth. Whitefield noted in his *Journals* that a Pennsylvanian who hawked his wares to Indians had been converted and was willing to become a lay exhorter among his Allegheny clients. The evangelist prepared a trea-

---

[16] Cited in Crawford, *Seasons of Grace*, 164. Through print, the revivals spread throughout the period 1737–1745. By viewing revivalism primarily in terms of the spoken word, historians have understated the scope of the Great Awakening. See Jon Butler, "Enthusiasm Described and Decried: The Great Awakening as Interpretive Fiction," *Journal of American History* 69 (September 1982): 302–325.

[17] Samuel Davies, "The State of Religion Among the Protestant Dissenters in Virginia" (1751), in *The Great Awakening: Event and Exegesis*, ed. Darrett Rutman (New York, 1970), 46–51.

[18] Ibid.

tise especially for the Indians and gave it to the trader. "I laid down the principles of our Holy Religion," he wrote, "wherein I . . . told them the promises of the Gospel, that had especial reference to them, and cautioned them against such things as I thought might be a hindrance to their embracing Christianity." In the letter, Whitefield couched the gospel in language familiar to native Americans, avoiding ecclesiastical jargon. However, the revivalist believed that little success could be expected in evangelizing Indians without developing lay exhorters among the various tribes. Toward that end he supported Eleazor Wheelock's Indian School and solicited English funds to provide theological education for native Americans.[19]

• Used everything he could to spread his beliefs around colonial America

WHITEFIELD AS NEWS

The November 15, 1739, *Pennsylvania Gazette* report of Whitefield's arrival in Philadelphia indicates that Franklin viewed the evangelist as news. Describing one of the revivalist's first services, the article noted that he "preached from the Court-House Gallery to 6000 [who] stood in an awful Silence to hear him." Announcing his intercolonial itinerary for the next twelve month, the account added that Whitefield "designs to preach the Gospel in every Province in America."[20] Thus Franklin reported what he considered to be an important current event: the arrival, preaching, and plans of a young Anglican minister who had made a stir in England.

Almost two years earlier Franklin had introduced Whitefield to his readers in a news account. William Seward, Whitefield's traveling companion and press agent, had paid for an announcement to be printed on the front page of the London *Daily Advertiser*. The September 19, 1737, edition indicated that Whitefield was about to sail for America to preach the gospel in Georgia. The article appeared in other London papers including the *Grub Street Journal*. Perhaps James Ralph, a writer in Grub Street, sent the paper to his friend Franklin. More likely Franklin, a subscriber to several London newspapers, noticed it himself. Two months after it appeared in London, Franklin reprinted the story in the *Pennsylvania Gazette*, a paper "Containing the freshest Advices Foreign and Domestick."[21] As publisher, Franklin deemed the story worthy of notice. To him the piece qualified as news, the eighteenth-century meaning of "advices."

[19] *Whitefield's Journals*, 428.
[20] *Pennsylvania Gazette*, November 15, 1739.
[21] Ibid., December 22–29, 1737.

Viewed from the present, the announcement hardly qualifies as news. To us the notice seems unexceptional; surely Whitefield was not the only Anglican minister to sail for America. But news, as "the reporting of current public occurrences," is contingent upon the social context of time and place.[22] To Franklin in mid-eighteenth-century Philadelphia, it was newsworthy. Perhaps the word "voluntarily" caught the entrepreneur's eye. Here was a gentleman traveling to the colonies who was not a missionary sponsored by the Society for the Propagation of the Gospel in Foreign Parts (SPG) or any other organization; rather, he was embarking with no apparent financial support other than his own resources—a religious entrepreneur. Maybe it was the destination that attracted Franklin's attention. Georgia was the newest colony, only four years old and struggling. Or the name "Whitefield," with daily references in London papers, represented a current metropolitan fad that aroused Franklin's curiosity. Whatever the reason, Whitefield became news in America soon after his name first appeared in English newspapers.

For six months prior to Whitefield's arrival, Franklin carried stories of Whitefield and the evangelical revival he had sparked in England. Perusing English papers for news, Franklin reported those aspects of Whitefield's ministry which were novel. Readers of the *Pennsylvania Gazette* noted the extraordinary crowds that gathered to hear the evangelist: "at Rose-Green [near Bristol] there were upwards of 20,000," and at Kennington Common outside London similar throngs assembled. Franklin reported unusual circumstances surrounding Whitefield's services: strange pulpits for delivering outdoor sermons such as "a Tomb-Stone in Islington Church Yard" and equally bizarre pews such as tree limbs. Colonists learned of the growing opposition to Whitefield, who accused Anglican clergymen of renouncing Protestant doctrines. To Pennsylvanians, Whitefield had become the center of a major news story they followed in Franklin's *Pennsylvania Gazette* and in the rival *American Weekly Mercury*, published by Andrew Bradford.[23]

Whitefield qualified as news because his ministry was current, that is, occurring in the present. He presented himself as an instrument of God to declare the necessity of a new birth to a generation he depicted as being in a deep spiritual sleep. As he attracted great crowds, Whitefield reported successes in newspaper reports of a "great awakening." After itineraries that took him throughout England, Scotland, Wales,

[22] The discussion on news is based on and enriched by insights developed in David P. Nord, "Teleology and News: The Religious Roots of American Journalism, 1630–1730," *Journal of American History* 77 (June 1990): 9–38.

[23] See *Pennsylvania Gazette*, May 31 and June 28, 1739.

and America, Whitefield proclaimed that a great awakening had spread all over the Atlantic world.[24]

Whitefield's ministry as presented in newspapers was more than novel and unique; it was also recurrent, an "intermingling of past and present."[25] As he sailed across the Atlantic on his first American preaching tour, Whitefield linked current evangelical revivals with the fervent religious faith of the seventeenth-century Puritan founders of New England. He associated his mission with that of "the venerable Cotton, Norton, and Elliot, and that great cloud of witnesses, which first crossed the Western ocean for the sake of the gospel, and faith once delivered to the saints." Many gave currency to the frequent jeremiads denouncing the decline of faith; "by reading the newspapers," they once again encountered "the good old Puritans."[26]

For readers of the *Pennsylvania Gazette*, accounts of Whitefield also meant anticipation. In addition to being a newsworthy event in England, Whitefield's ministry was exportable: it was coming to the colonies. The man who was attracting enormous crowds and defining a new expression of religion-out-of-doors had announced his intention to conduct a preaching tour of British America. Expectant Philadelphians must have been disappointed in summer 1739 to read that the evangelist had been delayed when merchant crews all along English coasts had been impressed into His Majesty's service. Finally, the November 8, 1739, issue of the *Pennsylvania Gazette* reported Whitefield's landfall at Lewistown, Delaware.[27] For the next fourteen months, Franklin would shift accounts of Whitefield's activities from "Foreign" to "Domestick" advices.

When Whitefield arrived in the colonies on October 30, he had already shaped a public perception through the press. He had fashioned a message that placed him in the Reformation tradition in opposition to the Church of England, which he depicted as betraying Reformed theology. Whitefield had carefully crafted his public persona as a special instrument selected by God to proclaim anew the necessity of the new birth. Writing in promotional language as well as in theological discourse, Whitefield presented himself as a well-publicized success. Just as colonists read about an expanding choice of consumer goods "recently arrived from England," they read about one who came offering them a new religious experience, a choice in a marketplace of religion that he extended beyond parish borders.[28] And by promoting

---

[24] Gillies, *Works of Whitefield*, 1:366.
[25] Nord, "Teleology and News," 10.
[26] Gillies, *Works of Whitefield*, 1:255–256.
[27] *Pennsylvania Gazette*, August 16–23 and November 8, 1739.
[28] For a colonial view of Whitefield as recently arrived English import, see [Herman

his revivals in all the colonies, Whitefield helped unite men and women from disparate regions in a common experience.

Whitefield's preaching tour rivaled England's declaration of war against Spain as the leading intercolonial news story of 1739–1740. His revivals enjoyed extensive newspaper coverage. Seventy-five percent of the *Pennsylvania Gazette*'s issues during the fourteen months he spent in America devoted space to Whitefield, often including reports of his successes and itineraries, reprints of his publications, and advertisements for his writings. The April 17, 1740, issue, for example, followed the evangelist's progress as he approached Philadelphia from Savannah on his spring preaching tour. It summarized his activities before his departure from Charleston, South Carolina, noting that he had "preached five times and collected seventy pounds sterling at one sermon for the [Georgia] orphan house." The account noted that Whitefield had exhorted a crowd of three thousand in Wilmington, Delaware, before arriving in Philadelphia where he addressed eight thousand on Society Hill. The next issue, April 24, reported fully on his previous week, indicating that he had preached twice on Sunday at Society Hill, attracting fifteen thousand in the evening and collecting more than £230 for the orphanage. The article concluded with an appraisal of Whitefield's effectiveness, declaring that "the congregations were much melted."[29]

Newspapers also published Whitefield's itineraries, an important means of promoting the revivalist as well as his services. The May 8, 1740, issue of the *Pennsylvania Gazette* set forth the evangelist's schedule for the following week: "Whitefield preaches in Philadelphia every day this week. Then he preaches at Darby and Chester where he plans to collect for the Orphan House. On Tuesday at precisely 10:00 in the Morning he preaches at Wilmington. Then Four O'clock in the Afternoon at Whiteclay Creek. Wednesday noon at Nottingham. Then to New Castle to sail for Georgia."[30] Seward provided Franklin with accounts of Whitefield's previous week's activities and the following week's plans, presenting a portrait of an industrious itinerant whose parish really was the entire British Atlantic world.

In addition to the frequency of newspaper coverage, Whitefield benefited from space allotted him within single editions, attesting to widespread interest. William Bradford often devoted the entire front page of the *New York Gazette* to the evangelist's letters, journals, endorsements, and testimonials. In the November 19, 1739, issue, Bradford

Husband], *Remarks on Religion, with the Author's Experience in Pursuit thereof* (Philadelphia, 1761), 207–210.

[29] *Pennsylvania Gazette*, April 17 and 24, 1740.

[30] Ibid., May 8, 1740.

allotted three and a half of the newspaper's six pages to Whitefield, who had recently arrived from Philadelphia. The publisher reserved two-thirds of the next week's edition for the itinerant. All of the front page plus one inside contained reprinted portions of Whitefield's *Journals*, describing his successes prior to New York. Additional space was given over to Whitefield's texts for sermons preached in New York, a favorable assessment of his exhortations, and a poem proclaiming him "commission'd from on high." A year later, after Whitefield returned to New York from his New England tour in late 1740, Bradford continued his extensive coverage. The front page of November 6 included a lengthy letter of recommendation from William Cooper, a prorevivalist Boston minister, and an endorsement of the evangelist's character from Josiah Smith, a supporter from Charleston.[31] During the Great Awakening, Britain's war with Spain was the only other event that commanded as much attention in colonial newspapers as Whitefield's revivals.

Although remote from population centers, newspapers in the Chesapeake and Lower South also found Whitefield newsworthy. The *Virginia Gazette* carried stories of the itinerant in a third of its 1740 issues despite Whitefield's being in the colony for less than one week during the year.[32] In seventeen of the *South Carolina Gazette*'s fifty-two issues published between the summers of 1740 and 1741, the major, front-page story was a heated controversy between Whitefield and his supporters and their opponents. The disputes centered on whether Whitefield's "enthusiasm" was acceptable behavior for an Anglican minister. Its persistence as a news item suggests that revival controversy was good business for the newspaper. Indeed, the *Gazette*'s publisher, Peter Timothy, expanded his paper, printing full-page inserts submitted by Whitefield supporters.[33]

News-hungry newspaper publishers facilitated Whitefield's construction of an intercolonial revival. Preaching imposed obvious restrictions on the itinerant: at any given time he could appear at only one place. Print allowed him to extend the spatial and temporal dimensions of his mission, giving him an audience reaching far beyond the sound of his voice. While he preached in one location, men and women throughout the colonies participated in the revivals by reading newspaper accounts of his progress, scanning advertisements of his printed works, following pamphlet wars between supporters and opponents, or

[31] *New York Gazette*, November 19, 1739 and November 6, 1740.

[32] See 1740 issues of the *Virginia Gazette*.

[33] For the religious controversy, see *South Carolina Gazette*, May 17, June 26, July 5, 12, 19, August 1, 23, September 13, 20, 26, October 2, 16, 30, and November 6, 1740. For special edition, see January 15–22, 1741.

reading one of his sermons. Whitefield's exploitation of the press was central to his making the Great Awakening a national event, binding "the separate revival movements into a great unified effort."[34]

Jonathan Edwards's invitation to Whitefield to visit Northampton provides a clue illuminating the itinerant's publicity strategy.[35] Twice Edwards mentioned "Mr. Seward," a reference to William Seward, who routinely sent news of the awakening's progress to leading evangelical clergy and laity throughout the Atlantic world, including Edwards, Colman, and Tennent.[36] Seward and Whitefield not only fashioned a publicity campaign unprecedented in revivalism; they also developed an intercolonial evangelical network through which they distributed printed works, especially newspaper articles.

A group of antirevivalist laymen attributed Whitefield's tremendous reception in Boston to advance publicity. Referring to the volume of newspaper reports and to their exaggerated claims, they noted that "his Name and Character were very great among us before his Arrival. He had made such a Noise and Bustle in Europe and America," they continued, "that the Expectations of the People and their Curiosity were very much rais'd both to see him, and hear him preach." Whitefield's self-promotion after his arrival represented to the laymen "a somewhat crafty Improvement of the Advantageous Circumstances and Character under which he arriv'd."[37] Although they opposed the evangelical's ministry, the laymen acknowledged Whitefield as a shrewd and artful manipulator of public opinion, especially skilled in exploiting the press.

Chauncy and Whitefield differed in their interpretations of the revivalist's newspaper advertisements. Chauncy found the weekly publication of Whitefield's itineraries "ostentatious and assuming." He objected to the evangelist's "proclaiming his Intentions in the public Prints to preach such a Day in such a Parish, the next Day in such a one, and so on" on the grounds that in most places neither pastors nor people had invited him. To Chauncy, such advertisements suggested that the regular ministry was not meeting their parishioners' spiritual needs and reflected Whitefield's presumption that his brand of religion represented success where settled ministers had failed. Whitefield re-

[34] Jerald Brauer, *Protestantism in America: A Narrative History* (Philadelphia, 1965), 50.

[35] Henry Abelove, "Jonathan Edwards' Letter of Invitation to George Whitefield," *William and Mary Quarterly* 29 (July 1972): 488–489.

[36] For Seward's role as press agent see Seward, *Journal of a Voyage*. Other traveling companions who handled Whitefield's press affairs included John Syms, Robert Cruttenden, and Whitefield's wife, Elizabeth.

[37] *The Testimony and Advice of a Number of Laymen Respecting Religion, and the Teachers of It* (Boston, 1743), 3.

plied to Chauncy's published charges with a pamphlet of his own. Whitefield acknowledged his advertising in the "publick Prints" but denied that his practice "proceeded from Ostentation. As I was a Stranger passing thro' the Country," he explained, "and so many either out of Curiosity or some other Principle were desirous to hear me, it was judged expedient by my Friends to give People previous and publick Notice of my Intention to preach among them."[38] Just as merchants employed newspaper advertising to alert customers to newly arrived merchandise, Whitefield announced his plans to proclaim what he considered to be a timely message.

In addition to enabling men and women to anticipate Whitefield's preaching, his intercolonial newspaper coverage allowed local evangelicals to participate in the intercolonial revival after his departure from a given town. Following his second trip to New England in 1744–1745, New Englanders read of the itinerant's activities when he embarked on a journey that would end at Bethesda, his orphanage near Savannah. Whitefield forwarded to the *Boston Gazette* and other newspapers accounts of his successes in New York, Pennsylvania, Maryland, Virginia, and Carolina. For example, Boston evangelicals read about the "great Acceptance and Success [Whitefield experienced] in some Parts of Virginia." They also followed the controversies surrounding Whitefield's ministry, such as accusations of misappropriation of funds raised for the orphanage. The *Boston Gazette* published a reprint of Whitefield's "attested" audit of the orphan house funds, which had first appeared in the *Pennsylvania Gazette*.[39] Through the press men and women participated in a national event that extended far beyond their meetinghouse seats.

Whitefield forged an intercolonial news exchange that united evangelicals from disparate regions. By reporting results of the revivals in a common language, Whitefield provided a means for his followers to express shared experiences throughout the colonies. Whitefield himself, as well as traveling companions such as Seward, John Syms, and Robert Cruttenden, wrote accounts of local awakenings and circulated them throughout the colonies. The Grand Itinerant operated at the center of a voluntary network of evangelicals who disseminated revival news by reprinting reports in local newspapers, relating progress to ministers, and distributing Whitefield's latest writings. Key members of this correspondence chain included James Habersham and Jonathan Barber in Georgia; Josiah Smith, Isaac Chanler, and Hugh Bryan in

---

[38] George Whitefield, *A Letter to the Reverend Dr. Chauncy, On Account of Some Passages Relating to the Reverend Mr. Whitefield, in His Book Entitled Seasonable Thoughts on the State of Religion in New England* (Boston, 1745), 4.

[39] See *Boston Gazette*, May 6 and 27, and June 3, 10, 17, 1746.

South Carolina; Benjamin Franklin, Samuel Finley, and James Blair in Pennsylvania; Gilbert and William Tennent in New Jersey; Ebenezer Pemberton and Thomas Noble in New York; Jonathan Parsons in Connecticut; and Benjamin Colman and William Cooper in Massachusetts.[40] On January 31, 1740, Whitefield sent a typical letter with enclosures of printed materials to Gilbert Tennent: "My journal, which I have sent to Philadelphia, will tell you what God has done in Maryland and Virginia. A foundation of great things I believe is laying there."[41] Often acting as both newspaper publishers and booksellers, printers forged a print network that facilitated intercolonial reporting. Whether motivated by profits or by religious convictions, printers eagerly reprinted news of Whitefield and the revivals in every part of the colonies.[42]

[handwritten annotation: Before he even came to America whitefield was in the papers]
[handwritten annotation: helped unite the colonies by setting up post office.]

WHITEFIELD AS GOOD BUSINESS

Franklin's report of Whitefield's arrival in Philadelphia suggests that the entrepreneurial printer viewed the evangelist as good business as well as good news. In addition to describing Whitefield's first preaching services, Franklin printed two advertisements relating to the revivalist, each of which suggests that the market provided a common bond between men who shared few other apparent interests. Whitefield himself placed the first advertisement. He announced that he had brought a cargo of the latest English manufactured goods for sale at auction with proceeds supporting Bethesda. By all accounts, the sale was a success.[43] Franklin's reaction to Whitefield's commercial savvy, or that of Seward, is unknown. Perhaps it encouraged him to suggest the proposition he announced in the second advertisement.

Franklin announced his intentions to print for subscribers Whitefield's *Journals* and sermons provided he received "sufficient Encouragement." Underlying that statement was an agreement between Franklin and Whitefield. After discussing the proposition with Whitefield and gaining the evangelist's approval, Franklin announced that "The Reverend Mr. Whitefield having given me Copies of his Journals and Sermons with Leave to print the Same, I propose to publish them

[40] Whitefield discusses the colonial correspondence network throughout his *Journals*.

[41] *Letters of Whitefield*, 145.

[42] In particular, Franklin maintained a financial interest in newspapers he helped start from Boston to Charleston, and through them afforded Whitefield access to intercolonial press coverage.

[43] *Pennsylvania Gazette*, November 8, 1739. For Whitefield's profitable sale of consumer goods, see Gillies, *Works of Whitefield*, 2:90.

Sloop Frances, Benjamin Butterfield, to St. Chriftophers.
Sloop Deborah, Richard Pidgeon, to Surrinam.
Brigt St. Stephen, John Henderfon, to Londonderry.

THE Rev. Mr. WHITEFIELD having
given me Copies of his Journals and Sermons, with Leave
to print the fame ; I propofe to publifh them with all Expedition, if I find fufficient Encouragement. The Sermons will
make two Volumes in twelves, on the fame Character with this
Advertifement, and the Journals two more, which fhall be delivered to Subfcribers at 2 s. each Volume, bound. Thofe therefore
who are enclined to encourage this Work, are defired fpeedily to
fend in their Names to me, that I may take Meafures accordingly.
                                             B. FRANKLIN.
            TO BE SOLD,
THE following Particulars, viz, 1500 Acres of good
Land in or near Piles-Grove, in Salem County, New-
Jerfey. 1200 Acres in the County of Hunterdon and Town-
fhip of Amwell. A Plantation containing 200 Acres, where-
on Neill Grant now liveth, with a good Houfe, Barn and Or-

6. Franklin's proposal to publish Whitefield by subscription.

with all Expedition."[44] Who initiated the proposal remains unknown.
By temperament and experience either man was capable of advancing
such a deal. Whitefield had already published more than a hundred
works in Britain: sermons and *Journals* that circulated throughout the
Atlantic world, including America.[45] Whitefield viewed the printed
word as an extension of the spoken word, applying the language of
itinerancy to books: "works [that] walk abroad."[46] Thus Whitefield and
Seward may have approached Franklin with the idea of a subscription
publication as a means of widening his American audience.

Of course, Franklin, as a printer seeking new avenues for profit,
would just as likely have approached Whitefield. A shrewd business-

[44] *Pennsylvania Gazette*, November 8, 1739.

[45] For a chronological listing of Whitefield imprints, see Roberts, *Whitefield in Print*. In
his biography of Whitefield, *The Divine Dramatist*, Harry Stout contends that "Franklin
taught Whitefield the power of the popular news sheets" (223), an argument that ignores
Whitefield's two-year newspaper publicity campaign in England prior to his American
arrival.

[46] Tyerman, *Oxford Methodists*, 257.

man locked in competition with rival printer and newspaper publisher Andrew Bradford, Franklin had proven himself an aggressive innovator. Noting that Bradford's *American Weekly Mercury* was "profitable to him" despite its being "a paltry thing [and] wretchedly manag'd," Franklin had a few years earlier lured subscribers to his *Pennsylvania Gazette* by giving it "a quite different Appearance . . . a better Type & better printed," as well as ensuring that it contained "spirited Remarks." He had won "a very profitable Job" from the Pennsylvania Assembly after writing a pamphlet supporting paper currency. The bill's supporters, "who conceiv'd [Franklin] had been of some Service, thought fit to reward [him], by employing [him] in printing the Money." Perhaps Franklin's most profitable innovations came in marketing and distribution. By investing in print shops from Charleston to Boston, he developed an intercolonial network to expand his sales beyond Pennsylvania.[47] Hence, to Franklin, who had closely followed Whitefield's popularity in England, the evangelist represented a marketable product and a competitive edge.

The *Pennsylvania Gazette* heralded Whitefield's disembarkation as a well-publicized English import. The November 8, 1739, issue announced that "the Rev. Mr. Whitefield landed from London at Lewes-Town [aboard] . . . the Ship Elizabeth, Nicholas Stevenson [Captain]." To emphasize the parallel between Whitefield's arrival and that of the "latest English fashions," the same edition reported that the evangelist had brought a shipload of manufactured goods "To Be Sold at the House of the Rev. Mr. Whitefield, In Second Street." The notice included a lengthy list of items for sale from brass candlesticks to gunpowder, an assortment similar to that displayed in merchant Samuel Samson's advertisement on the same page, alerting readers to merchandise "Lately imported from London and Britain."[48]

Over the next fourteen months Whitefield himself became a "commodity," offering himself to evangelicals in all the colonies. By traveling on horseback through every colony, Whitefield was an itinerant salesman of his message. Through open-air sermons the revivalist urged his auditors to "secure the pearl of invaluable price."[49] Moreover, Franklin and other newspaper publishers were eager to "sell" Whitefield to Americans.

To Franklin, Whitefield was a gifted salesman, capable of overcoming even a skeptic's sales resistance. The Philadelphia printer reached that conclusion while attending the itinerant's services, more from cu-

---

[47] Lemay and Zall, *Autobiography of Franklin*, 63–64, 67, 95.

[48] *Pennsylvania Gazette*, November 8, 1739.

[49] Gillies, *Works of Whitefield*, 5:233.

riosity than from conviction. In an oft-cited account, Franklin related how he went to one of Whitefield's sermons resolved to contribute nothing to the evangelist's plea for support of his Georgia orphanage. Franklin disapproved of locating the charity in "Georgia then destitute of Materials & Workmen," preferring instead that it be built in Philadelphia. However, as Whitefield pleaded for funds, Franklin's resolve began to weaken. With successive rhetorical flourishes, Whitefield melted the printer's determination to withstand the preacher's importunities, and Franklin "empty'd [his] Pocket wholly into the Collector's Dish, Gold and all."[50]

While attending Whitefield's outdoor services, Franklin had been impressed by more than the revivalist's oratory. He had also been struck by the "enormous . . . Multitudes of all Sects and Denominations that attended [Whitefield's] Sermons." Although he had reprinted in the *Pennsylvania Gazette* accounts of the preacher's London services, attracting crowds exceeding twenty thousand men and women, Franklin was skeptical of the reported figures. One evening as Whitefield preached from the courthouse steps at the intersection of Market and Second Streets, Franklin conducted an experiment to see how many auditors could hear the evangelist preach. Starting at the base of the steps, Franklin counted his paces along a line to the point where street noise began to obscure the sound of Whitefield's voice. Imagining a semicircle of the radius he had measured and allotting two square feet per person standing, Franklin calculated that Whitefield might be heard by more than thirty thousand people. The experiment "reconcil'd [Franklin] to the Newspaper Accounts of his having preach'd to 25000 People in the Fields."[51] Franklin's observations at Whitefield's services convinced the printer of two things: Whitefield was a persuasive orator, and he could attract huge crowds. Or, translated into language more suited to an entrepreneur, Whitefield was a powerful salesman who commanded an enormous market.

Franklin sought to exploit the revivalist's salesmanship and popularity by entering into a joint venture: a subscription publication of Whitefield's sermons and *Journals*. Franklin announced on November 15 his "proposal to publish by subscription [Whitefield's] journals and sermons each in 2 volumes in twelves at a cost of 2 shillings per volume."[52] Six months later Franklin claimed that "the whole number of Names far exceeds the Number of Books printed, [and that] those Subscribers who have paid or who bring the Money in their Hands will

[50] Lemay and Zall, *Autobiography of Franklin*, 105.
[51] Ibid., 106–107.
[52] *Pennsylvania Gazette*, November 15, 1739.

have the Preference."[53] Thousands of men and women from Boston to Charleston purchased volumes in what one scholar concluded "must have been one of [Franklin's] first large business ventures and certainly a lucrative one."[54] It also extended Whitefield's message of the new birth far beyond the reach of his voice. The subscription publication provides a window on Whitefield's technique of employing print, Franklin's role in promoting the evangelist, and the works' consumers. The result is a fresh look at how the impersonal market brought together persons of different religious orientation to pursue common interests.

Although an innovator and an aggressive salesman, Franklin was a prudent businessman who calculated risks as well as profits. Seeking, therefore, to reduce his risk, Franklin proposed a multivolume subscription publication. Subscription as a method of selling books represented a mutual obligation between the publisher and a group of readers. According to Ephraim Chambers's 1728 *Cyclopedia*, "subscription, in the Commerce of Books, particularly, signifies an Engagement a Person enters, to take a certain Number of Copies of a Book going to be printed; and the reciprocal Obligation of a Bookseller or Publisher, to deliver the said Copies on certain Terms." Subscription reduced the publisher's risk by shifting much of the burden to consumers. By the late seventeenth century, London booksellers "were regularly using such as a method of publishing expensive books." Alexander Pope published by subscription his multivolume translations of Homer's *Iliad* (London, 1712–1721) and *Odyssey* (London, 1725–1726). In the colonies, William Bradford announced in 1688 his intention to publish "a large house-Bible," but the project failed because of undersubscription. Then in 1726, a group of six Boston booksellers succeeded in publishing Samuel Willard's *A Compleat Body of Divinity* as five hundred subscribers agreed to purchase the "largest book printed in British North America to that time."[55] When Franklin proposed to publish Whitefield's works by subscription, he borrowed a technique that had produced uneven results.

Success was not guaranteed. Franklin had proposed subscription publications before that had failed to attract a sufficient number of subscribers. In July 1738, Franklin had advertised a work by John Tennent, a Virginia medical doctor who had already published several

[53] Ibid., May 22, 1740.

[54] For assessment of Whitefield's impact on Franklin's printing business, see C. William Miller, *Benjamin Franklin's Philadelphia Printing, 1728–1766; A Descriptive Bibliography* (Philadelphia, 1974), 85.

[55] Donald Farren, "Subscription: A Study of the Eighteenth-Century American Book Trade" (D.L.S. diss., Columbia University, 1982), 2–8.

works, on the "Disease of Virginia," stating that printing would begin "after 1000 copies [were] subscribed." Apparently the requisite number never materialized; no publication record exists. Then in November 1739, at the same time Franklin advertised the Whitefield subscription, he participated in a consortium of printers proposing to publish by subscription *A Collection of Divinity from Several Famous Authors* by Magnus Falconar. Although booksellers from Boston and New York joined Franklin in soliciting subscribers, the project failed.[56] Demand was the key to success in subscription publications.

William Parks, a Williamsburg printer and Franklin's business partner, demonstrated that a successful subscription depended on aggressive, intercolonial canvassing. In 1733, Parks proposed to publish a *Collection of All Acts of Virginia*, a compilation of the province's legislation. Recognizing that he needed subscribers from outside Virginia, the printer solicited residents of other colonies and persons doing business in the colony; he relied upon traveling merchants and planters as well as ships' captains to generate demand up and down the seaboard. He succeeded, and the list of subscribers indicates that Parks had indeed widened his market considerably. Although a majority of subscribers were Virginians, the list contains names of merchants and lawyers engaged in intercoastal trade. Individuals from Edenton, North Carolina, to New York City along with others from such ports as Baltimore and Philadelphia purchased the collection of statutes. Traders in London, Bristol, York, and Glasgow also bought copies. More than one-third were ships' captains, merchants, or attorneys who desired the volume as a guide to their trade with Virginia.[57]

In his proposed subscription, Franklin had the advantage of a cooperative author who had already demonstrated his market acumen in the London print market. Whitefield's sermons and journals reflect a calculated view of audience. In writing for masses, including poorer folk, Whitefield consciously wrote brief works. He considered the attention span and reading ability of those who had neither leisure nor skills to benefit from long treatises. A comparison of Whitefield's publications and Cotton Mather's a half century earlier illustrates the revivalist's penchant for brevity. The most prolific American writer of the seventeenth century, Mather published fifty-two titles during the 1690s with an average length of eighty-two pages. By comparison, Whitefield's American-printed publications during the Great Awakening, 1739–1745, averaged forty-six pages or 56 percent the length of

---

[56] *Pennsylvania Gazette,* July 27, 1738, and November 22, 1739.

[57] [William Parks], *A Collection of All the Acts of Assembly, Now in Force, in the Colony of Virginia* (Williamsburg, 1733), 623–626.

Mather's works. One-fourth of Mather's writings were works of more than one hundred pages; fewer than one in twelve of Whitefield's attained this length. And more than half of Whitefield's publications—but less than a fifth of Mather's—were under forty pages. A similar comparison of Whitefield's works with those of the revivalist Jonathan Edwards reveals the same pattern. Edwards wrote much longer, sustained analyses of the revivals and their theological implications. By writing brief publications, Whitefield made his works readable and affordable for large numbers of people.[58]

Whitefield also attempted to make his printed works accessible to people who had not benefited from much formal education. Again, a comparison of Whitefield's writing style with that of Cotton Mather is revealing. Almost any printed sermon of either author illustrates the wide stylistic divergence between the two. In his *Triumphs over Troubles* published in 1701, Mather adorned the title page with Latin quotations from Origen and Augustine. Targeting the more learned in England as well as New England, Mather sprinkled Greek and Latin throughout the text. He also displayed his scholarship with liberal citations of theological treatises drawn from patristic writers, Reformers, and Enlightenment thinkers. By contrast, Whitefield's *The Almost Christian* paints a word picture of the "almost Christian" in language unadorned by Latin and Greek quotations and references to works other than the Bible. After depicting the almost Christian as "one who halts between two Opinions, that wavers between Christ and the World," Whitefield held the account up to his readers as a mirror. Addressing his readers in the familiar second person, Whitefield wrote, "you can observe some Features in this Picture, odious as it is, too near resembling your own." Drawing upon his readers' daily experiences of participating in a market economy, Whitefield declared that the almost Christian had made a bad bargain by exchanging eternal life for transitory riches. Whitefield pictured the almost Christian as viewing religion much as one would perceive the latest fashion. The revivalist said that they looked upon "Religion merely for Novelty—as something which pleased them for a while; but after their Curiosity was satisfied, they have laid it aside again." Whitefield asked his readers, "Is Eternal Life so mean a Purchase as not to deserve the temporary Renunciation of a few transitory Riches?"[59] Whitefield confronted his readers with straightforward, poignant language that called for immediate self-examination rather than theological discourses designed for reflection and debate.

[58] Comparisons calculated from information in Evans, *American Bibliography*, 1:86–138, 2:149–303.

[59] Comparison based on Cotton Mather, *Triumphs over Troubles* (Boston, 1701), 1–5, 15–17; and George Whitefield, *The Almost Christian* (Boston, 1739), 8–11, 14–16.

Thus Whitefield promoted the subscription indirectly by preaching the message of the proposed books to enormous crowds. He also helped generate demand by differentiating between "good books" and "bad books." Much as competing merchants sought to distinguish their merchandise from that of competitors, Whitefield presented his version of the gospel in sharp contrast to other expressions. As he traveled through the colonies in 1739 and 1740, Whitefield warned crowds against being seduced by such popular works as Archbishop Tillotson's sermons and Richard Allestree's *The Whole Duty of Man*, second only to the Bible in colonial book sales. While those books contained useful ethical instruction, according to Whitefield, they demonstrated no understanding of experimental religion. Hence, prior to his intercolonial preaching trip in spring 1740, Whitefield published a polemic determined "to open People's Eyes . . . to shew them that the Writings, which for some Years past have been so much admired, are directly contrary to the Gospel of Jesus Christ." He charged that *The Whole Duty of Man* was "calculated to civilize, but . . . never was a Means of converting a single Soul." And Whitefield published a "publick Testimony against the Writing of Archbishop Tillotson . . . to point out the fundamental Error" of the author. He warned that Tillotson's theology was "founded on the Arminian Scheme," which was the "chief Cause that so many . . . have built their Hopes of Salvation on a false Bottom." In his most inflammatory language, Whitefield concluded that Tillotson knew "no more of true Christianity than did Mahomet."[60]

Whitefield distributed his attack on Tillotson in the British and American press. The revivalist argued that "Tillotson [had] been more instrumental of corrupting the Clergy of the present Generation, and propagating Arminianism amongst us, than any Book in England." As part of his goal to replace "good books for bad books," in 1740 Whitefield published his polemic in Charleston, Philadelphia, and London.[61] Seward sent copies to colonial newspapers. The *Pennsylvania Gazette* and the *New York Gazette* reprinted Whitefield's criticism of Tillotson, reproducing the document on their front pages in successive issues.[62] Whitefield's anti-Tillotson pamphlet served to distinguish more sharply the itinerant's message from that of his detractors. At the same time the work created greater controversy and deepened divisions as opponents responded angrily to his attack on a revered figure.

Whitefield customarily recommended sound evangelical books to his audiences. Noting his practice of publicizing his and other Pietists'

[60] See Whitefield, *A Letter From Whitefield . . . Shewing Fundamental Error of . . . The Whole Duty of Man* (Charles-Town, 1740), 4. *Pennsylvania Gazette*, April 10, 1740.

[61] Austin, "Bibliography of Works of Whitefield," 172.

[62] *Pennsylvania Gazette*, April 10 and 24, 1740; *New York Gazette*, May 19 and 26, 1740.

works, Whitefield described his custom: "After I had been preaching to a very large auditory . . . on the Continent of America, as is my usual custom [I] recommend[ed] the book of Homilies." Whitefield believed that the work had languished in the hands of unconverted clergymen and should be restored to a central place in Anglican worship. His efforts to promote the homilies extended beyond recommendation; he followed up to see if his followers indeed purchased copies of their own and discovered that "numbers were stirred up to go to the stores to purchase" the books.[63] Upon learning that booksellers and shopkeepers did not stock the volume, Whitefield pledged his assistance in procuring them.

Franklin must have been encouraged by the crowds Whitefield attracted and the evangelist's ability to stir crowds to purchase books. But the entrepreneur did not rely solely on Whitefield to ensure the project's success; Franklin became an aggressive promoter of the subscription and of Whitefield. Franklin's coverage of Whitefield's ministry in the *Pennsylvania Gazette* was extensive and glowing. During the evangelist's fourteen months in the colonies, Franklin carried either accounts of his services, reprints of his works, or advertisements for his books and pamphlets—and sometimes all three—in forty-five of sixty issues of the *Pennsylvania Gazette* during that period. The scope of coverage was as extensive as the frequency. Franklin devoted the entire front page of eight different issues to Whitefield. In one six-week period in spring 1740, as Franklin solicited subscriptions, Whitefield dominated the front page in five of the editions in addition to being represented by lengthy accounts of his preaching in Philadelphia and surrounding towns.[64]

Moreover, Franklin allowed Whitefield and Seward great latitude in shaping the material published. Seward supplied Franklin with a constant stream of news accounts for the printer to insert into the *Gazette*. Seward's reports appeared in the newspaper without attribution. One account he sent to a New York paper began, "We hear from Philadelphia that since Mr. Whitefield's Preaching there, the Dancing-School . . . has been shut up." The use of first-person plural suggested that the publisher was printing what he had received on good faith without disclosing the author's identity. It was the reader's problem to determine the writer's identity and perspective. As he "wrote and examin'd sundry Things for the Press," Seward placed the most favorable interpretation on Whitefield's ministry.[65] In short, he presented and re-presented Whitefield to Franklin's readers.

---

[63] George Whitefield, *A Letter to the Reverend Dr. Durell, Vice-Chancellor of the University of Oxford; Occasioned by a Late Expulsion of Six Students from Edmund-Hall* (Boston, 1768), 31.

[64] See *Pennsylvania Gazette*, April 10 through May 15, 1740.

[65] Seward, *Journal of a Voyage*, 10–18.

As they had done in England, Whitefield and Seward manufactured events in order to promote their work. On April 16, 1740, Seward rented a ballroom frequented by Philadelphia's upper crust for balls and concerts. He then proceeded to "shut up the Door of that private Concert Room," believing the establishment's entertainment promoted sin and violated the gospel. Upon discovering his deed, "some of the chief Persons in Town . . . caus'd the door to be broke open again."[66] Having rented the hall for an unexpired term, the gentlemen demanded answers from the hall's proprietor, William Bolton. However, the first explanation of this private dispute came not from Bolton but from Seward, who published his interpretation in the *Gazette*. What began as a local, private dispute soon became an intercolonial topic of public discourse.

Seward's account in the May 1 edition of the *Gazette* incensed Bolton and his gentlemen patrons. Written as a third-party, objective article, the account claimed that "since Mr. Whitefield's preaching here, the Dancing School, Assembly, and Concert Room have been shut up, as inconsistent with the Doctrine of the Gospel." Implying that the revival had diminished demand for worldly entertainments, Seward added that although the door had been reopened, "no Company came to the last assembly night."[67] Bolton responded in the newspaper's next issue, charging that Seward had misrepresented the case and insisting that the closing resulted from the evangelical's unlawful act rather than a change in public opinion of dancing. Moreover, Bolton accused Seward of manufacturing the whole event as a publicity stunt. Bolton concluded that "after this account of Seward's behaviour, no one can wonder at his low craft, in getting this paragraph foisted into the News papers just before his departure for England, in order to carry it along with him, and spread his Master's Fame, as tho' he had met with great Success among the better sort of People in Pennsylvania."[68] Although a harsh assessment of Seward's tactics, Bolton's evaluation of the press agent's practices was perceptive.

Bolton's suspicions were well founded. As Seward apologized to Bolton and the gentlemen who had rented the hall, the zealous press agent had already forwarded copies of his article to newspaper editors in New York and Boston where Whitefield would next appear.[69] And Whitefield's advance publicity worked to prepare distant strangers to hear his spoken message. Supporters and opponents attested to the powerful effect that the steady flow of newspaper articles had on New

[66] *Pennsylvania Gazette*, May 1, 1740. For Seward's explanation of the dancing school incident, see Seward, *Journal of a Voyage*, 21–22.

[67] *Pennsylvania Gazette*, May 1, 1740.

[68] Ibid., May 8, 1740.

[69] See Seward, *Journal of a Voyage*, 16.

Englanders. One observer noted that "no one Man more employs the Press" than does Whitefield, and the antirevivalist Charles Chauncy claimed that Boston's ministers refrained from expressing opposition to the itinerant because of his enormous popularity generated in part by favorable press coverage.[70]

After Seward departed for London on a fund-raising mission, Whitefield himself supplied Franklin with reports on the revival. On November 26, 1740, Whitefield sent Franklin a letter detailing his activities. After discussing ideas for upcoming publications, Whitefield described his recent New England preaching tour. "I think I have been on shore 73 days," the evangelist wrote, "preached 170 sermons and collected 700 pounds" for the Georgia orphan house. He added that "great and visible [were] the fruits" of his preaching. On December 4, Whitefield's account appeared in the *Pennsylvania Gazette*.[71] Through Franklin, Whitefield had access to a public newspaper that "puffed" the revivals in words chosen by the evangelist himself.

Franklin printed his own assessment of the revivals as well. In the June 12, 1740, issue of the *Pennsylvania Gazette*, Franklin published an account of the salutary effects of Whitefield's preaching tour in Philadelphia. While the article's authorship is uncertain, its sentiments were Franklin's. "The Alteration in the Face of Religion here is altogether surprizing," Franklin printed, an evaluation he included forty years later in his *Autobiography*. He noted that people attended sermons with more willingness and that ministers performed their duties with greater zeal and diligence. Commenting on how the revivals had influenced the way people spent their time and money, Franklin reported from the perspective of a bookseller that "only books of piety and devotion [were] demanded. Psalms and Hymns replace[d] idle songs and ballads." As Franklin saw it, Whitefield was the agent of change: "All which, under God, is owing to the successful Labours of the Reverend Mr. Whitefield."[72] He could have added that Whitefield was also good for the print business.

Franklin's prorevivalist editorial stance brought criticism from some Philadelphians. When a group of antirevivalists charged Franklin with "showing partiality to the revivals," the publisher retorted that the allegation was false. The evidence he offered for his evenhanded treatment of the revivals, however, must have been as unconvincing to contemporaries as it appears today. Franklin's first line of defense was to represent himself as part of the Philadelphia print trade, which, he

[70] Chauncy, *Letter From a Gentleman in Boston*, 3.
[71] *Pennsylvania Gazette*, December 4, 1739.
[72] Sentiments expressed in the *Pennsylvania Gazette*, June 12, 1740, are paraphrased in Lemay and Zall, *Autobiography of Franklin*, 103.

contended, printed both sides. He first cited Andrew Bradford's publication of an Anglican priest's attack on Whitefield's theology; he then
added that he himself had printed a pamphlet written by some Presbyterians criticizing certain passages in Whitefield's sermons and *Journals*.[73] The weight of Franklin's pro-Whitefield newspaper coverage
and the sheer number of Whitefield works he published undermined
the printer's case.

In addition to promoting the subscription publication through the
Gazette, Franklin created an ad hoc intercolonial sales force to solicit
and enlist subscribers. In his November 15 advertisement, Franklin
listed seven persons engaged in the print trade who would take subscriptions. Having learned from Seward Whitefield's itinerary for the
remainder of his American visit, Franklin organized the names according to the evangelist's schedule. First came those located in south-
eastern Pennsylvania and Delaware, where the revivalist preached after
leaving Philadelphia: Aubray Bevan of Chester, Mr. Curtis of New
Castle, and John Read of Christiana Bridge. Then followed the names
of agents in the Chesapeake: Jonas Green of Annapolis and William
Parks of Williamsburg. Recognizing that Whitefield already had contacts in Charleston and Savannah near his orphan house, Franklin
listed no one from the Lower South. But anticipating a New England
tour in 1740, Franklin designated Timothy Green of New London,
Connecticut, and John Franklin of Boston as printers accepting
subscriptions.[74]

Franklin must have been greatly encouraged at Whitefield's reports
after the evangelist departed from Philadelphia. At Chester, the itinerant preached to "near five Thousand People" from a balcony. Crowds
continued to follow the revivalist as he traveled farther south in Pennsylvania, attracting two thousand each at New Castle and Christiana
Bridge. Although Whitefield failed to draw large crowds in the Chesapeake because of a dispersed population, he challenged the "polite Part
of the World . . . [where] Ladies [were] as much wedded to Quadrille
and Ombre as Gentlemen [were] to their Bottle and their Hounds."
Employing a market discourse of exchange, Whitefield urged his auditors to substitute for their "Self-pleasing, Self-seeking" pursuits the
new birth—"the one Thing needful"—as a "product" that would bring
"Satisfaction and Profit" to many.[75] In the absence of towns where
large crowds could congregate, Whitefield would rely more on the

[73] For charges against Franklin's editorial practices and his reply, see *Pennsylvania
Gazette*, July 24, 1740.

[74] Ibid., November 15, 1739.

[75] George Whitefield, *A Continuation of the Reverend Mr. Whitefield's Journal* (Philadelphia, 1740), 156–165.

distribution of his sermons and *Journals* to convey the gospel to men and women in the Chesapeake.

As he traveled, Whitefield developed his own network of merchants and clergy who assisted him in selling and distributing his books. For example, on his third American tour, Whitefield published a continuation of his spiritual autobiography in Philadelphia and sold it through the following voluntary distribution chain:

James Habersham	merchant	Savannah
Josiah Smith	minister	Charleston
Mr. Branson	merchant	Philadelphia
William Bradford	printer	Philadelphia
William Shurtleff	minister	Portsmouth, N.H.
Rev. Pemberton	minister	New York
John Smith	merchant	Boston[76]

Together and separately, Whitefield and Franklin forged intercolonial ties that helped create a community drawn together by a shared message standardized in printed *Journals* and sermons.

By all accounts, the subscription was an unqualified success. On May 22, 1740, Franklin announced that the first volume each of the *Journals* and sermons would be ready the following Monday. Unlike his other ventures in subscription publication, this one was oversubscribed. Three months after the first volumes were available, Whitefield informed a London correspondent that his *Journals* and sermons were "bought off exceedingly" in America. In another letter the evangelist gave the triumphant report that his printed works were "now in the hands of thousands in these parts."[77]

Although no list of subscribers is available, Franklin's ledgers confirm the large sales he and Whitefield reported. The printer's Ledger "D" contains credit purchases of customers maintaining open accounts at the print shop. Sales of the *Journals* and sermons appear under the accounts of fifty of the more than two hundred customers who bought books, paper, printed forms, and ink from Franklin. That number probably represents only a small fraction of the total number who bought the volumes. After only two weeks of soliciting subscribers, Franklin reported to Whitefield that he "had taken above two Hundred Subscriptions for printing [the] Sermons and Journals."[78] Further, Ledger "D" does not reflect cash sales, and Franklin's Shop Book kept

[76] Whitefield employed his network most fully on his third American visit. See George Whitefield, *A Further Account of God's Dealing with the Reverend Mr. George Whitefield, From the Time of His Ordination to His Embarking for Georgia* (Philadelphia, 1746).

[77] Gillies, *Works of Whitefield*, 1:507.

[78] *Whitefield's Journals*, 360.

by his wife ends in August 1739, just before the subscription began. And no doubt more than fifty credit customers subscribed. Some entries for sales bear a generic designation, such as "miscellaneous books," and could well have included Whitefield volumes. However small a fraction of the total subscribers, the fifty identifiable subscribers purchased a total of almost twenty-five hundred volumes of sermons and *Journals*. While most bought entire sets, some acquired only sermons or only *Journals* or just the first volume or just the second volume of each. At any rate, the ledger points to a huge success for Franklin and Whitefield in their joint publishing venture.[79]

While Franklin's Ledger "D" reflects primarily the printer's commercial customers and therefore hardly represents a cross section of Philadelphia society, it does reveal that people from a wide range of professions and occupations purchased Whitefield's works. Both retail and wholesale customers bought the *Journals* and sermons. Subscribing for a single set or a few sets, retail customers included representatives of the following occupations: merchant, joiner, shopkeeper, portrait painter, organ maker, glazier, brickmaker, turner, craftsman, bricklayer, minister, lawyer, shoemaker, breeches merchant, staymaker, ship's captain, and mathematician. Wholesale purchases included the following: 200 volumes to John Read of Christiana Bridge, 250 sets to Benjamin Elliot of Boston, 150 volumes to Anne Franklin in Newport, 150 volumes to Mrs. Timothy in Charleston, and 1,000 volumes to Charles Harrison in Boston.[80]

The shipment of a thousand volumes to Harrison warrants closer attention. In his published analysis of Ledger "D," George Eddy speculated that Franklin obtained more profitable terms for binding the volumes in Boston than he could negotiate in Philadelphia. Hence, Eddy assumed that Franklin sent the volumes to Harrison, a bookbinder as well as a bookseller, only for binding and not for sale. If that were the case, the volumes would have to be subtracted from the total shipped by Franklin to credit customers. Franklin did note in his account book that he was sending the books to Harrison "to bind." However, there is no evidence that Harrison returned the bound books to Franklin. Instead Harrison advertised to sell the Franklin edition out of his own stock. Throughout Whitefield's New England tour, Harrison, along with most other Boston booksellers, took advantage of the

---

[79] Sales data taken from manuscript copy of Benjamin Franklin's Ledger "D" located at the American Philosophical Society, Philadelphia. The manuscript version provides a much fuller account of Franklin's sales of Whitefield works than that extracted in George S. Eddy, ed., *Account Books Kept by Benjamin Franklin*, 2 vols. (New York, 1929). Vol. 2 contains Ledger "D," 1739–1747.

[80] Ibid.

itinerant's enormous popularity and vigorously promoted the evangelist's publications.[81]

Boston printers sold Whitefield's works with the same sort of aggressive and creative promotion exhibited by Franklin. First they set Whitefield's revivals in a larger context by publishing testimonials from Britons as well as Americans from other provinces. The publisher of the *Boston Weekly News-Letter*, John Draper, placed on the front page a Scot's millennialist interpretation of the evangelical revivals. In the September 18, 1740, edition issued just as Whitefield arrived in New England, Draper printed an "extract of a letter from a gentleman in Scotland to his friend in New England." The writer expressed his opinion that "the People of [Whitefield's] Way in England [were] the best People in it." But he viewed the revivals as being of more than local or even national importance. "The Lord seems to be gathering in his Elect from all Nations," the Scot declared, "bringing in his People out of Babylon . . . and hastening his SECOND COMING."[82] According to that perspective, New Englanders awaited nothing less than the herald of Christ's return to earth.

Boston publishers timed releases of particular Whitefield works to coincide with the evangelist's New England preaching tour. Two months before his arrival at Newport, Rhode Island, on September 14, 1740, booksellers Benjamin Eliot, G. Rogers, and Daniel Fowle advertised for sale their edition of a Whitefield discourse, *Directions how to Hear Sermons*. Whitefield wrote the sermon as a vehicle for preparing men and women to receive the message of the new birth. Now booksellers introduced the volume in its third edition to set the stage for the revivalist's arrival. At the same time Eliot also announced the availability of Franklin's two-volume set of Whitefield sermons. About one month before Whitefield reached New England, Eliot and Joseph Edwards advertised Whitefield's latest volume of his *Journals* containing his journey from England to Philadelphia and including his American itinerancy before leaving Savannah for Newport.[83] As noted by Thomas Prince, Timothy Cutler, and others, these advertisements proved effective advance publicity, heightening readers' eagerness to hear the renowned preacher.

During Whitefield's New England tour, Boston booksellers competed vigorously with each other to satisfy demand for his works. According to a study of publishing and bookselling in colonial Boston, approximately fifteen individuals engaged in the trade in 1740. The

[81] Ibid. For Harrison advertisement, see *Boston Weekly News-Letter*, October 16–23, 1740.

[82] *Boston Weekly News-Letter*, September 18–25, 1740.

[83] Ibid., July 10–17, 17–24, and August 14–21, 1740.

7. Whitefield as a commodity in Franklin's account books.

most prolific booksellers such as Daniel Henchman, Daniel Fowle, and Samuel Kneeland published the itinerant's works in large numbers. Smaller shopkeepers such as Samuel Eliot and Joseph Edwards enjoyed their highest volume of business during and after Whitefield's New England visit. Edwards, for example, averaged publishing or selling about six books each year from 1735 through 1744. His most productive year was 1741, following Whitefield's New England itinerancy. Of the thirteen volumes he sold, six were titles written by the revivalist. Booksellers, many of whom were also publishers, sought a competitive advantage by releasing distinctive versions of Whitefield's works. At least six different editions of his *Journals* appeared in Boston newspaper advertisements. Edwards and Eliot published Whitefield's most recent *Journal* and appended the evangelist's answer to the bishop of London's pastoral letter charging the revivalist with enthusiasm. After Whitefield's departure from New England, Kneeland and Green appealed to local interest by publishing a New England version of Whitefield's *Journals* containing entries from his Newport arrival to his departure from Stamford, Connecticut, on October 29. The five editions issued in about six months suggest tremendous demand for the regional account. Similarly, Franklin announced in the November 5, 1741, issue of the *Pennsylvania Gazette* intentions to publish a version highlighting Whitefield's preaching activities in the Middle Colonies. Although the edition extended from the evangelist's departure from New England to his March 11, 1741, landing at Falmouth, England, Franklin billed it as "an account of the Work of God at New-York, Pennsylvania, and South Carolina."[84]

The relationship between Whitefield and Boston's printers was mutually beneficial. Not only did Whitefield benefit from the print trade's merchandising the evangelist and his books; printers exploited Whitefield's popularity to sell their wares. In his advertisement for Henry Scougal's *The Life of God in the Soul of Man*, bookseller Hopestill Foster cited Whitefield's testimony concerning the book's influence in his own salvation. In a footnote to his advertisement, Foster added: "N.B. The Rev. Mr. Whitefield was pleased to say of the above Book, 'That tho' I had Fasted, Prayed, and received the Sacrament so long, yet I never knew what True Religion was till God sent me that Excellent Treatise.' "[85] Charles Harrison capitalized on Whitefield's popularity with evangelical readers in his advertisement of Ralph Erskine's *Gospel Sonnets, or, Spiritual Songs*. Harrison appended an endorsement: "N.B. The above is recommended by the Reverend Mr. Whitefield and the Reverend Mr. Tennent."[86] In 1740 and 1741, Whitefield's name was as well known as that of anyone else in the colonies, and printers attempted to exploit his popularity.

Whitefield's works conveyed various meanings to those who bought and sold them. To buyers, the evangelist's *Journals* and sermons represented an opportunity to participate in the revivals when there was no chance to hear him preach. Indeed some people knew Whitefield only through his publications. When he traveled through the Chesapeake in 1739 and 1740, he preached in Annapolis and Williamsburg but bypassed much of the countryside. However, a Scottish merchant put in the hands of some Virginians "some of [Whitefield's published] Sermons, such as he had not revised, but had been taken down in shorthand at Glasgow." A Virginia evangelical reported that the books "were so useful that the People . . . sent to Scotland for 250 of 'em," and William Parks, the Williamsburg printer, "reprinted 400 and odd of

---

[84] Ibid., March 19–26, 1741. *Pennsylvania Gazette*, November 5, 1741.
[85] *Boston Weekly News-Letter*, January 8–15, 1741.
[86] Ibid., May 21–28, 1741.

them, and now there's not one of them to be had." When Whitefield returned to Virginia in 1746 to preach, his printed sermons continued to be in demand. One enterprising tradesman, "knowing Mr. Whitefield was to preach [and] had some books to sell, went with them and sold the worth of 17 pounds Sterling near the Meeting-House."[87]

For those expecting to hear Whitefield preach, printed accounts of the revival heightened anticipation. Jonathan Edwards wrote to Whitefield that "the Success of your Labours in other places [aroused my] desire to see and hear you in this Place."[88] Edwards and other New Englanders followed with anticipation Whitefield's progress as he moved through the Chesapeake and Middle Colonies before his arrival in New England. Jonathan Parsons, the pastor at Lyme, Connecticut, observed that the "frequent Accounts of the Success [Whitefield] had in many Places were serviceable among us."[89] And the Boston evangelical Thomas Prince noted the cumulative impact of Whitefield's advance publicity on New Englanders. Prince testified that printed "Accounts of the Reverend Mr. Whitefield as they *successively* arrived before his appearance here . . . prepar'd the Way for his Entertainment and successful Labours among us."[90]

For many, Whitefield's published works were symbolic, testimony to a revived faith that lingered long after Whitefield moved on. Demand for Whitefield's printed works remained high in Boston for more than nine months after his departure. Booksellers published a steady stream of books and pamphlets by and for the itinerant. Reading of evangelical publications was so widespread that antirevivalists requested assistance from the bishop of London. Timothy Cutler asked specifically for Samuel Weller's scathing polemic against Whitefield, which had been well received by London antirevivalists. Ridiculing claims of success made in the evangelist's fourth journal, Weller singled out Whitefield's self-promotion as particularly offensive. "The conduct of this gentleman in publishing the daily occurrences of his life," the author wrote, "is without example and unjustified by any precedent among the saints of God." Like Cutler, Weller objected to the volume and nature of Whitefield's publicity of himself and his ministry. To them, the evangelical presented himself as the instrument of revival, motivated by "a solicitude about what the crowd thinks or says of his preaching." It was not until October 1741—a full year after Whitefield's

[87] *Boston Gazette* , May 6, 1746.

[88] Abelove, "Jonathan Edwards' Letter," 488–489.

[89] Jonathan Parsons, "Account of the Revival at Lyme," in *The Great Awakening: Documents Illustrating the Crisis and Its Consequences*, ed. Alan Heimert and Perry Miller (New York, 1967), 40.

[90] *Christian History*, January 5 and 12, 1744/45.

departure—that Cutler received Weller's book and advertised it for sale.[91] Meanwhile evangelicals continued to purchase and read readily available works by the Grand Itinerant.

To colonial printers, Whitefield was a hot commodity representing profits in the print market. Franklin's ledgers reveal the evangelist as fast-moving inventory. The journal's pages spanning the years 1740 to 1746 are filled with charges for purchases of various Whitefield publications. Most entries include the author's name and a short title to indicate what customers bought: "Whitefield's Life," "Whitefield's Journal," "Whitefield's Sermons," "Whitefield's 1st Journal Bound," "Whitefield's Answer to the Querists," "Whitefield's Orphan House Account," etc. However, during May–July, 1740, when the first volumes of Franklin's four-volume edition of Whitefield's sermons and *Journals* were shipped, brisk sales introduced a shortened ledger notation. Entries now read, "5 sets of Whitefield," "2 vols. Whitefield," "2 $\frac{1}{2}$ Doz. Whitefields." Whitefield was a commodity! a best-seller in Franklin's intercolonial market. Like other merchandise the printer offered for sale, Whitefield represented revenue. The account of Thomas Rogers, shoemaker, illustrates the point. He made two purchases from Franklin in 1740: two volumes of Whitefield at four shillings and an ad for sale of a "Negroe Boy" at five shillings.[92] While Whitefield as subject turned the power of the print trade to his own designs, as object he was transformed into a vendible commodity. Whitefield spiritualized the metaphor as he pledged to "spend and be spent" for the Lord.[93] Franklin's account book suggests that many would appropriate Whitefield and the message he represented through a market transaction.

Whitefield represented sales to other colonial printers. Each year from 1739 through 1745, American publishers released more works by Whitefield than by any other writer. The total number of publications printed in the colonies increased 85 percent from 1738 to 1741, with most of the increase attributable to the Grand Itinerant. In the peak revival year, 1740, Whitefield wrote or inspired thirty-nine titles, or 30 percent of all works published in America. For many printers, Whitefield's writings constituted a significant proportion of their business. For instance, from 1739 to 1742, one of the largest publishers in the colonies, Daniel Henchman of Boston, spent more than 30 percent of his printing budget on producing the evangelist's books.[94] Whitefield

---

[91] Quotation from *The Trial of Mr. Whitefield's Spirit. In Some Remarks upon his Fourth Journal* (London, 1740), cited in Luke Tyerman, *The Life of George Whitefield*, 2 vols. (New York, 1877), 1:456. *Boston Weekly News-Letter*, July 9–16, 1741.

[92] Rogers's entry is located in the manuscript version of Ledger "D," 151.

[93] Whitefield, *Sermons on Important Subjects*, 69.

[94] Evans, *American Bibliography*. Rollo G. Silver, "Publishing in Boston, 1726–1757:

not only profited from the sale of his works; he benefited from generous contributions that printers such as Henchman and Franklin donated to the Georgia orphan house.

[handwritten marginal notes:
• Whitefield constantly in News
• He along w/ Franklin kept his name on papers/editorials
• win/win situation w/ he + printers
• Preached to the common men + rich men, knew his audience.]

WHITEFIELD AS TEXT

Whitefield also presented himself through the colonial press as a text to be "read" by men and women. Indeed Whitefield shared Franklin's identification of text and life. Franklin's immersion in the mid-eighteenth-century print culture provided a powerful metaphor for his own self-perception. In an epitaph he wrote for himself when he was still young, Franklin reveals himself as text:

> The Body of
> B. Franklin,
> Printer;
> Like the Cover of an Old Book,
> Its Contents torn out,
> And stript of its Lettering and Gilding,
> Lies here, Food for Worms.
> But the Work shall not be wholly lost.
> For it will, as he believ'd, appear once more,
> In a new & more perfect Edition,
> Corrected and amended
> by the Author.[95]

As one scholar has noted, Franklin draws his readers into "a fantasy of being-in-print." Composing the piece when he was twenty-two, Franklin "wrote the epitaph not for a gravestone but for a page." The printer and writer had presented himself "as a text that lies here" on the printed sheet.[96]

Upon reading the epitaph, Whitefield wrote a letter in reply that recognized the metaphor of print as a valid expression of life. In a 1755 letter to Franklin, Whitefield wrote: "I have seen your *Epitaph*. Believe on Jesus, and get a feeling possession of God in your Heart, and you cannot possibly be disappointed of your expected second edition, finely corrected, and infinitely amended."[97] For some time Whitefield

---

The Accounts of Daniel Henchman," *Proceedings of the American Antiquarian Society* 66 (April 1957): 17–36.

[95] Labaree, *Papers of Benjamin Franklin*, 1:109–111.

[96] Michael Warner, *The Letters of the Republic: Publication and the Public Sphere in Eighteenth-Century America* (Cambridge, Mass., 1990), 73–74.

[97] Cited in Labaree, *Papers of Benjamin Franklin*, 5:475–476.

had "read" his friend's life and expressed concern that Franklin had not experienced the new birth. Thus he hoped the printer would make revisions.

Although Franklin rejected Whitefield's plea for a spiritual alteration, he had confidence his friend would always give him a fair "reading" even when Franklin came under public attack. On one occasion Whitefield wrote Franklin: "I have read the Libels writ against you . . . but they rather gave me this good Opinion of you that you continued to be useful to the Publick: For when I am on the Road and see Boys in a Field at Distance, pelting a Tree, though I am too far off to know what Tree it is, I conclude it has *Fruit* on it." Whitefield's point was that the character of Franklin's life was a more reliable text than what was printed about him.[98] The anecdote not only suggests that Whitefield perceived human events as texts to be read but indicates the degree of his immersion in the world of print.

Whitefield's theology also informed his understanding of the relation between life and text. The evangelical viewed salvation itself as God's imprinting his grace upon the hearts of men and women. Christians "are made partakers of a divine nature, and from Jesus Christ, they receive grace; and every grace that is in Christ, is copied and transcribed into their soul." The condition of one's heart determines the clarity of imprints. Deepest impressions are made on hearts prepared to receive God's grace. But even God is thwarted by hard hearts. To Whitefield the text inscribed within the souls of converts represented the most valid testimony to the new birth, far surpassing works of learned divines.[99]

In his writings Whitefield poured himself into the texts. In 1740, the evangelist granted Franklin permission to print his "life." Whitefield's goal was a realistic portrayal, "an account of [his] failings as well as [his] virtues," in order that readers might encounter the revivalist on the printed page.[100] His *Journals* were detailed, personal reports of his daily activities, providing readers with an opportunity to accompany him on his evangelical mission. Masterful pieces of self-promotion, Whitefield's autobiography and *Journals* gave Franklin—who printed both—a model for his own self-representation.[101]

[98] Ibid.
[99] *Select Sermons of Whitefield*, 102, 138.
[100] *Whitefield's Journals*, 35–36.
[101] See Stout, *Divine Dramatist*, 223.

o know about relationship b/tw life & text

EVANGELICAL COMMUNITY

Whitefield employed the evangelical news exchange to create an imaginary evangelical community. Through printed works revivalists participated in awakenings throughout the Atlantic world. Even when Whitefield was absent from the colonies, he kept American evangelicals informed of the revival's progress. For example, the Grand Itinerant forwarded newspaper articles, pamphlets, and books from English presses to Jonathan Edwards and others to "shew you what the Lord is about to do in Europe."[102] Whitefield's opponents noted that through print the evangelist had indeed forged a national community of revivalists. Edward Wigglesworth, a Boston antirevivalist, identified Whitefield as the leader and "blameable Cause" of the religious disorders spread in the colonies. When Whitefield protested that he did not know many of the itinerants Wigglesworth cited as disseminating confusion among the churches, Wigglesworth retorted, "nor will it much alter the Case, tho' some who may have had a Hand in [the disorders] are Men whom you never knew. For tho' you are unacquainted with them, yet they are but too well acquainted with your Writings and Bad Example."[103]

By printing and preaching throughout the colonies Whitefield standardized evangelicalism. He created a common language of the new birth that evangelicals everywhere employed to distinguish themselves from those who had not undergone a spiritual conversion. Through publicizing testimonials of the new birth, Whitefield provided a model that tended toward a uniform response to his message. Such uniformity extended to publicity itself. As Whitefield approached Charleston, South Carolina, for the first time, local evangelicals wondered how they should publicize his coming. They decided that their welcome should be similar to that accorded him in other places. Submitting an announcement to the *South Carolina Gazette*, Josiah Smith indicated that "the Publick will naturally expect some Account of Mr. WHITEFIELD, an imitation of other Places where he has preached."[104]

As a result of Whitefield's knitting together disparate awakenings, by 1740 evangelicals began viewing local revivals in an intercolonial and even transatlantic context. Thomas Prince's *Christian History* widened the context of New England revivalism by offering readers accounts of similar outpourings in New York, New Jersey, Pennsylvania, South

---

[102] Gillies, *Works of Whitefield*, 1:121.

[103] Edward Wigglesworth, *A Letter to the Reverend Mr. George Whitefield By Way of Reply to His Answer to the College Testimony against him and his Conduct* (Boston, 1745), 53.

[104] *South Carolina Gazette*, January 5, 1740.

Carolina, and Georgia. He also published "extracts of the most remarkable Pieces in the weekly Histories of Religion . . . printed both in England and Scotland," a reference to the revivalist publications that had inspired the *Christian History*. Justifying his devotion of almost 20 percent of his first year's issues to the Scottish revival, Prince observed that "our pious people were last Summer greatly refreshed with the glad Tidings arrived and reprinted here of a remarkable Revival of Religion at Cambuslang." Reproducing large portions of James Robe's *A Faithful Narrative of the Extraordinary Work of the Spirit of God at Kilsyth*, Prince noted for his readers that Robe "describes the deplorable Declension of vital Religion in New England as well as Scotland." By interweaving revival accounts from different parts of the Atlantic world, Prince underscored the vast geographic scope of the awakenings. In one reportorial shift from Scotland to America, Prince drew his readers' attention to the revival's spatial dimensions. "Having at present closed our religious Accounts from Scotland," he wrote in January 1744, "we now return to America, and Begin at the Westernmost End of the British Colony of Georgia, about four Thousand Miles to the Westward of Scotland."[105] Through his magazine, evangelical readers found kindred spirits in every corner of the Atlantic world.

Prince's account of the Scottish revivals illustrates the reciprocal exchange of evangelical publications across the Atlantic. Revivalists in America and Britain swapped accounts of awakenings to provide encouragement and inspiration for further evangelistic successes. Robe patterned his conception of revivalism after that of Jonathan Edwards. Edwards's work had been reprinted at Glasgow and circulated among Scottish revivalists. The widespread distribution in Britain of sermons, journals, and newspaper articles showing the revival's advance in America gave a sense of community to evangelicals at great distance from each other. After reading an account of American revivalism, Rev. Willison of Scotland explained how print united remote awakenings into a common experience. Willison exulted in "seeing the extraordinary Work there [New England] at present (tho' several Thousands of Miles distant from Scotland) is of the same Kind with that at Cambuslang and other Places about." Robe also viewed the American and British revivals as one. Remarking on the tremblings, faintings, and convulsions wrought in some undergoing the new birth, Robe observed that "there were the very same Appearances accompanying such an Effusion of the Holy Spirit in some of our American Colonies."[106]

[105] *Christian History*, March 5, 1743, and January 14, 1744.
[106] Ibid., March 5 and May 14, 1743.

In addition to placing the revivals in an intercolonial and transatlantic context, Prince situated them within Reformation history. He promised that the *Christian History* would, "in the Intervals of fresh Occurrences, . . . give the Reader the most famous Old Writers, both of the Church of England and Scotland from the Reformation, as also the first Settlers of New England and their Children: that we may see how far their pious Principles and Spirit are at this Day revived." By citing such evangelical divines as Richard Baxter, John Cotton, and Increase Mather, Prince sought to demonstrate the "great and lamented Decay of Religion in the succeeding Generations." After establishing the deplorable condition of vital Christianity, the editor encouraged his readers by relating the history of American revivals. Prince viewed Whitefield's arrival as a watershed in revivalism. Prior to his arrival, awakenings such as that at Windham, Connecticut, in 1721 had been transient and local. Although Prince depicted the revival led by Edwards in the Connecticut Valley as "more extensive," he represented the Great Awakening as more enduring and widespread, linking Whitefield and his followers with seventeenth-century Puritans.[107]

[107] Ibid., March 5, April 23, and June 4, 1943.

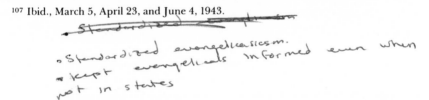

Interpreting the New Birth:
Audience Response

THE IMAGE of Whitefield as a producer of revivals suggests that his auditors were consumers of religion. For some, such a characterization contains more than a kernel of truth, as the case of Herman Husband illustrates. A fifteen-year-old boy living with his family in Maryland, Herman passed his leisure time entertaining himself with goods purchased from itinerant salesmen who peddled their wares in his community. He recalled "playing at cards," a popular pastime among "old men as well as young" made possible by "some Pedlars, bringing some Packs and selling in the Neighbourhood." His pleasure diminished, however, when his mother objected to his playing for money, rum, or pins—the latter two items no doubt also procured from the chapmen's packs. The young boy turned to reading for diversion, preferring romances such as *The Famous and Renowned History of Valentine and Orson* and a book of Robin Hood ballads, again available from the traveling salesmen.[1]

Then, in 1739, "there came news of a man, a preacher, newly come from England, that both men and women were ready to leave all their livings to follow him." Within days, a notice, perhaps a broadside or maybe a messenger, informed the Husbands and their neighbors that George Whitefield would be preaching within fifteen miles of their home. Herman attended that service and became "convinced that [the new birth] was the way to happiness, [but he] longed to see some of Whitefield's Writings, that [he] might more certainly know his opinion in this matter." In other words, he wanted to reflect on the itinerant's teachings and reach his own conclusions. Herman in fact acquired copies of the revivalist's works, perhaps from Scottish peddlers who hawked them or more likely from one of Whitefield's assistants who customarily lingered in a community dispensing the evangelist's sermons and *Journals*.[2] Thus Husband found the means of his conversion through the market, purchasing a commodity—in this case, a religious work that was, like most of the baubles consumed by colonists, touted as "recently arrived from England."

[1] Husband, *Remarks on Religion*, 207–210.
[2] Ibid., 220.

One of the risks in characterizing Whitefield as a salesman of religion is that of depicting his auditors as passive consumers. While Herman Husband's experience indicates that men and women did appropriate Whitefield's revivals through market exchange, it also suggests that, though consumers, they were active producers of meaning. To clarify how his audiences read Whitefield, the focus must shift from text to context—from the message he created to the many meanings his readers and listeners constructed as they filtered the words through their own circumstances. Roger Chartier and others have pointed out that texts do not convey a universal, transhistorical message understood in the abstract. Rather, people adapt a discourse to fit their own historical and social situations. Whether printed or spoken, "texts are not deposited in objects—manuscripts or printed books—that contain them like receptacles, and they are not inscribed in readers as in soft wax." Interpretations depend in part on how the text is presented and on how it is read, "silently or aloud, as sacralized or secularized, in community or singly, in public or in private." The result is "plural uses and multiple meanings" crafted by diverse readers to suit their own understanding of themselves and their place in the world about them.[3] For an understanding of Whitefield's message, then, it is necessary to examine both his presentation of the new birth's necessity and the re-presentation of his audiences.

When Husband attended the preaching service, he did not merely accept Whitefield's message at face value. While the evangelist had stirred a longing for the new birth within him, the inquisitive young man was not satisfied, feeling that Whitefield "in his discourse . . . had not explain'd adequately" the concept of the new birth. And Husband's definition of his conversion represented a departure from Whitefield's intentions. Husband equated the new birth with the "light within" as taught by Quakers, a competing claim in the marketplace of religious ideas that Whitefield vehemently opposed, claiming it led to pride.[4] Certainly Husband's defiance of political as well as religious authority, as evidenced by his becoming an apologist of the North Carolina Regulators and the western Pennsylvania Whiskey Rebels, ran counter to Whitefield's teaching of obedience to constituted rulers.[5] Although a

[3] Roger Chartier, *Cultural History: Between Practices and Representations*, trans. Lydia G. Cochrane (Ithaca, N.Y., 1988), 4–14.

[4] Husband, *Remarks on Religion*, 226–228. For Whitefield's views of Quakers, see *Whitefield's Journals*, 341.

[5] Husband participated with the North Carolina Regulators, a group of western North Carolina farmers protesting against the eastern-dominated legislature, in the Battle of Alamance in 1771. He also took part in the Whiskey Rebellion, a revolt of western Pennsylvania farmers that George Washington put down in 1794.

consumer of the word, Husband was also a producer of the revival's meaning for his own life.

Rather than viewing reading as "simply submission to textual machinery" that prescribes a single interpretation, Husband and other evangelicals saw reading as a response, a "poaching" of the text as readers produce unintended meanings. Writers attempt to guide the process, sometimes explicitly through prefaces, commentaries, and notes. But readers reconstruct texts sometimes singly when reading alone and sometimes in community when listening to reading in a group. In group readings, prevalent among evangelicals, meanings are determined by "interpretive communities, whose members share the same reading style and the same strategies of interpretation."[6]

Further, printers insinuate themselves into the interpretive process, creating a gap between writer and reader. By the size, format, quality, price, appearance, and promotion of the works they manufacture, printers influence meaning. The eighteenth century witnessed a hierarchy of books determined by size. Lord Chesterfield described the scheme: "Solid folios are the people of business with whom I converse in the morning. Quartos are the easier mixed company with whom I sit after dinner; and I pass my evenings in the light, and often frivolous chitchat of small octavos and duodecimos." The very size of a volume could suggest the density of its contents.[7]

To understand the meanings his audiences produce, then, one must examine the interaction between Whitefield's texts and the multiple contexts in which they were appropriated. Such an exploration must include the readers themselves: their identity, numbers, motivations, and capacities. It must also consider how revivalist and antirevivalist leaders attempted to guide reader interpretation. However skilled writers and speakers were in influencing audiences, men and women read evangelical ideas and practices within their own social circumstances and perceptions and produced variant meanings.

In particular the focus here is on the growing consumer market that expanded individual choices by making available broader assortments of goods and wider ranges of ideas. Increased competition for consumer attention, whether to sell a product or preach a doctrine, freed individuals from being captive to a single source. By the mid-1700s, persons in colonial towns and villages weekly read advertisements for a profusion of new items on the market. Even remote settlers had access to country stores or itinerant peddlers. Whitefield extended choice to

---

[6] Roger Chartier, "Texts, Printing, Readings," in *The New Cultural History*, ed. Lynn Hunt (Berkeley and Los Angeles, 1989), 156–158.

[7] Ibid., 167.

religion. By preaching outside parish boundaries in the marketplaces and communicating to a mass, public audience through newspapers, Whitefield expanded the range of possible meanings men and women could construct concerning spiritual matters. The result was a new sense of individualism by which lay people challenged not only their parish ministers but often Whitefield himself.

[handwritten annotation: ◦ Some audience did not reach well to Whitefield's sermons.]

READING AND REVIVALISM

Contemporaries for and against the revivals testified to the enormous crowds Whitefield attracted. Estimating the size of his reading public, however, is more problematic. Whitefield intended his message for a mass audience, never aiming for one defined by denominational affiliation. Although any attempt to estimate the number of people who bought and read Whitefield's works is more impressionistic than statistical, publication facts give some indication of the number of readers. Between 1737 and 1745, printers on both sides of the Atlantic published more than three hundred editions of his works.[8] While information on print runs is fragmentary, data from printers' ledgers and Whitefield's records suggest that the *average* minimum run was in excess of one thousand copies and perhaps as high as fifteen hundred. At the lower figure, printers made available at least three hundred thousand Whitefield publications in a population totaling about six million in Britain and America combined in 1740—in other words, a copy for every twenty men, women, and children. In the colonies alone, in the same period printers published eighty publications, or a minimum of eighty thousand copies in a population of nine hundred thousand in 1740—a ratio of one copy for every eleven people. While numbers of documents printed do not translate into readership and ratios do not represent actual readers, they do indicate an enormous demand for Whitefield's publications.

Opponents noted with alarm the flood of evangelical literature circulating in the American colonies. Timothy Cutler of Boston lamented the abundance of "Books of this unhappy tendency, Books Calvinistic, Enthusiastical, and Antinomian." Commenting on the unprecedented volume of evangelical works, Cutler claimed that "the Press here never had so full employ before, nor were people ever so busy in reading."

[8] Publication data taken from Roberts, *Whitefield in Print*. Of particular conceptual importance in analyzing the production and distribution of Whitefield's printed works is Robert Darnton, *The Business of the Enlightenment: A Publication History of the Encyclopédie, 1775–1800* (Cambridge, Mass., 1979).

Cutler's letters to the bishop of London indicate a greater concern over Whitefield's voluminous publications than over his preaching services. Even after Whitefield's departure from New England in late 1740, Cutler was dismayed that the itinerant's "pernicious doctrine and printed libels" continued to create a "flood of confusion" among men and women.[9]

In Britain and British North America, Whitefield disseminated his message among a highly literate population. Margaret Spufford's study of seventeenth-century English popular culture reveals a world of growing literacy as thousands of "humble readers" purchased inexpensive chapbooks distributed by itinerant peddlers. She estimates that by the late 1700s, 65 percent of East Anglian yeomen could read and eagerly bought books on courtship, sex, and song as well as historical and chivalric novels. However, the rate of literacy was uneven. "Widespread literacy and cheap print to satisfy it" arrived late in northeastern Scotland, not until the 1770s.[10]

Why literacy expanded in the seventeenth and eighteenth centuries is the subject of much investigation. David Creasy sees a strong link between the spread of commerce and literacy, noting that in the 1700s those most fully engaged in trade—retailers, distributors, specialist craftsmen, manufacturers, and processors—developed literacy rates from two-thirds to 90 percent. Persons in occupations further from the market, such as village crafts and manual labor, continued to reflect literacy rates of less than 50 percent.[11] Stephen Foster sees religious orientation as a strong influence on reading. Because of its emphasis on lay participation, Puritanism and the sects it influenced promoted literacy as essential to understanding divine purpose.[12] Whitefield attracted large numbers from the groups of readers defined by both Creasy and Foster: merchants and traders as well as dissenting evangelicals.

Studies of colonial literacy suggest that reading rates increased in every region throughout the eighteenth century. New England, and particularly Boston, began as highly literate because of the influences of Puritanism and commerce. Kenneth Lockridge sees the greatest change occurring among "back-country farmers" because of increased

[9] Perry, *Historical Collections*, 3:367.

[10] Margaret Spufford, *Small Books and Pleasant Histories: Popular Fiction and Its Readership in Seventeenth-Century England* (Athens, Ga., 1981), xviii, 12, 46.

[11] David Creasy, *Literacy and the Social Order: Reading and Writing in Tudor and Stuart England* (Cambridge, Eng., 1980), 136.

[12] Stephen Foster, *The Long Argument: English Puritanism and the Shaping of New England Culture, 1570–1700* (Chapel Hill, 1991), 7–8.

exposure to schools and newspapers.[13] Linda Auwers has discovered that women made dramatic strides in learning to read and write in the eighteenth century. Because of increased female education in New England, the percentage of women who could sign their names jumped from less than 30 in late 1600s to almost 90 percent in the third quarter of the 1700s.[14] Even in Virginia, where literacy rates lagged far behind those in New England, reading slowly spread among the "common planters"—ironically, in part because of "ignorant" itinerant evangelists who distributed revivalist pamphlets to backcountry people.[15]

Evangelicals promoted literacy even among those denied opportunity to read by law and circumstances. In 1740, Seward paid two thousand pounds as a down payment on five thousand acres of land on the Forks of the Delaware in Pennsylvania in order for Whitefield to "erect a Negroe School there." While in Wales raising money for the school, Seward was killed by a band of rock-throwing toughs hired by antirevivalists to disrupt his services. Although the stone that proved fatal to Seward also curtailed Whitefield's dream for his Pennsylvania school, it did not end the evangelist's efforts to educate slaves.[16] Through the support of the wealthy South Carolina convert Hugh Bryan, Whitefield opened a school in Charleston to teach black children to read. And in the frontier parish of St. Helen's, an SPG (Society for the Propagation of the Gospel in Foreign Parts) missionary conceded in 1740 that "there are two or three families in the Parish who have been lately prevailed upon to have their Negroes Instructed in the principles of the Christian faith by the Earnest Persuasions of Mr. Whitefield."[17]

African Americans demonstrated great interest in becoming literate when offered opportunities by evangelicals. When William Bolton, the former proprietor of the Philadelphia ballroom, experienced the new birth, he converted his assembly hall into a "School for teaching children to read." The *Boston Weekly News-Letter* reported response to Bolton's enterprise: "Upon notice that he would teach Negroes also, in 23 Days no less than 53 Black Scholars" enrolled in the program. White opposition was swift as opponents accused Bolton in court of violating

---

[13] Kenneth Lockridge, *Literacy in Colonial New England: An Enquiry into the Social Context of Literacy in the Early Modern West* (New York, 1974), 13, 21.

[14] Linda Auwers, "Reading the Marks of the Past: Explaining Female Literacy in Colonial Windsor, Connecticut," *Historical Methods* 13 (Fall 1980): 204.

[15] Isaac, *Transformation of Virginia*, 149–150.

[16] See *Pennsylvania Gazette*, December 4, 1740.

[17] Cited in Frank J. Klingberg, *An Appraisal of the Negro in Colonial South Carolina: A Study in Americanization* (Washington, D.C., 1941), 71.

the "Negroe Law." However, Bolton prevailed and continued the school without interruption.[18]

Virginia slaves also responded with courage and diligence to the chance to become readers. Samuel Davies, a Presbyterian prorevivalist who more than any other carried evangelical revivalism into Virginia, sought to instruct slaves in the Christian faith. In an address to slaveholders, Davies expressed his conviction that African Americans had the capacity to learn if given the opportunity. "Your Negroes may be ignorant and stupid as to divine Things," Davies wrote, "not for want of Capacity, but for Want of Instruction." Reflecting on his personal experiences in teaching blacks to read, Davies continued, "I have Reason to conclude that making Allowance for their low and barbarous Education, their imperfect Acquaintance with our Language, their having no Opportunity for intellectual Improvements, and the like, they are generally as capable of Instruction as the White People."[19]

When allowed by a few slaveholders to learn to read, African Americans demonstrated their desire and ability. Like Whitefield, Davies relied upon the Society for the Promotion of Christian Knowledge (SPCK) to supply devotional books and pamphlets to distribute among those who could not afford them. His letters to the SPCK reflect his interest in acquiring books for slaves. He expressed his compassion for "the poor *Negroe Slaves*, who are so far from having money to purchase books, that they themselves are the property of others." In thanking the organization for previous shipments and requesting others, Davies noted that slaves had viewed books "as a *Reward* of their *Industry*." Davies wrote, "I am told, that in almost every house in my congregation, and in sundry other places, they spend every leisure hour in trying to learn, since they expect Books as soon as they are capable of using them." His statement suggests that the acquisition of marketable commodities—books—may have been as great a motivator of blacks seeking education as the desire for salvation. Davies himself acknowledged that slaves wanted to read for their own purposes, including "curiosity, ambition, [and] vanity." Whatever the motivation, Davies continued to advocate literacy among slaves because "it render[ed] them more capable of Instructions in the great concerns of Religion."[20]

Backcountrymen along the Carolina and Virginia frontiers also had access to the print trade, and many could read. During his surveying expedition along the Virginia–North Carolina border, William Byrd

[18] *Boston Weekly News-Letter*, August 21, 1740.

[19] Cited in Winthrop Jordan, *White over Black: American Attitudes toward the Negro* (Chapel Hill, 1968), 188.

[20] Cited in George Pilcher, "Samuel Davies and the Instruction of Negroes in Virginia," *Virginia Magazine of History and Biography* 74 (July 1966): 295–296.

discovered literacy in the most unlikely places. He described a visit to Cornelius Keath, a Scots-Irish settler who "liv'd rather in a Penn than a House with his Wife and 6 Children." Byrd was appalled at the family's circumstances. "I never beheld such a Scene of Poverty in this happy part of the World," he recorded in his diary, adding, "the Hovel they lay in had no Roof to cover those wretches from the Injurys of the Weather; but when it rains, or was colder than Ordinary, the whole Family took refuge in a Fodder Stack." But to Byrd's surprise, the man could "read & write very well."[21]

The evangelical practice of reading aloud extended Whitefield's printed works beyond the literate. Within religious societies, Whitefield instituted what he and his associates termed "Letter Days" for the purpose of reading aloud news about the revival. John Wesley recorded in his journal one such occasion upon Whitefield's return to England in 1738 after his first American visit. Wesley reported that "George Whitefield read his journal at our Society," referring to the Fetter Lane Society in London.[22] John Lewis, publisher of the *Weekly History*, described a typical Letter Day conducted by Whitefield at his London Tabernacle: "Monday, February 14, was the Monthly Letter-Day at the Tabernacle; where letters were read from many correspondents concerning the success of the Gospel in various parts, and a verse or two sung at the end of each letter. The Reverend Mr. Whitefield read the letters; and begun, and concluded with an exhortation suitable to the occasion."[23] Through Letter Days, society members participated in the revival's successes in remote places, joining through print thousands of distant strangers in celebrating the revival of experimental religion.

Antirevivalists feared that most readers of Whitefield's works lacked sufficient education and discernment to resist the seduction of his teachings. One SPG missionary worried about his parishioners' uncritical acceptance of Whitefield's claims. He reported that "the generality of my hearers not only run after him but adore him as an oracle from heaven," looking upon his words as "the immediate dictates of the holy Ghost." Another Anglican clergyman in Pennsylvania expressed dismay over "how fond the common people are of novelties in religion, how easily they become a prey to seducers." Whitefield was able to "seduce" many readers because the "generality of the Common sort

[21] *William Byrd's Histories of the Dividing Line*, 305.

[22] Nehemiah Curnock, ed., *The Journal of the Rev. John Wesley, A.M. Sometime Fellow of Lincoln College, Oxford*, 8 vols. (London, 1938), 2:118.

[23] *The Christian History: Or, A General Account of the Progress of the Gospel, In England, Wales, Scotland, and America: So far as the Reverend Mr. Whitefield, his Fellow-Labourers, and Assistants are Concerned* (London, 1744), 73–81.

here are . . . a fickly, inconstant people." William Beckett, of Lewiston, Delaware, was taken aback by the reception of Whitefield's doctrines from pulpit and press. "It is surprising," Beckett wrote, "to observe how the vulgar every where are inclined to enthusiasm."[24] In short, Whitefield's opponents thought little of the evangelist's followers and of their capacity to read with discrimination.

Antirevivalists in Virginia petitioned the House of Burgesses to provide legal remedies against evangelicals who preyed upon the poor, disrupting the social order. One remonstrant in 1751 expressed particular concern over the practice of reading Whitefield's sermons to those with undeveloped powers of reasoning. He cited reports from the counties of Hanover, Henrico, and Goochland that had prevailed for years concerning "numerous assemblies, especially of the common people" who met under religious pretexts. He objected to the practice of "merely lay enthusiasts, who, in those meetings, read sundry fanatical books" to introduce their listeners to evangelicalism. Addressing the legislature during Whitefield's fourth American visit, the complainant feared the spread of Whitefield's influence by preachers and readers. He especially protested the itinerancy of John Cennick, who had accompanied Whitefield to America and conducted preaching services in Amelia and Albemarle counties. Virginia's House of Burgesses did pass a law mandating licensure for itinerant preachers, as did the legislatures in Massachusetts and Connecticut.[25] Behind the burgesses' fear was the idea that ordinary people might indeed read revivalist writings and reach conclusions threatening to the social order.

- Literacy bloomed in New World
- Anti-revivalists feel evangelicals preying on poor.

ATTEMPTS TO GUIDE READERS

Whitefield and his auditors did not make sharp distinctions between hearing and reading the gospel. To most, both exercises represented means of encountering God and receiving his grace. Whitefield's own conversion resulted from his private reading of a Puritan sermon. Print represented a powerful form of mediating God's word, allowing one to linger over the page in a sustained reflection of what the message meant to the reader. When converts described their experiences, the language was the same whether the individual had listened to a sermon or read a text. The Bible or other devotional works contained "the living speech of God, the 'voice' of Christ, a text that people 'heard.' "

[24] Wiliam Beckett to the secretary of the SPG, April 25, 1741, in Perry, *Historical Collections*, 5:83.
[25] Whitefield accused the Virginia commissary of using his political influence as a member of the colony's council to restrict itinerancy. See Gillies, *Works of Whitefield*, 2:419.

Responses to hearing and reading were interchangeable: "a rush of feeling, a moment of sharp self-awareness, a new sense of obligation, and all because . . . people thought of sermons [spoken or printed] as equivalent to the very speech of God."[26] Some of Whitefield's listeners literally transcribed his utterances into written statements by taking notes of his sermons.

Although evangelicals believed in the centrality of the proclaimed word, they also valued the printed word as a means of spreading the gospel. The seventeenth-century English Puritan Richard Baxter viewed "the Writings of Divines [as] nothing else but a preaching of the Gospel to the eye, as the voice preacheth it to the ear." While "vocal preaching . . . hath the preeminence in moving the affections, . . . Books have the advantage in many other respects." Through print every congregation has access to "the most judicious or powerful Preachers" even though their own pastors may not be gifted in the pulpit. And books are more enduring than sermons. Baxter observed that "if Sermons be forgotten, they are gone. But a Book, we may read over and over till we remember it: and if we forget it, may again peruse it at our pleasure." Concluding his endorsement of reading "well chosen" writings, Baxter wrote that "Books are domestick, present, constant, judicious, penitent, yea, and powerful Sermons."[27]

For more than thirty years prior to Whitefield's first arrival in America, Anglican missionaries had relied upon books to spread the gospel. Concerned about the lack of sufficient numbers of trained, conscientious ministers in the colonies, Thomas Bray shipped hundreds of books to Anglican clergymen and their parishioners. In 1700, Bray, founder of the SPG, sent a collection of 291 volumes to Christ Church in Philadelphia as the "foundation of a provincial library." Stating his faith in the efficacy of good books in promoting the gospel, Bray wrote "that nothing can so directly tend to encourage Good Men, and Lovers of Souls, to venture themselves in the Labours of the Gospel abroad, as good Books." He added that "nothing can so immediately tend to render them "Good and useful when they are there, as the same."[28] Although Whitefield and the early Methodists challenged Bray's canon, they agreed that good books would compensate for bad preaching.

From his association with the Holy Club, Whitefield followed the practice of distributing books. One of John Wesley's principles was that of "visiting and relieving the Prisoners and the Sick, and giving away

[26] David D. Hall, *Worlds of Wonder, Days of Judgment: Popular Religious Beliefs in Early New England* (Cambridge, Mass., 1990), 24, 42.

[27] Richard Baxter, *A Christian Directory* (London, 1673), 60.

[28] Cited in Edwin Wolf, *The Book Culture of a Colonial American City: Philadelphia Books, Bookmen, and Booksellers* (Oxford, 1988), 13–14.

Bibles, Common-Prayer Books, and the *Whole Duty of Man* . . . and explaining the Necessity and Usefulness of those holy Books at all Opportunities to those to whom they gave them." Whitefield, Hervey, Ingham, Broughton, Grimshaw, and others were more than distributors. To those who could read, the young evangelicals explained what "they don't understand." As for the illiterate, especially children, the Holy Club taught them how to read, taking care "that they be taught the Catechism."[29] That beginning in propagating the gospel through print had a lasting influence in the early Methodists' ministries. Thomas Broughton became secretary of the SPCK, which distributed thousands of religious books and pamphlets in Britain and America. Some of the others, such as Hervey, the Wesleys, and Whitefield, wrote scores of volumes, and in many cases published their own works. John Wesley and Whitefield operated Book Rooms located in their respective London headquarters, distributing their works throughout the Atlantic world.

Whitefield and other evangelicals were not content with merely distributing books and tracts; they attempted to make certain that readers arrived at correct—i.e., the authors'—interpretations. Thus, evangelicals attempted to direct their followers' reading. The first goal was to influence *what* people read by differentiating between good and bad works. Good works reflected experimental religion, while bad ones promoted formalism, or worse, rationalism. Whitefield provided readers with a list of acceptable volumes either by recommending or by publishing titles. Throughout his autobiographical works and travel *Journals*, the revivalist mentioned books helpful to him and worthy of his followers' perusal. He also published a number of low-cost works and wrote recommendatory prefaces in others.

Consistent with his emphasis on experience as the keystone of true religion, Whitefield recommended to his readers devotional works that had influenced his own faith. He mentioned most of those titles in his most personal writings, especially his autobiography and *Journals*. Some were works written by seventeenth-century Dissenters who stressed the necessity of a spiritual new birth, including Scougal's *The Life of God in the Soul of Man* and Baxter's *Call to the Unconverted*. Whitefield also recommended volumes by Catholic writers who emphasized spiritual transformation over doctrinal obedience—titles such as Juan de Castaniza's *Spiritual Combat* and Thomas à Kempis's *Imitation of Christ*. Whitefield recommended works by both German and English Pietists, including Francke's *Against the Fear of Man* and Law's *Serious*

[29] Whitefield, *Several Discourses Upon Practical Subjects*, 8, 12–14.

Call to a Devout Life, On Christian Perfection, and *The Absolute Unlawfulness of the Stage Entertainment.*[30]

Whitefield did more than recommend titles to his readers; he also offered to act as their guide in interpreting those works. In 1759, Whitefield wrote a preface to an edition of the Bible prepared by the Anglican minister Samuel Clarke, aiming his remarks "at the Serious Reader." Assuming the role of the New Testament character Philip the Evangelist, Whitefield asked his unseen audience, "Understandest thou what thou readest?" Whitefield urged his readers to assume a "teachable and child-like disposition" in approaching the Scriptures. He insisted that commentators like Clarke are necessary guides for the laity. "For though the grand lines of our Christian faith and practice are written in such plain and legible character," Whitefield cautioned, "we shall find many things both in the Old and New Testaments, into the due knowledge of which, we have need of some men, or of some good men's works to guide us." In addition to Clarke's analysis, Whitefield recommended that readers consult Matthew Henry's "incomparable comment upon the Bible." He concluded with an admonition for diligence in biblical study. He expressed his hope that whether Christians "read this or any other comment, or the pure scriptures, without any comment, . . . [they] may in such wise read, mark, learn, and inwardly digest them."[31]

To ensure that his followers had available good books, Whitefield published works he deemed worthy of reprinting. For instance he published a sermon by the martyrololgist John Foxe, *A Sermon of Christ Crucified.* He also assisted in "bringing out" a two-volume edition of John Bunyan's works, to which he added a recommendatory preface. In explaining why he helped make these writings available, Whitefield linked seventeenth-century Puritanism and eighteenth-century revivalism. "Puritans of the last century," he wrote, "[were] such burning and shining lights. Though dead, by their writings they yet speak: a peculiar unction attends them to this very hour." Noting the reception of Puritan writings among evangelical revivalists, Whitefield observed "that the more, true and vital religion hath revived at home or abroad, the more the good old puritanical writings . . . have been called for." Displaying an awareness of what evangelicals purchased at bookshops, Whitefield noted that such works as "the unparalleled commentary of the good Mr. Matthew Henry, the pious and practical writing of the excellent Mr. Flavel, and the critical and judicious commentaries and

[30] *Whitefield's Journals,* 43–79.
[31] Preface to Samuel Clarke's edition of the Bible in Gillies, *Works of Whitefield,* 4:275–277.

tracts of the accurate Doctor Owens, I hear are enquired after, and bought up, more and more every day."[32]

Concerned that the church failed to instruct its own members in Protestant principles, Whitefield published editions of Anglican liturgical documents such as catechisms and homilies. He expressed dismay at the "dreadful ignorance, as to the fundamentals of our holy religion, that almost every where abounds amongst the members of our established church." To make the church's devotional works available to a large number of readers, Whitefield "selected a few of the most essential homilies, with a suitable collect and a hymn [for] each, at a very small price, on purpose for the instruction and edification of the poorer sort, who are generally chiefly attacked by the parties of the Romish communion." His model for distributing the homilies was that of the Scottish church. According to Whitefield, "Her confessions of faith . . . are printed so frequently and so cheap that they are almost in every hand."[33]

But Whitefield did more than reprint works; he also edited them. In 1748, he published an abridgement of William Law's *Serious Call*. Always concerned about the length and cost of books, Whitefield shortened the work by "excluding whatever is not truly Evangelical," thereby hoping to render the volume "more useful to the children of God." After reducing the original to only "truly Evangelical" passages, Whitefield then added his own interpretations, "illustrating the subject more fully from the Scripture."[34]

Some readers followed Whitefield's recommendations in adding volumes to their libraries. In his study of private libraries in the colonial south, Richard Beale Davis discovered many evangelicals who owned not only Whitefield's own writings but works recommended by the revivalist. An ardent Whitefield supporter, Isaac Chanler, a Baptist minister in Charleston, "had six of the twenty books especially recommended by that evangelist" and a five-volume set of Whitefield's works. Peter Porcher, a wealthy South Carolina rice planter, also included in his collection "several [titles] recommended by Whitefield."[35] Thus, for some of his followers, Whitefield's recommendations succeeded in helping shape evangelicals' reading habits.

[32] Recommendatory preface to the works of Bunyan in ibid., 303–308. Whitefield's preface for the martyrologist's work in Foxe, *A Sermon of Christ Crucified*, ii–iii.

[33] For Whitefield's preface to his edition of the homilies, see Gillies, *Works of Whitefield*, 4:441–443.

[34] See n. 106 to chapter 2, above. For Whitefield's rationale for editing, see Gillies, *Works of Whitefield*, 4:375.

[35] Richard Beale Davis, *Intellectual Life in the Colonial South, 1585–1763*, 3 vols. (Knoxville, Tenn., 1978), 2:572–573.

Other noted evangelicals recommended Whitefield's works to lay revivalists. Gilbert Tennent was one of Whitefield's warmest admirers and strongest supporters. In 1746, when Whitefield's foes attacked him as an enthusiast and an antinomian, Tennent prefaced a volume of Whitefield's sermons, "recommend[ing] them to the World, as sound, seasonable, and solid Composures." In praising the book, he noted that the sermonic themes were "so well suited to the Times, . . . the Stile is easy and natural, [and the message] . . . equally fitted to alarm Sinners and comfort the Saints of God." Tennent admitted that Whitefield had invited charges of heterodoxy through "some exceptionable, unguarded Expressions in some of his former Writings." However, he urged readers to consider that the errors resulted from "young years, strong Passions, [and] Education in Arminian Principles." Concluding his recommendatory preface, Tennent claimed that "Charity should induce us to put a favourable Construction on [Whitefield's early writings], at least on his Designs; especially considering that his after Writings set many Things in a better Light."[36]

Whitefield's critics also attempted to guide readers, cautioning readers to examine the revivalist's works with a critical eye. In a pamphlet published by Franklin in 1740, George Gillespy, an antirevivalist Presbyterian minister in Philadelphia, challenged men and women "to read, and seriously to weigh, without Prejudice" Whitefield's sermons and *Journals*. Selecting the evangelist's "own Words, taken out of his Printed Pieces, . . . [as] the Grounds of [his] Remarks," Gillespy invited readers to "Examine Mr. Whitefield by the Word of God." The author believed that reasonable people would therein conclude that Whitefield was "quite inconsistent with himself . . . [and] a man under a delusive Spirit." Gillespy knew that many would overlook flaws in Whitefield's writings because they believed the Grand Itinerant was a divine instrument of good. Cautioning against the blinding effect of Whitefield's publicity, which highlighted successes, Gillespy warned: "Let not his . . . Success, in God's doing some Good to Souls preached by him, be your Rule." He concluded with a jab at the accuracy of Whitefield's press coverage, suggesting that "the Success is not so great as is boasted of, if truly considered."[37]

Newspaper publishers also influenced reader perceptions of Whitefield by their editorial comments. Samuel Kneeland, the prorevivalist publisher of the *Boston Gazette*, attempted to support the evangelist while increasing sales of his publications. The December 10, 1754,

[36] George Whitefield, *Five Sermons; With a Preface by the Rev. Gilbert Tennent* (Philadelphia, 1746), iii–iv.

[37] George Gillespy, *Remarks Upon Mr. George Whitefield, Proving Him a Man under Delusion* (Philadelphia, 1740), 2.

edition reported Whitefield's Boston farewell sermon, emphasizing the preacher's declaration that he "never intended to harm ministers or colleges," a reference to charges first leveled a decade earlier. Attempting to lend credence to Whitefield's claim that he had publicly renounced unguarded expressions criticizing Harvard and Boston clergymen, Kneeland gave readers a brief history of the matter. Kneeland wrote, "The Printer hereby informs the Publick that in 1749 Mr. Whitefield, then in London, sent over a Pamphlet he printed there, wherein he freely owns the exceptionable things in his Journals; with his Desires that it might be Re-Printed here, which was accordingly done by me." Combining an interest in commerce with his concern for justice, Kneeland added that he had "a Number of them still by me to dispose."[38] Kneeland attempted to assure readers that Whitefield was a changed person, and should be "read" not as an intemperate youth but as a mature evangelical leader.

Antirevivalist newspaper publishers also attempted to guide reader interpretation of Whitefield. Thomas Fleet, editor of the *Boston Evening-Post*, reprinted a letter from a Charleston revivalist, chronicling the itinerant's preaching activities in the Lower South during the winter of 1752. The report ended with Whitefield's spring itinerary, including the announcement that the evangelist would "shortly embark for Bermudas, from whence he will go to New-England." Fleet could not resist editorializing on Whitefield's plans in brackets immediately following the letter. "If he comes upon the OLD ERRAND," Fleet wrote, "'tis great Odds he misses his Aim."[39]

Whitefield himself attempted to shape reader interpretation by selecting only favorable newspaper articles for distribution among evangelicals. While traveling in America on his second preaching tour, Whitefield instructed James Read, a bookseller in New-Castle, Delaware, to "send all the parts of the late newspapers concerning me . . . by private hand to [John] Lewis in Bartholomew Close." Once in the prorevivalist Lewis's hands, the articles would be reprinted in the *Christian History*. Whitefield instructed his followers to reprint and distribute only those newspaper accounts favorable to the revivals. In 1747, he asked Thomas Prince to send to England and Scotland "such paragraphs that are printed in Kneeland and Green concerning me. Many at home will be glad to know where and how I am."[40] Kneeland and Green were publishers of the *Boston Gazette* who championed Whitefield's cause in a newspaper war with Thomas Fleet. Whitefield wanted

[38] *Boston Gazette*, December 10, 1754.
[39] *Boston Evening-Post*, April 13, 1752.
[40] George Whitefield to Thomas Prince, May 21, 1747, Etting Collection, Historical Society of Pennsylvania.

APRIL 10. 1740.   NUMB. 591.

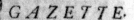

The Pennsylvania GAZETTE.

Containing the freshest Ad-   vices Foreign and Domestick.

A *Letter from the Rev. Mr.* WHITEFIELD, *at* Georgia, *to a Friend in* London, *wherein he vindicates his Asserting,* That Archbishop *Tillotson* knew *no more of Christianity than* Mahomet.

Savannah, January 18. 1739,40.

My Dear Friend,

THO' that Saying of the Psalmist, *Thou shalt answer for me, O Lord my God,* has generally been a Rule for my Conduct, in respect to my Adversaries; yet when the Glory of God and the Welfare of his People are concern'd, I think it my Duty to maintain whatever I have asserted in any of my Discourses, either publick or private.----My affirming *That Archbishop* Tillotson *knew no more of Christianity than* Mahomet, has been look'd upon as one of the most unjustifiable Expressions that ever proceeded out of my Mouth: For this I am not only look'd upon as a greater Monster than ever by my Enemies, but also have been secretly despised and censured by some, who, otherwise, were my Friends. Indeed, I dare not say this Expression came originally from me: No; my dear and honoured Friend Mr. *John Wesly,* if I mistake not, first spoke it in a private Society, when he was expounding Part of St. *Paul's* Epistle to the *Romans,* and proving the Doctrine of Justification in the Sight of God, by Faith alone, in Contradistinction to good Works. It is in this particular (not to mention others) that I have and do now join Issue with my honour'd Friend, and upon the maturest Deliberation, say again what I have often said before, *That Archbishop* Tillotson *knew no more about* true *Christianity than* Mahomet. — Whatever high Opinion others might have of that great Man and his Works, I must confess he was never a Favourite of mine. My Sermon on *the Eternity of Hell Torments* was directly level'd against a Discourse of his on that Subject, before I left the University: And since I came from thence, my Dislike of him has been much encreas'd, because I have observ'd all natural Men generally speak well of Archbishop *Tillotson's* Works. — And if we may judge of Men's Writings as well as themselves, by our Lord's Rule, we cannot but pronounce a Woe against those Books which natural Men generally speak well of. Did he teach the Truth as it is in Jesus, Thousands, who now admire, would throw

aside his Discourses as waste Paper. --- But I would not lay all the Stress of my Objections here — Out of his own Writings will I prove my Assertion. — Any spiritual Man that reads them, may easily see that the Archbishop knew of no other than a bare historical Faith: And as to the Method of our Acceptance with God through Jesus Christ, and our Justification by Faith alone (which is the Doctrine of the Scripture and the Church of *England*) he certainly was as ignorant thereof as *Mahomet* himself. — It would be endless to produce all the Passages out of his Sermons, that prove this; I shall only refer every impartial Reader to *Vol.* 2*d. Serm.* 52*d.* 53*d.* 54*th.* 55*th.* 56*th.* The Title of which runs thus — "On the Nature of Regeneration, " and its Necessity, in order to our Justification and " Salvation." So that according to this Title, His Grace intended to prove, that we must first be regenerated and sanctified, and then on Account of that Regeneration or Sanctification, that God will justify, i. e. acquit, accept and reward us. --- That I do not wrong the Archbishop, is plain from this Passage in *Sermon* 52*d. page* 325, *Folis.* " All that the Gospel requires as " necessary to these Purposes (i.e. to Man's Justification " and Salvation) is that we perform the Conditions of " the Gospel, that so we may be capable of being made " Partakers of the Blessing of it." And at the End of *Sermon* 56, which is the last on that Subject, and as the Summary of what he had before been delivering, He writes thus — " You see then what it is that must " recommend us to the Favour of God. The real " *Renovation* of our Hearts and Lives after the Image " of him that created us, before ever we can hope to be " restored to the Grace and Favour of God, or to be " capable of the Reward of eternal Life: And what " could God have done more reasonable than to make " those very Things the Terms of our Salvation, " which are the necessary *Causes* and Means of it? " How could he have dealt more mercifully and " kindly with us, than to appoint that to be a Conditi- " on of our Happiness which is the only Qualification " that can make us capable of it?" Had St. *Paul* been alive and read this Passage, I am persuaded he would have pronounced an ANATHEMA against the Writer of it, as he did against the *judaizing Teachers* in the Church of *Galatia.* — For what can be more contradictory to the Gospel of Jesus Christ: Here is not a Word mention'd about the all-sufficient, perfect and everlasting

8. Colonial newspapers afforded readers extensive revival coverage.

his readers to have access to interpretations that placed the revivals in a positive light.

However, Whitefield and other evangelical writers realized their limitations in presenting the gospel in print. A prolific author of devotional works, John Wesley stressed the role of readers in interpreting evangelical tenets. "It must be remember'd that the great practical truths of religion," he wrote, "cannot be fully discerned but by those readers who have read the same things in their own souls." In other words, revivalists believed that proper understanding involved the heart as well as the head, experience *and* reason. Only by realizing that the new birth meant changes in attitudes and behavior could readers understand the revivalists. Gospel truths eluded all but those who derived their knowledge "not from commentaries, but experience. . . . This is that inward, practical, experimental, feeling knowledge, so frequently commanded by our [Lord]."[41] The message was clear: readers, not writers, produced understanding not simply by viewing words on a printed page but by sifting texts through a changed heart.

• Books used to spread truth

THE NEW BIRTH IN SOCIAL CONTEXT

Although Whitefield preached a universal message as he traveled through the colonies, his audiences filtered his sermons through local circumstances, producing a variety of meanings. When he arrived in Philadelphia in 1739, Whitefield unwittingly acted as a catalyst for deepening divisions already existing among Pennsylvania Presbyterians. When almost thirty thousand Scots-Irish immigrated to America in the early 1700s, they brought with them a controversy over the church's institutional structure. Although all embraced Calvinism with its emphasis on election, original sin, and the covenant of grace, they differed over the clergy's role and authority. So-called Old Lights favored a "highly skilled, academically trained ministry" presiding over a "formal, hierarchical structure of Presbyterian government." New Lights advocated an active laity, and while insisting on an educated ministry, emphasized personal piety, demanding that individuals "participate actively in their own conversion."[42] Through their diverse reactions to Whitefield's preaching, contending factions widened their rift.

While Whitefield adhered to Calvinism, the Old Light Presbyterians

[41] John Wesley, *The Christian's Pattern* (London, 1735), xix–xx.

[42] Marilyn J. Westerkamp, *Triumph of the Laity: Scots-Irish Piety and the Great Awakening, 1625–1760* (New York, 1988), 184.

in Pennsylvania accused him of embracing Arminianism with its emphasis on human agency in salvation. In 1740, some Philadelphia clergy questioned Whitefield's orthodoxy in an anonymous pamphlet, *The Querist*. Written from a Calvinist perspective, the document cited and challenged several extracts from Whitefield's writings. The authors found particularly objectionable Whitefield's allusions to universal salvation and the "efficacy of sincere repentance." His detractors believed he attributed an unwarranted role to men and women in their own redemption—ironically, the identical charge Whitefield had leveled at Wesley. Whitefield had become a Calvinist in America, probably because of his intense contact with the New Light Tennents. But the Querists thought that Whitefield had moved beyond orthodoxy, attacking him for rejecting an "intellectually correct theology in favor of experimental piety." One opponent, George Gillespy, portrayed Whitefield as "a man under a delusion of spirit . . . a strengthener of erroneous persons, as Arminians, Moravians, and a puller-down of a Reformation work."[43] New Light ministers and laity approved the itinerant's preference for experimental religion and applauded his support of Gilbert Tennent and his "Log College," a training school for revivalists, including laymen.[44] Hence, a long-standing dispute among the colony's Presbyterians influenced how his auditors interpreted Whitefield's message. Never an advocate of denominationalism, he found himself in the center of a theological debate that split the Philadelphia synod. And, favoring a genuine conversion experience over "head learning," Whitefield opted to admit his theological errors and reaffirm his allegiance to the Westminster Confession, the creed of Calvinist orthodoxy.

In addition to preaching within a context characterized by religious disputation, Whitefield found that his auditors and readers placed social interpretations on the revivals. From the outset, the early Methodists practiced a democracy that disregarded social standing, a stance that both attracted and repelled men and women in Britain and America. In their London tabernacles Wesley and Whitefield insisted that "none were suffered to call any place their own, but the first comes sat down first." While they separated men and women during worship, rich and poor commingled. Groups of colonial worshipers attending out-of-doors revival meetings took on a democratic character that unsettled some contemporaries interested in maintaining social boundaries. In Philadelphia, a Whitefield supporter writing under the pseudonym Obadiah Plainman accused an antirevivalist of denouncing

43 Ibid., 188.
44 Ibid., 185–186.

revivalists as "the Mob, or the Rabble." Plainman reminded the spokes-man for the "Better Sort" that writers such as Demosthenes, Cicero, Algernon Sydney, and John Trenchard had "never approached [the lower orders] but with Reverence: *The High and Mighty Mob, The Majesty of the Rabble, The Honour and Dignity of the Populace*, or such like Terms of Respect."[45] Although Whitefield addressed a mass audience without making class distinctions, colonists read him within a social context where rapid demographic and commercial growth meant that individuals constantly renegotiated their position in society.

Whitefield's arrival in Boston in 1740 coincided with an economic crisis that had divided the city, influencing how men and women viewed his message. As one of the busiest colonial ports, Boston depended on trade for its vitality, and recent events had disrupted New England's commerce. After twenty years of peace, war erupted in 1739 between England and Spain, drawing colonists into the struggle for empire. While some benefited by shipping provisions to British armed forces, most suffered from sharp curtailment of Atlantic trade. Adding to social unrest, Whitehall responded to complaints of English merchants by insisting on retirement of the province's highly inflated paper currency. Defying ministerial instructions, colonists proposed two solutions, one a Land Bank favored by farmers who could receive bills of credit for their land, and the other a Silver Bank organized by wealthy Boston merchants who advocated a less inflationary medium tied to silver.[46] In a study of church records and membership lists of Land and Silver banks of 1740, one scholar found that "Land Bankers worshiped preponderantly at New Light Congregational churches or at Congregational churches that had both Old Light and New Light elements, [and] Silver Bankers worshiped mostly at Anglican and Old Light Congregational churches."[47] While Whitefield's supporters and opponents did not divide neatly along lines of the currency controversy, they nevertheless interpreted the evangelist's message to defend their positions.

Although Whitefield's message focused primarily on personal salvation, it concealed powerful social implications that his Boston audience seized. Echoing words of Jesus, Whitefield preached against love of money and underlined how difficult it was for the rich to enter the Kingdom of God. He maintained that "God has chosen the poor of this

---

[45] *Pennsylvania Gazette*, May 15, 1740.

[46] Gary B. Nash, *The Urban Crucible: Social Change, Political Consciousness, and the Origins of the American Revolution* (Cambridge, Mass., 1979), 212–214.

[47] Rosalind Remer, "Old Lights and New Money: A Note on Religion, Economics, and the Social Order in 1740 Boston," *William and Mary Quarterly* 37 (October 1990): 566–567.

world" and contended that "the rich [failed to] believe or attend on [Christ]."[48] Rather than advocating that those with abundant material resources give up their wealth, Whitefield encouraged them to earn and spend for advancing the gospel by contributing to those less fortunate. However, other itinerants, such as James Davenport, followed Whitefield in Boston, proclaiming a strong antimarket, antimaterialist bias. Maintaining that Boston's problems stemmed from commerce and consumption, Davenport dramatized his opposition to worldly goods by publicly burning his own possessions and encouraging his auditors to do the same.[49] Because he was the recognized leader of revivalism, Whitefield received much blame for fomenting economic discontent. What he had intended as a religious awakening became embroiled in economic and social unrest. Opponents of the Silver Bank scheme, for example, couched their protest in religious epithets, calling merchants "carnal Wretches, Hypocrites, Fighters against God, Children of the Devil, cursed Pharisees." And antirevivalists denounced Whitefield's preaching in social terms, lamenting that "such an enthusiastic, factious, censorious spirit was never known here." One Whitefield opponent wrote sarcastically: "Every low-bred, illiterate person can resolve cases of conscience, and settle the most difficult points of divinity, better than the most learned divines."[50]

Whitefield's American preaching tour also coincided with a time of racial tension from South Carolina to New York. Whitefield's audiences constructed interpretations of his message in racial terms. To the Philadelphia slaves Whitefield encouraged to read, revival represented enlightenment in the form of literacy as well as salvation.[51] But to South Carolina slaveholders offended by Whitefield's attack on their cruel treatment of slaves, revivalism signified a "sinful and dangerous [threat] to the publick safety."[52] In South Carolina's Stono Rebellion of September 1739, sixty people died as "a group of slaves struck a violent but abortive blow for liberation."[53] Whitefield's preaching the message of the new birth to Charleston's blacks and whites two months later prompted some whites to view his ministry as incendiary. One antirevivalist accused Whitefield of promoting "Felo de se among the

[48] Whitefield, *Sermons on Important Subjects*, 358–359.
[49] *Boston Weekly Post-Boy*, March 28, 1743.
[50] Cited in Nash, *Urban Crucible*, 215–216.
[51] *Whitefield's Journals*, 422.
[52] Alexander Garden, *Six Letters to the Reverend Mr. George Whitefield . . . Together with Mr. Whitefield's Answer to the first Letter* (Boston, 1740). The sixth letter contains remarks on Whitefield's 1740 letter concerning treatment of slaves.
[53] Peter Wood, *Black Majority: Negroes in Colonial South Carolina from 1670 through the Stono Rebellion* (New York, 1974), 308.

Slaves and Insurrection against their Masters." Upon reading White-field's 1740 pamphlet attacking slaveholders' treatment of their slaves, William Douglass, a Boston physician, wrote a South Carolinian: "considering what usage your Slaves commonly meet with, I wondered they did not put an End to their own Lives or yours, rather than bear such Usage."[54]

Whitefield understood the importance of contextualizing his message. He preached gospel principles in language drawn from everyday life. To understand Whitefield's sermons, then, it is necessary to examine not just texts but contexts in which his audiences read and heard them. Whitefield knew the importance of framing his message in language familiar to his hearers. He endeavored to clothe his ideas in "such plain language that the meanest negro or servant . . . may understand," believing that if the "poor and unlearned can comprehend, the learned and rich must."[55] Consequently he preached the necessity of a spiritual conversion in the language of ordinary people's daily experience, often casting his theology in mercantile terms. Whitefield admired those evangelical preachers who, like one Dr. Marryat of London, employed "market language" to preach the gospel. In Marryat's usage, market language included tropes drawn from agriculture, commerce, and manufacturing.[56]

Whitefield's auditors appropriated his message in many different contexts—large crowds, private homes, times of crisis, moments of meditation—with the result that a variety of meanings was produced. Some listened to the persuasive orator as part of a mass audience. The German Lutheran Henry Melchior Muhlenberg observed that mechanics and other uneducated hearers often responded only to the "preacher's person, posture, voice, . . . bodily motions, gestures, facial expressions, etc." He told of a German woman who, after attending one of Whitefield's services, asserted that never in her life had she had "such a quickening, awakening, and edifying experience as when she listened to this man." Muhlenberg pointed out that she "understood nothing of his English sermon, but from his gestures, expressions, looks, and voice," she gained the "vivid impression that he was serious and sincere in what he said."[57] In other words, she viewed Whitefield himself as a text, and her reading of him was favorable.

---

[54] William Douglass, *A Summary, Historical and Political, of the first planting, progressive Improvements, and the present State of the British Settlements in North America*, 2 vols. (Boston, 1748 and 1753), 2:141.

[55] Gillies, *Works of Whitefield*, 2:265.

[56] *Select Sermons of George Whitefield*, 193.

[57] *The Journals of Henry Melchior Muhlenberg*, trans. Theodore Trappert and John Doberstein, 2 vols. (Philadelphia, 1942), 2:696.

The former slave Olaudah Equiano also viewed Whitefield's preaching as a text, interpreting the evangelist's performance through his own experiences in bondage. What captivated Equiano's attention as he listened to Whitefield in Philadelphia was how hard the preacher worked in delivering the gospel. "I saw this pious man exhorting the people with the greatest fervour and earnestness," Equiano wrote in his autobiography. He added that Whitefield "sweat[ed] as much as I ever did while in slavery on Montserrat beach." The itinerant's performance left a deep impression on Equiano as he compared Whitefield with other ministers he had heard. "I was very much struck and impressed with this [performance]," he recalled; "I had never before seen divines exert themselves in this manner before."[58] For at least one auditor, Whitefield had become a laborer, toiling in his business of evangelism.

Others appropriated Whitefield through reading about his successes or perusing his works in private. Catherine Bryan, wife of one of the evangelist's most ardent supporters, the South Carolina planter Hugh Bryan, testified to the effect of reading Whitefield's sermons. In a letter to her sister, Mrs. Bryan wrote that "there was a particular providence in sending those sermons to me when I stood so much in need of instruction." She claimed that the character of Whitefield came through in his printed discourses. She added, "it gave me a great opinion of the author for I thought it was impossible he should treat of those things as he does if he had not experienced them and that in a more extraordinary manner than I had." She encouraged her sister to read Whitefield's sermons and *Journals*, testifying that from them she had received "great advantage."[59] She was aware that the new birth could occur at any time, for the solitary reader of the revivalist's sermons as well as for his auditor at a crowded service.

• People interpreted Whitefield's sermons depending on the region,

READER-RESPONSE

Most scholars have depicted Whitefield as a master of the spoken word, insisting that his success as a preacher rested on his sheer oratorical ability. For some, Whitefield's appeal was a function of his extemporaneous sermons, of their "channeling the full heart and soul of the speaker into the actual moment of delivery and fusing a unique bond

[58] Paul Edwards, ed., *Equiano's Travels: His Autobiography, The Interesting Narrative of the Life of Olaudah Equiano or Gustavus Vassa the African* (Oxford, 1989), 92.

[59] *Living Christianity Delineated in the Diaries and Letters of Two Eminently pious Persons lately deceased; viz. Mr. Hugh Bryan, and Mrs. Mary Hutson, Both of South Carolina* (London, 1760), 21–22.

between speaker, audience, and the immediate solution."[60] The spontaneity and enthusiasm of his performances, they argue, disappeared when reduced to the printed page. Indeed, some contemporaries saw little to praise in Whitefield's writing abilities. One antirevivalist, Rev. James Honeyman of Newport, claimed that while Whitefield aped the "sublety of [George] Fox," he lacked the great Quaker's "sophistry of a pen."[61] From Franklin's perspective, Whitefield's publications distracted contemporaries from his powerful oratory, serving only as a target for his enemies' attacks on his theology.[62]

Yet many other voices of the mid-eighteenth century testify to the power of Whitefield's printed works. Favorable readings by leading colonial ministers predisposed many toward the evangelist. As Whitefield embarked on his American itinerary in 1739, he sent copies of his printed *Journals*, sermons, and letters to leading colonial divines as a means of convincing them of his orthodoxy. Whitefield forwarded copies to such New England evangelicals as Benjamin Colman of Boston and Jonathan Edwards of Northampton. In a letter to Whitefield acknowledging receipt of a packet of printed documents, Colman wrote, "I lov'd and honour'd [you] from the first Sight I had of your Journal to Gibraltar." He added, "when I saw your nine Sermons printed in 1738 . . . I saw more Reason to admire the Work and Grace of God in your Rise and Progress." Confessing that he had worried about Whitefield's claims to direct divine inspiration and the charges of enthusiasm they drew, Colman expressed satisfaction "by what [he had] since seen from your Pen in your answer to the Lord Bishop of London."[63] One of the leaders of the revival in New Jersey, Gilbert Tennent, also testified to the correctness of Whitefield's theology. He wrote Whitefield, "your sermons have much confirmed the truths of Christ which have been preached here for many years."[64] Whitefield's familiar message of the new birth's necessity arrived first in print, preceding his preaching among Americans.

Scores of ordinary men and women testified that reading Whitefield's works played an important role in their conversions. In a representative letter to Whitefield, one correspondent captures the powerful moment of encountering God on the printed page: "On reading your account of what the Lord is doing for you and by you, I felt all my

[60] Stout, *New England Soul*, 190–192.

[61] Letter from Rev. James Honeyman to the bishop of London, June 23, 1746. Society for the Propagation of the Gospel Papers, B.14, Rhodes House, Oxford University.

[62] Lemay and Zall, *Autobiography of Franklin*, 107.

[63] Benjamin Colman, *Three Letters to the Reverend Mr. George Whitefield* (Philadelphia, 1739), 5.

[64] Ibid., Gilbert Tennent to George Whitefield, December 1, 1739.

chains broken, my mouth inwardly opened to praise in Spirit."[65] Others, such as a group of Presbyterian laymen in Hanover County, Virginia, who had no pastor, read aloud sermons by Martin Luther and Whitefield. For them, the reformer's works lacked the fire and immediacy that Whitefield's conveyed.[66]

English converts testified to the power of Whitefield's writings. In 1746, an English convert wrote in a letter reprinted in the *Weekly History* that many in his community were "much revived by the reading of Dear Mr. Whitefield's nine sermons and others of his writing." In a passage echoed by many similar testimonies, the letter-writer assessed the printed word's impact in language usually employed to describe the preached word's effect. "The spirit of the Lord is giving life to the words which drop'd from that dear man's pen," he wrote. Reading led to action. The writer explained that Whitefield's printed sermons "landed home with [such] power to some souls when we first received those nine sermons [that] it pleased the Lord to draw some few of us to gather in to a little society once a week," to read, exhort, and pray.[67] Whitefield's friend James Hervey credited a specific work with his own salvation: "[Your] Journals and Sermons, especially the sweet sermon upon 'What think ye of Christ?' had been a means of bringing me to a knowledge of truth."[68]

Some readers, however, discovered perplexity rather than enlightenment in reading Whitefield's works. After hearing the evangelist preach for the first time, Daniel Wadsworth, pastor at Hartford, Connecticut, recorded in his diary, "What to think of the man and his Itinerant preachings, I scarcely know." To answer his question, Wadsworth read Whitefield's *Journals* and sermons. Then, after perusing the revivalist's autobiography, Wadsworth expressed his continued confusion: "Met with the famous Mr. Whitefield's life and read it. But what is it?"[69]

Others were skeptical in their examination of Whitefield's works. Thomas Webb, clerk of the parish church in Worcestershire, wrote Whitefield concerning how a parishioner confirmed his salvation through reading an evangelical sermon, but only after checking its orthodoxy. A Tewkesbury glazier told Webb that after he had heard

---

[65] Howell Harris to George Whitefield, April 16, 1741, Trevecka Collection, National Library of Wales, Aberystwyth, Wales.

[66] Davies, "The State of Religion" 47.

[67] Richard Smith to John Lewis, March 17, 1746, in Whitefield Manuscripts Collection, Dr. Williams's Library.

[68] Tyerman, *Life of Whitefield*, 2:47.

[69] *Diary of Rev. Daniel Wadworth, Seventh Pastor of the First Church in Hartford* (Hartford, Conn., 1894), 56–58. The diary covers the period 1737–1747.

Whitefield preach, he acquired the revivalist's "sermon on the New Birth." Suspicious of Whitefield's theology, the man compared Whitefield's printed sermon with "an old Exposition of the Catechism, the Church Articles, and Book of Homilies" and discovered "that these old books spoke to the very same purpose as Mr. Whitefield did."[70] Though he eventually reached a conclusion favorable to the evangelist, the reader had withheld judgment pending his own investigation.

People of all backgrounds wrote Whitefield about their progress in experiencing the new birth. Apologizing for being "backward in righting," one correspondent from Stoke sent a letter to the revivalist in order to "comply with [his] desire in giving a strict account of the work of grace upon my sole."[71] Similarly, a hairdresser's wife from Southwark asked Whitefield to "excuse [her] writen for it is not spelt proper at toll."[72] Others expressed in evocative prose their joy in reading the preacher's works. Thomas Davidson of London wrote, "My soul has been comforted by the pamphlets relating to the work of God which my wife has brought with her. They were as oyl to my bones. They refreshed and filled me with joy."[73] The London evangelist John Cennick described his initial reaction upon reading part of Whitefield's *Journals* lent him by a friend in 1738. Referring to a specific passage, Cennick exclaimed, "my heart cleaved to him!"[74] Whether written in fractured phrases or eloquent lines, men and women documented the power of the printed page in their spiritual lives.

The most systematic contemporary attempt to gauge reader-response occurred in Scotland. T. C. Smout has analyzed the published testimonies of 105 converts in the Scottish revivals of 1742–1744 sparked by Whitefield's preaching.[75] A Presbyterian minister, Rev. William McCullough, conducted interviews aimed at examining the new converts, exploring their understanding of the new birth and the process by which they experienced conversion.[76]

Many of those interviewed testified that reading was an integral part

[70] *Whitefield's Journals*, 326–329.
[71] Anonymous letter to Whitefield from Stoke, n.d., in Whitefield Manuscripts Collection, Dr. Williams's Library.
[72] Richard Good to George Whitefield, August 1739, in Whitefield Manuscript Letters, Evangelical Library, London.
[73] Thomas Davidson to George Whitefield, October 26, 1742, in Whitefield Manuscript Letters, Evangelical Library, London.
[74] See preface to John Cennick, *Naaman Cleansed, With an Address to the reader signed: George Whitefield* (London, 1760).
[75] T. C. Smout, "New Evidence on Popular Religion and Literacy in Eighteenth-Century Scotland," *Past and Present* 97 (November 1982): 114–127.
[76] See D. Macfarlan, *The Revivals of the Eighteenth Century, Particularly at Cambuslang* (Edinburgh, n.d.).

of the process. Janet Jackson, an unmarried woman of twenty-four, related how she had been indifferent to religious duties during her early life. Then in September 1741, she heard Whitefield preach at Glasgow. As a result she began to spend "much of her time in prayer and in reading her Bible and Mr. Whitefield's sermons." Although she had received very little formal schooling, Janet could read. Over a period of weeks she "read more in the Bible and in Mr. Whitefield's sermons, and also the *Weekly History* after it began to be published."[77] Janet's quest for salvation alternated between attending public revival services along with thousands of others and reading devotional works in solitude. The printed and spoken word complemented each other.

Janet's nineteen-year-old friend Elizabeth Jackson also experienced a conversion to experimental religion, but by different means. Although McCullough did not indicate whether Elizabeth could read, her salvation came in part through the printed word. Like Janet, Elizabeth was first awakened to the necessity of a new birth through listening to Whitefield in Glasgow. Afterwards she attended McCullough's sermons at Cambuslang. At one of those services, Elizabeth "heard Mr. M'Cullough read some papers concerning the spread of the gospel in foreign parts, which moved [her] greatly." The "papers" were probably issues of the *Weekly History*, the evangelical magazine inspired by Whitefield and devoted to informing revivalists of successes throughout the Atlantic world. The readings contributed to Elizabeth's own search for salvation, "especially on observing how much good others were getting."[78] By hearing how disparate people shared the same experience in diverse parts of the world, Elizabeth's private quest became part of something much larger. The accounts also enabled her to see not only that others struggled as she did but that the outcome was often a triumphant conquest of sin.

One more example will suffice in demonstrating how individuals responded to the spoken and printed word. A worker and dyer at Busby, John Parker, had the advantage of a "good education," which meant that he could read, write, and work with numbers. Parker's new birth began when he heard Whitefield preach in September 1741, an experience that had a "powerful effect but left [him] confused." Upon hearing Whitefield a second time, Parker testified that his "heart melted." For weeks afterwards, Parker "remained in a state of comparative bondage of spirit, till reading a sermon of Mr. Whitefield's on the Evidences of Regeneration, [he] became again satisfied, and was so far

[77] Ibid., 117–119.
[78] Ibid., 123.

relieved."[79] In Parker's case, reading confirmed and reinforced what had first been awakened during Whitefield's services. He found assurance by contemplating in the private act of reading what had initially captured his attention in an open-air sermon.

To be fair, Whitefield's printed works did not move every reader to experience the new birth. Rather than discovering solace in the revivalist's writings, some either little understood what they read or found only frustration. The Virginia minister Devereux Jarratt testified that he gained little from his first reading of a volume of Whitefield's sermons. Having found "Mr. Whitefield's eight sermons, preached in Glasgow," in his host's backcountry Virginia home, Jarratt "had the curiosity to look into it." However, the young schoolmaster was yet "a poor reader, and understood little of what [he] . . . read."[80]

In addition to experiencing conversion through reading Whitefield's works, readers found encouragement in the evangelist's frequent reports of success. Whitefield and his followers presented accounts of revival success as signs of God's anointing their work. Throughout the colonies evangelicals welcomed news of Whitefield's success in remote places. A Boston revivalist, William Cooper, expressed his "pleasure [in reading] . . . a refreshing Account of the Success with which God has been pleas'd to crown the Ministry of . . . Whitefield in Charles-Town in South Carolina."[81] The minister who had reported to Cooper, Isaac Chanler, wrote that God had blessed people "in these Parts, as well as Multitudes of others elsewhere, with the Successful Ministrations of . . . [the] esteemed Mr. Whitefield." To Chanler, accounts of success represented concrete evidence of "some many Sinners [delivered] from Darkness unto Light, and from the Power of Satan unto the Living God; giving new life to Religion in so many parts of the World, both in Europe and America." He concluded that the "Facts [were] so visible and numerous, that [Whitefield's] very Enemies cannot deny them." To Chanler reports of large crowds and numerous conversions constituted "an irrefragable Argument that [Whitefield] is a Man sent from God, to be . . . a burning and a shining Light in the midst of a crooked and perverse Generation."[82]

Reports of Whitefield's success heightened New Englanders' anticipation of his visit. Upon receiving reports of Whitefield's ministry in England and later in the Middle Colonies and Lower South, Jonathan Edwards wrote the revivalist, inviting him to his church in North-

[79] Ibid., 177–178.
[80] Cited in Isaac, *Transformation of Virginia*, 126.
[81] See William Cooper's preface to Isaac Chanler, *New Converts Exhorted to Cleave to the Lord* (Boston, 1740), ii.
[82] Ibid., 2–4.

ampton. Edwards expressed his satisfaction that Whitefield preached sound doctrine, rejoicing in God's "rais[ing] up in the Church of England [one] to revive the mysterious, Spiritual, despised and exploded Doctrines of the Gospel, and full of a Spirit of zeal for the promotion of real vital piety." The focus of Edwards's letter was not theology, however, but the success that had attended Whitefield's labors. Six times in his three-paragraph letter, Edwards referred to Whitefield's "Labours [which] have been attended with such Success." He assured Whitefield that no place accorded the itinerant's "Labours and Success . . . with fuller credit" than did the people of western Massachusetts. Edwards interpreted the evangelist's "Swift Progress [as] . . . the work of God" and hoped "that Such a Blessing as attends your Person and Labours may descend on this Town." While the centerpiece of Whitefield's theology was the necessity of the new birth, the focus of his publicity was his ministry's success.[83]

Though Whitefield publicized his interpretation of the revivals, colonial men and women reached their own conclusions, choosing from multiple, often conflicting, versions. Prior to Whitefield's arrival in New England on his first preaching tour, Bostonians received at least three different reports of the evangelist's revival in Philadelphia during May 1740. One was the itinerant's own account, recorded in volume 6 of his *Journals*. Focusing on the spiritual manifestations of the services, Whitefield wrote that he had never seen "a more general awakening in any place." After his farewell sermon, delivered to a crowd of "very near twenty thousand hearers," the revivalist declared that "religion [was] all the talk," adding that "the Lord Jesus hath gotten Himself the victory in many hearts." In the few days he remained in Philadelphia, many came to him "under deep soul-concern," and others pressed him to baptize their infants.[84] From Whitefield's perspective, the revival meetings were divine means by which God wrought the new birth in hearts of men and women.

Benjamin Franklin offered a second reading of Whitefield's preaching in Philadelphia. While ignoring the revivals' spiritual dimension, Franklin, the architect of many of the city's civic reforms, applauded their salutary effects on citizen conduct. He exclaimed that "the alteration of the face of religion . . . [was] altogether surprizing." He approved of the assiduous performance of religious duties by laity and clergy alike, noting that "never did people show so great a willingness to attend sermons, nor the preachers greater zeal and diligence in performing the duties of their function." Motivated perhaps by self-

---

[83] Abelove, "Jonathan Edwards' Letter" 488–489.
[84] *Whitefield's Journals*, 422.

interest as Whitefield's printer, Franklin observed with satisfaction that "no books [were] in request but those of piety and devotion, and instead of idle songs and ballads, the people are everywhere entertaining themselves with psalms, hymns, and spiritual songs." He credited the "successful labours" of Whitefield with this reformation in manners.[85]

The third report presented a negative view, citing deleterious social effects of Whitefield's revivals in Philadelphia. In a letter printed in the *Boston Weekly Post-Boy*, an anonymous eyewitness claimed that the excessive number of services triggered by Whitefield's presence turned the "vulgar . . . [from] industry, honest labour, and care for their families." He charged Whitefield with "infatuat[ing] the common people with the doctrine of regeneration, free grace, conversion, etc. . . . as the essential article of salvation, tho' inconsistent with true religion, natural or reveal'd, [and] subversive of all order and decency." Warning Bostonians, the writer expressed his hope that Whitefield would not "divert and distract the labouring people," assuring readers that the evangelist was "qualified to sway and keep the affections of the multitude."[86]

The evangelical revivals divided colonial society, and how a reader interpreted Whitefield's works depended in part on his or her predisposition toward the revivalist. Some were prejudiced against his style, perhaps objecting to itinerancy or to extemporaneous preaching. Others found offensive what they considered to be arrogant claims of divine inspiration. His followers, however, believed that Whitefield was indeed an emissary from God whose successes made his shortcomings pale by comparison. A 1753 letter from one D. Schuyler to his nephew, William Bradford, the Philadelphia printer, illustrates how a charitable view of Whitefield colored the interpretation of his printed works. After reading Whitefield's published letter to Count Zinzendorff, a Moravian leader, Schuyler concluded that "the Count is not used well in that matter." Although he disagreed with the censorious attack on Zinzendorff, Schuyler did not blame Whitefield. He wrote, "I do not think that Dear Mr. Whitefield is so much to blame as these wicked people that put him upon it for I cannot think that dear man Mr. Whitefield would be the occasion of persecution to any people." Schuyler finished his letter with the confidence that Whitefield himself would soon disavow the printed letter's sentiments and "repent" of the matter.[87] Schuyler viewed Whitefield as favorably after reading the disagreeable pamphlet as he had before.

Whitefield's admirers tended to give his works a broad, generous

[85] *Pennsylvania Gazette*, June 12, 1740.

[86] *Boston Weekly Post-Boy*, June 23, 1740.

[87] D. Schuyler to William Bradford, September 14, 1753, in the Bradford Manuscripts Collection, Case 24, Historical Society of Pennsylvania, Philadelphia.

reading, while his detractors gave them a narrow, severe scrutiny. One of his most ardent defenders, Thomas Foxcroft, a Boston minister, acknowledged that Whitefield "may not always have so happily expressed himself, with that nice judgment, and care of exact distinction between different cases, which it were to be wished he had." But, Foxcroft asked, "Why should the accidental slips of a young pen, where so much of a Spirit of Christian Piety and Goodness so evidently breathes, be made that object of our severe reflections?" According to Foxcroft, part of Whitefield's problem in writing stemmed from the similarity between his styles of preaching and composing. The evangelist often resorted to "writing in haste, and as it were extempore," resulting in "illjudged expression." Foxcroft urged readers to consider the tone of Whitefield's works instead of searching for misstatements. Despite occasional injudicious phrases, the "whole Tenor" of the revivalist's writings suggests to "any impartial, attentive, and intelligent Reader" the work of one who preached the "gospel of grace."[88]

Although he found the tone of Whitefield's works objectionable, Andrew Eliot of Boston warned against allowing tone to obscure message. Responding to a critic of Whitefield's writings, Eliot, pastor of the New North Church, acknowledged that the evangelist's works bordered on enthusiasm. He wished that Whitefield would "guard against ye unhappy tendency of many passages in his Life and Journals." But having confessed that Whitefield "has not expressed himself in a way that is agreeable to me," Eliot concluded that "to call him a *rank enthusiast* is, I think, carrying the matter too far." His interpretation of Whitefield's claims led Eliot to believe that "Mr. Whitefield does not pretend to any extraordinary mysteries."[89] In other words, readers should heed what Whitefield wrote rather than dwell on occasional infelicitous expressions.

His detractors subjected Whitefield's writings to a much closer and more critical examination. SPG missionaries in the colonies read the revivalist's publications and sent their interpretations to the bishop of London. In some cases critics emphasized the tone of a Whitefield work. For example, George Ross wrote that Whitefield had "stirred up the people and inflamed them against the missionaries with the most opprobrious language." Ross added that Whitefield had "ruined his credit with thinking people by his malicious letters against Archbishop Tillotson and by his weak but ill-natured attack upon the Author of the *Whole Duty of Man*." It is difficult to determine if Ross's objections

---

[88] Thomas Foxcroft to Samuel Phillips, October 10, 1744, in the Gratz Manuscripts Collection, Historical Society of Pennsylvania, Philadelphia.

[89] Andrew Eliot to Richard Salter, April 15, 1745, in the Craig-Biddle Papers, Historical Society of Pennsylvania, Philadelphia.

stemmed primarily from Whitefield's assaults against Anglican men and ideas or from the evangelist's ungentlemanly expressions. At any rate, the whole tenor of Whitefield's works offended Ross and, in his opinion, other "thinking people."[90]

Evangelical books and pamphlets consisted of more than text to be interpreted; they were also consumer goods with physical characteristics and intangible value similar to that found in other items available in colonial markets. Thus printers recognized the need to make Whitefield's works appealing to buyers. In his volumes of Whitefield's sermons and *Journals*, Franklin sought to produce an attractive work. He selected a fine grade paper, "American, marked Pro Patria," and a handsome binding, "Sheep, blind-tooled."[91] Franklin's efforts reflect his understanding that buyers judged books by appearance as well as content.

Like other consumer goods, religious books are more than physical objects; they have symbolic meaning. Books embody ideas, reminding their owners of "values, goals, and achievements they seek to cultivate." Among revivalists, Whitefield's volumes represented new birth, advancing reformation, and evangelical community. Possession of religious books also points to "a complex mixture of a need to belong, a need for self-respect bordering on pride, all wrapped in a religious tradition."[92] Whitefield's works strengthened a sense of identity and belonging to a family of faith stretching across the Atlantic.

Individual readers viewed their copies of Whitefield's works as prize possessions. Many people autographed their Whitefield editions, recording pertinent information tying volume to owner. Ephraim Parker inscribed the title page of his copy of Whitefield's sermon *The Duty and Interest of Early Piety* with "Ephraim Parker, His Book. Anno Domini, 1739/40," signifying ownership and indicating a date of personal significance.[93] Louis Bovier, Jr., purchased a volume of a sermon he heard Whitefield preach in New Jersey during spring 1740. The inscription served as a reminder of the occasion:

[90] Letter of George Ross, August 5, 1740, Newcastle, Delaware, in the Read Manuscripts Collection, Historical Society of Pennsylvania, Philadelphia.

[91] See Miller, *Benjamin Franklin's Philadelphia Printing*, 85.

[92] Mihaly Csikszentmihalyi and Eugene Rochberg-Halton, *The Meaning of Things: Domestic Symbols of Self* (Cambridge, Eng., 1981), 69.

[93] The idea of gauging reader-response by examining reader comments within the volumes they read is set forth in Cathy Davidson, *Revolution of the Word: The Rise of the Novel in America* (New York, 1986). For current example, see George Whitefield, *The Duty and Interest of Early Piety Set forth In a Sermon* (Boston 1739). For Ephraim Parker's inscription, see title page of copy in Rare Book Collection, New York Public Library.

Morristown
April 22, 1740
Louis Bovier, Jr.[94]

Some buyers recorded the book's purchase price, indicating the volume's value expressed in market terms. Thomas Pickering recorded on the flyleaf of volume 2 of Franklin's collection of Whitefield sermons the book's six-shilling cost:

Vol. 2nd 6/.
Thomas Pickering 1741[95]

Others received books as gifts and recorded the particulars. William Tarbox inscribed his copy of a Whitefield sermon:

William Tarbox
his Book
giving [*sic*] to him
Mr. Ephraim Parker[96]

For some, Whitefield's books were cherished articles occupying privileged status among family possessions. One family passed Whitefield's 1745 publication *The Christian's Companion; Or, Sermons on Several Subjects* from generation to generation. The book also served as a repository of key dates in the life of the family much as births, marriages, and deaths are recorded in family Bibles. Inscribed on the flyleaf are the wishes of the book's original owner:

William Furnell His Book
God give him grace therein to look
and not to look. But understand that Larning
is better than House or Land.

Another inscription on the back flyleaf suggests that the volume continued to inspire subsequent generations:

Stratford April 19, 1761
my name this Book
Shall in it have when I am Dead and Laid
in Grave when gready worms my Boddy

[94] George Whitefield, *De Wyze en Dwanze Maagden Vertoont in Ein Predicatie Dvor* (New York, 1740). Bovier inscription appears on page 2 of copy located in Rare Book Collection, New York Public Library.

[95] Whitefield, *Sermons on Various Subjects*, vol. 2. Pickering's inscription is located on front flyleaf of copy at Van Pelt Rare Book Collection, University of Pennsylvania.

[96] See reference for Ephraim Parker in n. 93.

have eat. then hear my name doth
stand compleat.
Thomas Furnell

The front flyleaf contains a family record:

John Furnell Was Born May the 28 Day 1736
Humphrey Furnell Was Born September ye 17 day 1741
Thomas Furnell was Born June ye 17 day 1741
Humphrey Furnell departed this life 1748
The Last Day of Time[97]

Some book owners conversed with Whitefield's printed message through marginalia. In a society of blurred lines between oral and printed messages, readers sometimes engaged in dialogue with writers as if they were discussing the subject in a parlor. John Holmes of Exeter, England, sustained a running commentary in the margins of his copy of *The Reverend Mr. Whitefield's Answer to the Bishop of London's Last Pastoral Letter*. In that work, Whitefield acknowledged that youthful passion had colored some of his early writings and promised to confess any passages "blameable in any Respect." In a marginal note written in 1764, Holmes exclaimed, "Oh ho! And how do you know and distinguish your mistakes from verities? Supposing that there *are* any verities and realities." Defending field-preaching, Whitefield asked if "the best Sermon that was ever preach'd [was not] delivered on a *Mount*." Holmes reacted with a marginal question of his own: "Are your's at all like it?"[98] To Holmes the book afforded an opportunity to question and criticize the author.

Whitefield's followers also made notes in their copies of the evangelist's works. Through marginalia, an anonymous prorevivalist applauded Whitefield's polemic against the bishop of London, cheering each point scored like a spectator watching a sporting match. Reacting to Whitefield's charge that the bishop's teachings were "contrary to the Doctrines of the Church of England and the whole Tenor of the Gospel," the book owner scribbled in the margin: "fear ye Bp is so fast bound yt he Never can Rise with out acknowledging that he was in an Error and I fear his Pride in it is so great yt it will . . . [illegible]." Addressing the reader directly, Whitefield insisted that three things

[97] See George Whitefield, *The Christian's Companion; or, Sermons on Several Subject* (London, 1745). Furnell inscriptions appear on copy in the Van Pelt Rare Book Collection, University of Pennsylvania.

[98] See John Holmes's marginalia in *The Reverend Mr. Whitefield's Answer to the Bishop of London's Last Pastoral Letter* (London, 1744), 5–6, 22. Located in the Rare Book Collection at Garrett Evangelical Seminary Library, Evanston, Illinois.

were necessary for true religion: "sound Principles of divine Truth known; the Savour of that Knowledge in the Heart; and the Power of that Savour in a Man's Worship and Walk." The passage evoked approbation from the reader: "O yt every [one] that doubts [this] may have impressed [on] his Soul the Spirit of Christ."[99] Private readings were not passive events. Rather they afforded readers opportunity to express themselves more fully than they could at crowded outdoor services.

Whitefield's frequent use of commercial language and tropes and his frequent collections for charities invited readers and listeners to interpret his mission in market language. And indeed, the language of the marketplace was one discourse in which men and women interpreted Whitefield and his mission. He and his supporters presented the new birth as an expansion of choice, offering the gospel as the "pearl of great price" in comparison to the bankrupt notions of rationalism. John Lewis, publisher of the *Weekly History*, viewed mid-eighteenth-century religion in consumer terms: "It is not now the fashion to have any more religion than what will save us from a prison or the gallows, or maintain a good reputation in the world."[100] Whitefield's mission was to introduce a new "fashion."

Whitefield's opponents employed commercial metaphors to emphasize what they characterized as the itinerant's greedy and even fraudulent enterprise. Alexander Garden, the Anglican commissary of Charleson, singled out Whitefield's Georgia orphanage to illustrate the itinerant's false advertising. Garden claimed that the Georgia trustees as well as Whitefield had misrepresented the struggling colony in English and American newspapers as a means of raising money. He noted, however, that South Carolinians saw through the developers' exaggerated claims. "The whole Colony is accounted here one great Lie," he wrote in 1743, "from the beginning to this day." Shifting the culpability to Whitefield, Garden added that the "Orphan House . . . [was] a Part of the Whole—a scandalous Bubble!" This was no doubt a reference to the South Sea Bubble of 1720 when an "orgy of speculation and bribery [ended] in the worst stock-market crash in British history."[101]

---

[99] For pro-Whitefield marginalia, see *The Bishop of London's Doctrine of Justification, In His Late Pastoral Letter . . . In Vindication of the Reverend Mr. Whitefield's Assertions, relating to the Errors contained in the Book call'd the Whole Duty of Man and Archbishop Tillotson's Works* (London, 1740), vii, ix, 39. Copy located Rare Books Collections, Princeton Theological Seminary.

[100] *Weekly History*, May 2, 1741.

[101] "Letter from the Rev. Alexander Garden, about Whitefield and the Orphan House in Georgia—1742–3," *New England Historical and Genealogical Register* 24 (April 1870): 117–118. For discussion of the South Sea Bubble, see William Willcox and Walter Arnstein, *The Age of Aristocracy, 1688 to 1830* (Lexington, Mass., 1983), 88–91.

CHAPTER 4

Others compared Whitefield's ministry to another fraudulent financial scheme that had the added opprobrium of being French: the crash of the Mississippi Company's shares. In 1739 an antirevivalist accused Whitefield in *Read's Weekly Journal* of creating a frenzy among "the giddy Rabble," just as the Scot John Law had done among French investors in the 1722 speculative binge. Writing in verse, the anonymous author penned these lines: "Infatuated Crowds to hear him flock, / As once to France for Mississippi Stock."[102] In a rapidly expanding commercial world, antirevivalist writers were confident that their readers would understand the parallel between Whitefield's enthusiasm and market excess.

[102] *Read's Weekly Journal,* June 16, 1739.

- Whitefield attracted many, detracted some.
- People interpreted his sermons differently.

CHAPTER 5

Debating the Great Awakening
in a Religious Public Sphere

ON MARCH 14, 1740, Whitefield provoked a dispute with Alexander Garden in the Anglican commissary's Charleston, South Carolina, home. Whitefield put the church leader on the defensive by asking him if he had preached "against the assemblies and balls" in Charleston. Garden replied: "No, I have not exclaimed against them; I think there is no harm in them." Angered by the impudent young itinerant, the commissary ended the meeting abruptly, shouting at Whitefield, "Get you out of my house."[1]

The exchange would not be noteworthy had not the disputants made it public, engaging in a heated print war, exchanging salvos in newspapers and pamphlets. Whitefield initiated the debate by challenging Garden to an open airing of their differences. In his invitation to a public exchange, Whitefield wrote: "It would be endless to enter into a private Debate, as you, Reverend Sir, seem desirous of." Whitefield suggested to Garden that if the latter could find anything in the itinerant's printed sermons—public documents—"contrary to sound Doctrine, or the Articles of the Church of England," then he should "be pleased to let the Publick know it from the Press." Whitefield announced that he was content to "let the World judge whether you or my Brethren the Clergy have been rashly slandered."[2]

Garden retaliated by accusing the revivalist of failing to provide reasoned arguments supported by evidence. He charged Whitefield with appealing to readers on the basis of emotion and rhetoric instead of proof. "You know how to dispence [your attacks] to the Populace in a Vehicle of cant Terms, without Sense or Meaning," Garden wrote. Seeking to put Whitefield on the defensive, Garden asked, "Where are the Proofs of your Accusation? What Evidence have you therein brought to support your Charge?" The commissary concluded that Whitefield's polemics had "not the least Shadow or Appearance of [Proof] throughout the Whole."[3]

Theological debates were not new. What was different was the nature

---

[1] *Whitefield's Journal*, 400–401.
[2] Garden, *Six Letters to the Reverend Mr. George Whitefield*, 5–6.
[3] Ibid., 8, 33.

of the dispute. The disputants debated in public before a mass audience through a popular medium—the newspaper. While enabling Whitefield to construct a national evangelical revival, the press also made possible a new public discourse for revivalists and antirevivalists alike to debate the Great Awakening.[4] By addressing a mass audience through newspapers, Whitefield shifted religious discussion from a private sphere defined in denominational terms to a public arena where literate men and women employed their rational powers to judge among contending views. However, the same public context that Whitefield helped shape constrained the Grand Itinerant, forcing him to fashion arguments based on evidence rather than mere assertion.

Whitefield and his opponents sought to shape public opinion, a term that took on a new meaning in the eighteenth century. Jurgen Habermas has noted that men and women throughout Europe and England took advantage of new ways of communicating ideas.[5] After Parliament relaxed licensing regulations in 1695, political writers flooded the country with pamphlets and newspapers. By 1724, print shops increased from twenty in all of England to seventy-five in London alone.[6] Increased competition among printers resulted in an efficient, inexpensive means for writers to address an expanding reading public. Thus, persons wishing to shape public opinion "began during this period to map out an imagined public space, a mental realm separate from the intimate affairs of private or family life where increasingly confident and strident voices spoke for something called the 'public.' "[7]

What distinguished the eighteenth-century American public sphere from that of Europe was the character of ideas debated. Habermas and others have noted that Europeans in general and the English in particular contested political ideas. In coffeehouses and salons reasoning men and women read and discussed the latest proposals for political reform advanced in scores of pamphlets and newspapers. The writers debating political rights and liberties were not members of the court but outsiders who held no public office in government. According to Habermas, "a public sphere that functioned in the political realm arose first in Great Britain at the turn of the eighteenth-century. Forces endeavoring to influence the decisions of state authority appealed to the

[4] The conceptual foundation of this chapter is inspired by Breen, "Retrieving Common Sense." See also Frank Lambert, "The Great Awakening as Artifact: George Whitefield and the Construction of Intercolonial Revival, 1739–1745," *Church History* 60 (June 1991): 223–246.

[5] Jurgen Habermas, *The Structural Transformation of the Public Sphere: An Inquiry into a Category of Bourgeois Society*, trans. Thomas Bergen (Cambridge, Mass., 1989).

[6] Alvin Kernan, *Printing, Technology, Letters and Samuel Johnson* (Princeton, 1987), 59.

[7] Breen, "Retrieving Common Sense."

critical public in order to legitimate demands before this new forum."[8]
By 1740, Americans debated the great issues of the day in a public
sphere similar to that of England in all respects but one: the colonists
debated religion, not politics.

Whitefield's exploitation of the press to defend his message and
tactics against antirevivalist criticism contributed to the creation of
what T. H. Breen has aptly called a "religious public sphere, an intellectual space in which allegedly disinterested writers employing their reason in the name of the people might criticize and shape popular religious assumptions."[9] Drawing upon the work of Jurgen Habermas,
Breen has argued that religion, not politics, provided the subject matter debated in mid-eighteenth-century colonial newspapers by writers
who employed reason in claiming to speak for "a large, well-educated,
impressively literate population." Whitefield's use of print reflects
many of the elements Habermas attributed to "public discourse."[10]
First, the itinerant spoke to evangelicals through the press, a public
institution as opposed to a private organization such as the church.
Second, he wrote in the third person to present his account more as
impartial observation than as self-promotion. Third, Whitefield employed the language of reason, especially evident in statistical reports
that, endowing his activities with an objective, measurable aspect, addressed a readership growing more numerate in an age of expanding
commerce.[11]

• Debated the Great Awakening.

MANUFACTURING CONTROVERSY

George Whitefield had a history of creating controversy on his way out
of town. Upon leaving London for America in August 1739, he left with
his publisher James Hutton a manuscript attacking the bishop of London, who had indirectly criticized the revivalist for enthusiasm. Whitefield's pamphlet, printed and widely distributed on both sides of the
Atlantic, stirred supporters and opponents to engage in heated public
debate. Then as the evangelist prepared to depart from the colonies a
year and a half later, he denounced Harvard in his seventh journal,
accusing the rector and tutors of neglecting students' spiritual develop-

---

[8] Ibid. Habermas, *Structural Transformation of the Public Sphere,* 57.

[9] Breen, "Retrieving Common Sense."

[10] Ibid.

[11] For a discussion of growing numeracy in the eighteenth century, see Patricia
Cline Cohen, *A Calculating People: The Spread of Numeracy in Early America* (Chicago,
1983).

ment. "Bad books are become fashionable among the tutors and students," Whitefield wrote; "Tillotson and Clark are read, instead of Shepard, Stoddard, and such-like evangelical writers." When he returned to New England in 1744, Whitefield faced a firestorm of criticism spread primarily through pamphlets defending Harvard and Yale against the evangelical's polemics. The result of Whitefield's attacks was increased publicity and intensified debate regarding the revivalist and his ministry.[12]

In their dispute, the bishop of London, Edmund Gibson, and Whitefield represented themselves as theological centrists. Both agreed that enthusiasm and infidelity were polar opposites in the contemporary theological debate. The bishop fired the first printed salvo in 1739 accusing Whitefield of being an enthusiast—one who claimed direct divine revelation. He acknowledged that evangelical zeal had a place in "this profane and degenerate Age." The important question was the authority that ministers cited in speaking for Christ against a sinful people. He insisted that "Men should be called upon for some reasonable Evidence of a *divine* Commission" for their preaching. The bishop warned readers against accepting Whitefield's claims of a "special and immediate *Mission* from God." He pointed to passages in Whitefield's *Journals* where the evangelist boasted of "sudden and surprizing Effects as wrought by the Holy Ghost in Consequence of his preaching." By proclaiming a message based on direct revelation, Whitefield was "propagat[ing] a *new Gospel*, as unknown to the Generality of Ministers and People in a Christian Country." Thus the bishop of London characterized Whitefield as an extremist who lay outside Christian orthodoxy.[13]

Answering the bishop, Whitefield rejected the characterization of enthusiast and placed the cleric at the opposite extreme of the theological spectrum. After defending himself against the bishop's charges, the young evangelist proceeded to lecture the churchman on the greater sin of lukewarmness, a euphemism for infidelity. First, Whitefield took issue with the bishop's contention that unconverted church members were in "an *imperfect* state." The revivalist argued that those who content themselves "with a bare bodily attendance upon the Public Worship of God . . . as the whole of that Christianity requires of [them]" are in "no state of Christianity at all." Further, Whitefield extended his charge of lukewarmness to Anglican clergymen, charging them with

---

[12] *Whitefield's Journals*, 324, 462.

[13] See *The Bishop of London's Pastoral Letter To The People of his Diocese; Especially Those of the two Great Cities of London and Westminster: By Way of Caution Against Lukewarmness on one hand, and Enthusiasm on the other*, 5th ed. (London, 1741), 16–21.

being "*Indolent, Earthly-Minded,* [and] *Pleasure-Seeking.*"[14] If the bishop of London was going to make public accusations of enthusiasm against Whitefield, the revivalist made certain in his published answer that the bishop would have to defend himself against public attacks of lukewarmness.

Third parties engaged in the dispute by inserting commentary in newspapers. Most presented themselves as partisans, advocates of either Whitefield or the bishop. However, one letter-writer, assuming the pseudonym Philalethes, published a pamphlet purporting to be an objective, impartial assessment of the debate. He noted that both the bishop and Whitefield "set out together on the same foot," but they had arrived at opposite points. Having read both arguments, Philalethes offered to assist readers in deciding who was right. He concluded that Whitefield's contention was "more persuasive" because the evangelist had based his notion of orthodoxy on a strict interpretation of the Church of England's articles of faith. In other words, Whitefield had been more faithful to the primary texts under dispute. Philalethes suggested that if the doctrines do not have "some plain and determinate Sense," then they could not serve their intended purpose of preventing "Diversities of Opinions and establishing Consent [concerning] Matters of Religion." If the articles did not mean what they said in a strict sense, Philalethes envisioned theological anarchy with each "Man's being allowed to understand them in *his own* Sense."[15] Turning the bishop's argument on its head, Philalethes indicated that the cleric, not Whitefield, sought to substitute his own authority for that of the church.

Whitefield aimed his first public attacks in America at Anglican leaders as well, targets that aroused great suspicion in the minds of many dissenting colonists. Although no bishop resided on American soil, Dissenters feared the establishment of a colonial see. SPG missionaries sent a steady stream of requests to Lambeth Palace imploring the archbishop to appoint a resident bishop. The archbishop refused because he knew from other reports that colonists would view such an appointment as a threat to their liberties. Instead, he was content to continue with the present organization: Anglican rectors and missionaries reporting to the bishop of London. In cities including New York, Philadelphia, and Charleston, commissaries handled official

[14] George Whitefield, *The Reverend Mr. Whitefield's Answer to the Bishop of London's Last Pastoral Letter* (New York, 1739), 3, 19.

[15] [Philalethes], *A Letter to the Right Reverend the Lord Bishop of London Occasioned by His Lordship's late Pastoral Letter, And The Reverend Mr. Whitefield's Answer* (London, 1739), 5–6, 23.

church matters, exercising some oversight of church discipline. Aware of dissenting attitudes toward the Church of England, Whitefield knew that confronting Anglican officials would win him much public favor.[16]

After arriving in America on October 30, 1739, Whitefield wasted little time in accosting Anglican leaders. Two weeks after his disembarkation, the itinerant accepted Commissary William Vesey's invitation to a private audience in New York City. Perhaps prompted by the bishop of London, Vesey demanded to see Whitefield's Letters of Orders and license to preach. When the evangelist failed to produce the documents, Vesey charged Whitefield with "breaking the Canon which enjoins ministers and churchwardens not to admit persons into their pulpit without a licence." The meeting then degenerated into a series of charges and countercharges. The only surviving version of that exchange is Whitefield's account recorded in his *Journals*, a public piece of self-promotion designed to present Whitefield as a champion against a threatening hierarchy. "I told him I had [preached without license]," Whitefield wrote, "for the clergy and laity of our Church seemed to be settled on their lees." He continued, "My end in preaching was not to sow divisions, but to propagate the pure Gospel of Jesus Christ." When Vesey declined the itinerant's offer of assistance in preaching, Whitefield answered in words that colonial Nonconformists must have relished: "I replied, if they preached the Gospel, I wished them good luck in the Name of the Lord; but as he had denied me the church without my asking the use of it, I would preach in the fields for all places were alike to me."[17]

In his second visit to Philadelphia in April 1740, Whitefield challenged Commissary Archibald Cummings to a public debate in the press. At a private conference, Cummings informed Whitefield that Anglican churches in Pennsylvania would no longer be open to him. The commissary cited Whitefield publications as the basis of his barring the itinerant from the church. "He told me that he could lend me his church no more," Whitefield recorded in his *Journals*, "because I had not treated the Bishop of London well in my Answer to his late Pastoral Letter, and also, because I had misquoted and misrepresented Archbishop Tillotson in a letter published in the last week's [*Pennsylvania*] *Gazette*." Whitefield responded with a challenge: "I told him he had best shew that in public." Cummings replied that "the printers would

---

[16] William Howland Kenney has argued that Whitefield's appeal in the colonies lay in the fact that he was an Anglican attacking Anglicans. See William H. Kenney, "George Whitefield, Dissenter Priest of the Great Awakening, 1739–1741," *William and Mary Quarterly* 26 (January 1969): 75–93.

[17] *Whitefield's Journals*, 348–349.

not publish anything for [antirevivalists], and that the press was shut against them." Although Whitefield denied being aware of press bias, he knew that Franklin and Bradford had eagerly printed prorevivalist accounts and interpretations without fail. Bradford did publish a pamphlet for Cummings in which the commissary defended himself "from the false and rash reflections of the famous Mr. Whitefield."[18] But clearly, in Philadelphia, the 1740 public debate was dominated by the Grand Itinerant.

In Charleston, Whitefield met his match. Alexander Garden proved to be a willing, able combatant who accepted Whitefield's challenge to settle their dispute in the public sphere. By airing their differences in the press, both men conformed to John Caldwell's perspective on theological disputes. Caldwell, a Boston antirevivalist, dismissed the pulpit as a proper forum for debate because it was a private arena controlled by the clergy. He claimed that the pulpit was a place "where none dare (even after Service) offer to reason under less Penalty than hard Names and Threats." On the other hand, the "publick Prints [were] where Men may do themselves Justice." Caldwell advocated settling religious disagreements in a public forum, where "Men who will think" will decide the issue.[19] Arguing their positions in newspapers and pamphlets, Whitefield and Garden gave people plenty to think about. Often, however, the exchanges were more heated than enlightening.

Three years after it subsided, Garden published his reflections on the acrimonious debate. He wrote: "I could now indeed wish that my Pen against W____d had run in somewhat smoother style. But had you been here on the Spot, to have seen the Frenzie he excited 'mong the People;—the Bitterness and Virulency wherewith he raved against the Clergy of the church of England in general and how artfully he labored to set the Mob upon me in particular. . . ."[20] Whitefield countered in the seventh installment of his *Journals*. Of Garden's assault, Whitefield wrote: "Had some infernal spirit been sent to draw my picture, I think it scarcely possible that he could have painted me in more horrid colors." However, Whitefield maintained that Garden's vicious attack should prompt pity, not hatred, among evangelicals. The itinerant wrote, "I pitied, I prayed for him; and wished, from my soul, that the Lord would convert him, as He once did the persecutor Saul, and let

[18] Ibid., 406–407. Archibald Cummings, *Faith Absolutely Necessary, But not Sufficient to Salvation Without Good Works. Published in their own Vindication from the False and Rash Reflections of the Famous Mr. Whitefield* (Philadelphia, 1740).

[19] John Caldwell, *An Answer to the Appendix of the Second Edition of Mr. McGregore's Sermon on the Trial of the Spirits, etc.* (Boston, 1743), 3, 6.

[20] "Letter from the Reverend Alexander Garden," 117–118.

him know it is Jesus Whom he persecutes."[21] In other words, the unconverted Garden could not help himself.

In his lawsuit against Whitefield in early 1741, Garden escalated the public debate and, unwittingly, made the itinerant, in the eyes of his followers, a victim of arbitrary power and a champion of liberty. The commissary explained his decision to put "the Ecclesiastical Laws in Execution against [Whitefield]: my Conscience would give me no Peace had I neglected so bounden a Duty."[22] Thus, on January 10, a constable served Whitefield with a warrant citing the evangelist for contempt "of His Majesty and his laws [for] . . . a false, malicious, scandalous, and infamous libel against the clergy in this Province." The publication referred to was actually written by Jonathan Bryan, a prorevivalist planter, but Whitefield admitted that he had "revised and corrected [it] . . . for the press."[23] Although the case was eventually resolved in Whitefield's favor, he exploited the matter in his anticlerical attacks. The symbolic significance of the event is explored more fully in chapter 6.

Engaged in debate of other p. pastors/etc.

CONTROVERSY OVER FUNDING

No aspect of Whitefield's ministry attracted more public attention than did his fund-raising, in particular the enormous sums he collected for Bethesda. To assure existing and potential donors that their contributions were properly accounted for, Whitefield published accounts of his collections and expenditures in 1739, 1741, 1743, and 1746. Then, in 1765 and 1770, he made public sworn attestations to totals received and disbursed but did not provide supporting names and amounts of individual contributions. The first accounting—that of 1739—contained the greatest detail. Receipts include the following from Gloucester:

	£	s.	d.
The Rev. Mr. John Ratcliffe	01	01	0
The Rev. Mr. Alexander	01	01	0
The Dean of Gloucester	01	01	0
Mr. James Pitt, Lawyer	01	01	0
Thomas Ratcliffe, Esq.	01	01	0
Mr. Raikes, Printer	00	10	6
Madam Parsons	00	10	6

[21] *Whitefield's Journals*, 442.
[22] "Letter from the Reverend Alexander Garden," 117–118.
[23] *Whitefield's Journals*, 503.

The Rev. Mr. Webb	01	01	0
The Rev. Mr. Lloyd	01	01	0
Mr. Burroughs	01	01	0
Mrs. Ann Savage	00	10	6
Mrs. Paulin	00	05	0
Mrs. Bennett	00	10	6
The Rev. Mr. Savage	00	13	6
Mrs. Farmer	01	01	0
Mr. Alderman Hayward	00	10	6
Mr. Steel	00	05	0
Hon. Lady Selwyn	05	05	0[24]

The list provides a full, detailed disclosure of contributors and the amounts of their donations.

Whitefield also rendered a careful accounting of expenditures. For example, he published details of his December 27, 1737, purchases from a London shopkeeper, Mrs. Lydia Turner:

	£	s.	d.
6 Pieces of Holland Tape	0	4	0
6 Pieces ditto narrower	0	2	6
6 Pieces ditto	0	2	0
6 Pieces broad Manchester	0	6	6
6 Pieces narrower	0	3	3
6 Pieces coloured	0	4	6
2 Pieces Beggar's Tape	0	0	8
1 Dozen of Bobbin	0	2	8
8 Pieces of Quality Binding	0	7	10[25]

The evangelist's scrupulous record keeping was exactly the type that his severest critics demanded in the public newspaper attacks on his finances.

However, Whitefield's subsequent audits showing monies collected and spent for the Georgia orphan house are far less specific, with sums often lumped together rather than separated by donor. Entries of contributions include the following from 1740:

	£	s.	d.
Collections at Pennsylvania, New York and the Jerseys	438	4	8

---

[24] *An Account of Money Receiv'd and Expended by the Rev. Mr. Whitefield, For the Poor of Georgia* (London, 1739), 5.

[25] Ibid., 10–11.

Collections at Charlestown,
Georgia   99   19   9
Private Persons at Charlestown,
Rhode Island   11   4   3[26]

Absent are names of individuals with how much each contributed. The lack of detail indicates in part Whitefield's increased reliance on preannounced public offerings as opposed to private solicitations. The revivalist advertised in colonial newspapers his intentions to take collections for the orphanage at designated services. Critics charged that his reporting lump sums misled readers by failing to differentiate between amounts donated specifically for the charity and those given to Whitefield personally.

Similarly, absence of specificity made Whitefield's accounts a target for critics who charged the evangelist with diverting sums intended for the orphanage to his personal use. Rather than providing line-item purchases, Whitefield entered in 1739 such aggregate debits as the following:

	£	s.	d.
Philadelphia. To Cash for sundry Provisions, Family, and Sloop	186	4	10
Wm. Lasserre at Charleston for Sundrys laid out there	236	1	2
Thomas Noble of New-York. Sundry Provisions, etc.	255	13	4[27]

Whitefield's failure to provide frequent, full financial reports attracted criticism from his opponents and concern from his friends. An adversary, writing under the name Publicola, printed a series of letters in 1746 in the *South Carolina Gazette*, challenging Whitefield to disclose his accounts to the public. The writer called on the itinerant to satisfy the "publick's reasonable expectation and demand of your accompts, your full, faithful, sufficiently vouched, sworn to, authentickly audited, and attested accompts of the said House . . . from the beginning." The author stipulated a format including an accounting of receipts and disbursements, revenues from commodities produced at Bethesda, allowances per orphan, weekly and monthly expenses, and servants employed at the orphanage. The anonymous writer also demanded that Whitefield disclose "what sums he has all along received for his *own* use." In a subsequent attack, Publicola leveled particularly scurrilous

[26] George Whitefield, *An Account of the Money Received and Disbursed for the Orphan House in Georgia* (London, 1741), 29.
[27] Ibid., 28.

charges. Publicola chided Whitefield for not publishing an independently audited account of Bethesda receipts and disbursements. He then charged that the promised accounting was not forthcoming because of the certain embarrassment it would produce. Publicola offered a third-person summary of speculative malfeasance: "Some allege you have squandered away money on fellow itinerants; others that you have set it aside in a safe place for your own use; others that your increased entourage including your wife enhances your traveling charges and damages the poor House."[28]

James Habersham responded with a letter printed in the same newspaper indicating that because Whitefield raised and spent funds in Britain and America, it was impossible for him "to publish a full accompt, without knowing the particular transactions relating to the orphan house in America and England." The merchant asserted that the funds spent on Bethesda far exceeded the sums collected for the charity, adding that he and Whitefield had expended their own personal resources on the children.[29] Believing that Whitefield's detractors were more interested in besmirching the evangelist's character than in seeing an independent audit, Benjamin Franklin testified in print that he believed Whitefield was "a perfectly honest man" despite the fact that "some of Mr. Whitefield's enemies affected to suppose that he would apply . . . collections to his own private emolument."[30]

Although originating in Charleston, the debate became intercolonial as other newspapers reprinted the charges and countercharges. The *New York Post-Boy* published Publicola's initial challenge to Whitefield and Habersham to make a full, audited, public disclosure of Bethesda's receipts and expenditures. In Boston, rival newspapers added their own commentary on the dispute, with the *Boston Gazette* supporting Whitefield, and the *Boston Evening-Post* attacking him. The *Gazette* printed an announcement from the Charleston evangelical Josiah Smith that Whitefield "for the Satisfaction of the World has had his Accompts audited from the Foundation of that House."[31] The *Evening-Post*, however, sought to discredit Whitefield, referring to the itinerant as "the Retailer of Trifles."[32]

Charges and countercharges over funding led to a broader discussion of the commercialization of religion, with each side employing market language to attack the other's ministry and motives. In addition to calling Whitefield a "Retailer of Trifles" and "Pedlar of Divinity,"

28 *South Carolina Gazette*, July 4, 1743, and February 17, 1746.
29 Ibid., October 15, 1744.
30 Lemay and Zall, *Autobiography of Franklin*, 105.
31 *Boston Gazette*, June 17, 1746.
32 *Boston Evening-Post*, December 24, 1744.

antirevivalists suggested that the itinerant made "merchandize" of religion, citing the huge sums he collected for Bethesda. Whitefield responded in kind. He accused rationalists and formalists of "deal[ing] in the false commerce of unfelt truth." Of Anglican clergy, he wrote: "The truth is plain, they make a market of religion, and hirelings and slaves of their Brethren in the gospel."[33]

Charles Chauncy led a public attack in New England against Whitefield's fund-raising. The antirevivalist observed that Whitefield had "certainly made *large Collections*," and questioned whether the funds went to support their stated purpose, the Georgia orphan house. "No one, I believe besides himself," Chauncy wrote, "can tell the *Amount* of the *Presents* he received in this Town as well as in the other Places for his *own proper Use*." For Chauncy, the lack of accountability was as big a concern as the collections themselves. In his printed reply, Whitefield acknowledged that he had indeed received large offerings for the orphanage but that he had also "given a publick and fair Account of expending them." He added that if his "kind Benefactors would give [him] Leave," he would "freely acquaint [the public] with what [he] had received for [his] own private Use," implying that donors had made confidential gifts to the evangelist.[34]

Harvard's president and faculty made even more serious charges against Whitefield regarding fund-raising. In their 1745 polemic, they called Whitefield "a Deluder . . . [who] almost extorted from the People." They claimed that in pleading for funds, Whitefield had promised that the Georgia orphans would be under his direct tutelage and that upon graduation in four years many would preach the new birth in New England. Further, the academics charged that the accounts Whitefield had made public were "by no Means Satisfactory" because they provided too few details concerning receipts and disbursements, containing such general entries as "a *Thousand Pounds* our Currency charged in a very summary Way." Dismissing the extortion charges as absurd and groundless, Whitefield defended his public accounting. He asserted that he was being held to a far higher standard of public disclosure than other organizations, including Harvard College. Inviting detractors to compare his financial disclosure with those of other fund-raisers, Whitefield asked, "Did you ever see an Account of that Nature more particular? Is that of the Society for Propagating the Gospel more so?" Then counterattacking, the revivalist wondered if "you yourselves, Gentlemen, [would] be more particular, supposing an

---

[33] Gillies, *Works of Whitefield*, 2:45. *The True Character of the Reverend Mr. Whitefield; in a Letter from a Deist in London, to his Friend in the Country* (London, 1739), 13.

[34] Whitefield, *A Letter to the Reverend Dr. Chauncy*, 7.

9. Charles Chauncy, a leading antirevivalist.

Account of what has been received and disbursed at *Harvard-College*, should ever be required at your Hands."[35]

Although the public debate over Whitefield's finances abated after his second American tour, it never ceased until his death and the publication of his will. In his final sermon delivered at Bethesda, Whitefield told his audience, "I might have had a thousand a year out of this place if I had chose it; when I am gone to heaven you will see what I have got on earth."[36] Judging by his estate, Whitefield was indeed more a

[35] George Whitefield, *A Letter to the Reverend the President and Professors, Tutors and Hebrew Instructor, of Harvard College, in Cambridge, In Answer to a Testimony By Them Against the Reverend Mr. George Whitefield and his Conduct* (Boston, 1745), 13–14.
[36] Whitefield, *Sermons on Important Subjects*, 725.

prophet than a profiteer. His probated will indicates that the evangelist accumulated personal property in excess of £3,300, a significant sum in 1770, when an artisan's house and lot in Savannah cost £250 and a teacher at the orphan house received an annual stipend of £50. However, half of Whitefield's estate, excluding land, was cash recently bequeathed the itinerant following his wife's death. The remainder consisted of items he left to the orphanage such as his books, furniture, and carriage. In death as in life Whitefield expressed his desire to use the world, not succumb to the seduction of its baubles.[37]

"Drama over Finances.

DEBATING THE REVIVALS

When Whitefield returned to the colonies on his third American visit in late 1744, he found deep divisions among clergy and laity. Part of the dissension stemmed from Whitefield's earlier attacks, including those against clergymen who, in his opinion, failed to preach the necessity of a new birth, and his polemics against the colleges. Opposition had intensified in reaction to the itinerancies of Gilbert Tennent and James Davenport. After Whitefield departed New England in 1740, he had asked Tennent to "water the seeds" Whitefield had sown. Preaching in the first half of 1741, Tennent attacked antirevivalist ministers, prompting many men and women to separate from their congregations and start new evangelical fellowships. Davenport's tour stirred up even more controversy. A Presbyterian minister from Long Island, Davenport engaged in such bizarre behavior as publicly attempting to destroy his earthly goods, claiming that he was following a direct revelation from God. Prorevivalist ministers intervened, fearing that Davenport's extremism would hurt all evangelicals.[38] Although Davenport publicly renounced his excesses, Whitefield would have to contend with lingering hostility.

Whitefield's arrival ignited a major newspaper war as rival Boston printers filled their pages with pro- and antirevivalist sentiments, increasing revenues in the process. Two of the town's leading publishers, Samuel Kneeland and Timothy Green, had interests in several papers supportive of the evangelicals, including the *Christian History*, a "laudatory chronicle of the Great Awakening," and two newspapers, the *New*

[37] "The Letters of the Hon. James Habersham, 1756–1775," in *Collections of the Georgia Historical Society* 6 (1904): 118–119, 138.

[38] Davenport's public apology found in *The Reverend Mr. James Davenport's Confession and Retractions* (Boston, 1744).

England Weekly Journal and the *Boston Gazette*. Kneeland and Green advertised Whitefield's works in their papers, touting them by heaping praise on the author. In promoting a sermon, for instance, they referred to the discourse as being "occasioned by the late visit and uncommon labours in daily and powerful preaching of the Rev. Mr. Whitefield: the brother whose praise is in the gospel throughout all the churches." Kneeland and Green also printed favorable accounts of the revival's progress, often pieces submitted by Whitefield himself.[39]

Thomas Fleet led the opposition press in his *Boston Evening-Post*. He defended those who opposed the revivals, insisting that if they wished to "hear their own pastors instead of itinerants, . . . they ought not to be stigmatized as atheists, profligates, or very irreligious persons as they lately have been by many."[40] However, Fleet indicated that his primary interest in the controversy was financial, adding that he acted "purely as a printer, and would as soon serve one side as the other . . . [if he] had a prospect of getting a penny by it." In fact, religious printing accounted for more than a few pennies, constituting about 80 percent of Fleet's printing income from 1740 through 1745, with nearly one-half derived from the revival.[41]

Much of the debate in 1744 and 1745 occurred in the press as rival newspapers filled their pages with partisan attacks, and publishers flooded the colonies with pamphlets attacking and defending Whitefield. New England ministers spearheaded the debate. The "Associated ministers of the County of Windham" explained why clergymen chose to voice their views as a group and in a public forum. "Since private Endeavours have proved insufficient," the Windham ministers complained in a 1745 pamphlet opposing Whitefield's use of their pulpits, "we have lately united to give our publick Testimony against some Things."[42] Ministers presented arguments to the reading public setting forth their reasons for supporting or opposing Whitefield.

One pamphlet from each of the camps suffices to illustrate the opposing contentions of all the ministerial associations. The ministers of the county of New Haven listed their reasons for denying Whitefield use of their pulpits, beginning with their opposition to his itinerancy on the grounds that it did not constitute an "orderly call." They censured

[39] *New England Weekly Journal*, December 9, 1740.
[40] *Boston Evening-Post*, October 6, 1740.
[41] Cited in M. A. Yodelis, "Boston's First Newspaper War: A 'Great Awakening' of Freedom," *Journalism Quarterly* 51 (Summer 1974): 207–212.
[42] *A Letter From the Associated Ministers of the County of Windham, To the People in the Several Societies in said County* (Boston, 1745), 3–5.

him next as a "publisher of False Doctrines" from both pulpit and press. Citing "his writings, especially in his *Journals* and the *History of his Life*," the clergymen accused Whitefield of "uncommon Pride and Arrogance . . . [in publicizing] his great Success here and there." Again referring to his publications, the pamphleteers charged the revivalist with enthusiasm as evidenced by "his frequently receiving Messages from Heaven by the Holy Spirit." The polemic closed with what the authors considered an irreconcilable contradiction: Whitefield's "extemporaneous preaching in Congregational and Presbyterian Churches [and] his subscription and vows at the time of episcopal Ordination."[43] In similar language, other groups of antirevivalists echoed the New Haven themes.

A group of ministers convened at Taunton, Massachusetts, published typical explanations revivalists cited for inviting Whitefield to their meetinghouses. In what amounted to a point-by-point refutation of the New Haven pamphlet, the Taunton publication took no exception to Whitefield's itinerancy, applauding instead his extraordinary measures in proclaiming the gospel to non–church members. The authors found Whitefield's message orthodox, contending that it was "agreeable to the Standard of Truth" established in holy writ. Far from questioning the Grand Itinerant's claims for his ministry, the Taunton clergymen confirmed and applauded "the Remarkable Success that has attended his Labours." The writers conceded Whitefield's "Mistakes and Foibles" and lamented the "quarrels and contentions" surrounding the revival. They sought, however, to distance Whitefield from Davenport and other radical exhorters, noting that Whitefield had "reprov[ed] those that have gone too far this Way."[44]

Declaring their opposition to ministers on both sides of the debate, a group of Boston laymen styling themselves an "Association or Club of Laymen" published their own views of the controversy. The writers noted that "the Reverend Clergy [were] divided into two Classes, viz. the Friends, and the Opposers of Mr. Whitefield," and stated their intent to bear "this our publick testimony against the exceptionable Conduct" on both sides. Dismayed at the acrimony and scope of the print war, the authors observed that "scarce a Day pass[ed] but some envenom'd Pamphlet makes its Appearance for or against Mr. Whitefield." They objected to ministers' arrogating unto themselves "the sole Propriety in the Pulpit," and renounced the authority of ministerial associations to speak for the congregations they represented. Scolding

---

[43] *The Declaration of the Association of the County of New-Haven in Connecticut*, 2–6.
[44] *The Testimony of a Number of Ministers Conven'd at Taunton* (Boston, 1745), 4–12.

the clergy for their "railings," the laymen called for a resolution based on "Scripture, Reason, or the Law of the Land."[45] The laymen dismissed the clergymen's insistence that their views were indeed scriptural and rational. The debate raged unabated.

Another group of laymen published a pamphlet seeking to elevate the discussion to the level of reason and evidence. The authors, "a Number of Laymen [writing about] Religion and the Teachers of It," claimed that they should be heard because they were "disinterested Persons, which Ministers are not." The writers exhorted ministers to "not dread the free Inquiry of the Laity into Things and their Requests for the Proof of the Truth of what you assert and teach." In other words, the laymen insisted on logical argument and sound evidence rather than oracular pronouncements and assumed authority. They chided preachers for logical inconsistencies and warned pamphleteers, "Don't set out upon Calvinistical Tenets and conclude upon Arminian Principles, whereby the former Part is contradictory to the latter; and consider well with yourselves what Principles are rational and what not, and stick to those that are rational." They admonished pastors against "the use of Technical and Systematical Terms, by means of which neither you yourselves, nor your Hearers know what you mean." The publication concluded by insisting that ministers recognize lay readers as qualified to "understand the true Sense of the Holy Scriptures." Among the laity were "competent Judges of Reason and good Argument [who] are not to be turn'd off by bombast Fustian or Cant."[46]

The public sphere provided laymen with an opportunity to question clerical pronouncements, denying ministers the privileged place they enjoyed in New England meetinghouses. One writer to the *Boston Evening-Post* reminded an offended clergyman that he could expect to be challenged in the public sphere: "If Gentlemen of your Cloth will appear in Newspapers, they must expect to be treated as dress'd in coloured Cloaths, which is all the Excuse I have to make for being so free with you."[47] When Rev. Thomas Prince published a broadside announcing his intention to publish the *Christian History*, he faced instant ridicule in the newspaper. A letter-writer proposed to print yet another paper, but instead of showing the progress of evangelical religion, it would follow "the progress of Enthusiasm in all Ages and Na-

---

[45] *The Testimony of an Association or Club of Laymen Conven'd at Boston Respecting the Present Times* (Boston, 1745), 3–8.

[46] *The Testimony and Advice of a Number of Laymen Respecting Religion, and the Teachers of It*, 1–9.

[47] *Boston Evening-Post*, January 24, 1743.

tions with the Confusions consequent upon it." In public debate, all voices were heard, and few notions went unchallenged.[48]

At the heart of the 1745 print war was public debate over whether a religious revival had occurred at all, and, if so, what its nature and influence might be. Antirevivalists argued that whatever Whitefield had initiated in his 1740 visit, it was not beneficial to the state of religion. Rather than an outpouring of God's grace, the so-called awakenings had sown "Errors, Disorders and Confusions," all under the "Preaching and Management of Mr. George Whitefield." This oft-expressed view proclaimed the revivals as itinerants' orchestrations as opposed to divine outpourings. Indeed, Whitefield's artful writings and preachings were designed "rather to move the Passions of the Weak and Ignorant than to inform the Understanding." To many parish ministers, Whitefield's commercialization of religion put him in the same category as the quack medicine peddlers common in rural New England.[49]

Thomas Prince countered that the revivals had reversed the decline of New England religion, filling the pages of his *Christian History* with testimonials that Whitefield and Tennent did indeed revive the spiritual zeal for which New England's forefathers had been praised. Prorevivalist ministers convened for the express purpose of passing resolutions attesting to the awakenings' authenticity. In a typical affirmation, the ministerial association at Windham, Connecticut, testified that "there has been of late . . . a very great and merciful Revival of Religion in most of the Towns and Societies in this County, as well as in many other Places in the Land." The work was of divine origin as "God [sent] down the Holy Spirit to convince and convert Sinners." Acknowledging that extravagances and disorders had accompanied the revivals, the clergymen attributed those disturbances to the Devil. The "Prince of Darkness" had sown seeds of discord in the most insidious way: "by imitating, as nearly as he cou'd, the Work of the Holy Ghost, . . . by setting on imaginary Frights and Terrors." Those opposing the awakenings had fallen victim to Satan's ruse.[50]

Led by Boston ministers, New England clergymen sought to issue a quasi-official pronouncement on the revival's efficacy. Lacking authority in churches governed by a congregational polity, an association of Boston pastors issued an invitation in 1743 for New England ministers to convene and discuss the recent revivals. After deliberating, the body

[48] Ibid., March 14, 1743.

[49] *The Testimony of the North Association in the County of Hartford in the Colony of Connecticut convened at Windsor, February 5, 1744/45, Against the Reverend Mr. George Whitefield and his Conduct* (Boston, 1745), 2–3.

[50] *A Letter from the Associated Ministers of the County of Windham,* 3.

published a fifty-page apology for the awakenings "attesting to a remarkable Revival of Religion . . . in many Parts of this Land." To give weight to their statement, the council provided statistical evidence of concurrence, noting that 111 ministers had signed the statement and that "many more Attestations from our Brethren in Connecticut [would have been forthcoming] if the Proposal that was published had reach'd them seasonally." Although affirming the revivals, some conferees qualified their support by denouncing itinerancy as an intrusion "into other Ministers' Parishes without their Consent which [produced] great Disorder."[51]

In a dynamic transatlantic evangelical print market, public debate spread rapidly to other parts of the Atlantic world. New England's dispute sparked a similar public debate in Scotland that in turn further fueled the American contest. Prorevivalists seized the initiative by circulating throughout Scotland "Relations of the great Conversion in New-England." According to one antirevivalist pamphleteer, prorevivalists distributed reprints of Whitefield's successes through a print network stretching from Boston to London to Glasgow. "The *Weekly History* of the Methodists printed at London, and reprinted at Glasgow," the pamphleteer explained, "was every now and then giving us Copies of Letters from Reverend Ministers and others, containing joyful Accounts of the wonders of divine Grace wrought among you." Those reports "had never been contradicted" until 1743, when there appeared an opposing view of the state of religion in New England since Whitefield's arrival. After the document was published in Glasgow, "there was such a Run upon it that in a Week's Time a numerous Edition of it was sold off." A second edition printed "with larger and more Extracts" of antirevivalist testimony "stung" Whitefield. The war was on. Whitefield suspended his preaching schedule in Edinburgh and "shut himself up till he had an Answer ready for the Press." On the other side, sermons from several opponents of the revivals, including Charles Chauncy, were reprinted in Scotland. As a result, "the Press teemed with second Editions of . . . printed Papers from New England" as opposing sides waged public debate.[52]

In 1742 the evangelical revivals in New England continued to capture public attention even though Whitefield spent the entire year in England and Scotland. Supporters and opponents perpetuated heated discussion of the state of religion in America through the presses. "He must be a Stranger in Israel," a group of prorevivalist ministers wrote,

[51] *The Testimony and Advice of an Assembly of Pastors and Churches in New-England, At a Meeting in Boston July 7, 1743. Occasion'd By the late happy Revival of Religion in Many Parts of the Land* (Boston, 1743), 51.

[52] Chauncy, *Letter from a Gentleman in Boston*, 5–15.

"who has not heard of the uncommon religious Appearances in the several Parts of this Land among Persons of all Ages and Characters." Their reference to the geographic sweep of the revivals gains significance when one considers that their remarks were prefaced to the prorevivalist Jonathan Dickinson's account of God's grace in New Jersey. The writers concluded that "this is an Affair which has in some Degree drawn every One's Attention, and been the Subject of much Debate both in Conversation and Writing."[53] Even as they pointed out the extent of the controversy over evangelicalism, the clergymen publicized and contributed to the debate.

While he was participating in the New England controversy, Whitefield also challenged his London critics to public debate. Behind the controversy were "some anonymous papers against the people called Methodist . . . [which] have been for some weeks printed in a large edition and handed about and read in the religious societies of the cities of London and Westminster." Whitefield objected to the private, even secretive, nature of the circulation. He claimed that the document contained "strict injunctions to lend them to no one, nor let them go out of their hands to any." Having obtained a copy "accidentally," the revivalist discovered "many queries of great importance concerning" his ministry. He desired "a speedy open publication of the aforesaid papers in order that a candid, impartial answer may be made thereto by me."[54] The fact that he exposed the anonymous document by publishing his reaction in a widely circulated pamphlet put pressure on his opponents to engage in public debate.

When his opponents made their private attack public in a pamphlet, Whitefield responded in a publication charging the anonymous authors with cowardice and libel. He claimed that the writers attempted to deceive readers by representing the printed version as identical with the private document. According to Whitefield, "the Author ought to have added, *A New Edition, with several Alterations, Additions and Corrections*; for otherwise the World is made to believe that this is the self-same Composition which was handed about some Months ago." Because of the changes, Whitefield charged that the "Title-Page is not only injudicious, but false and scandalous." Continuing his dissection of the pamphlet, the evangelist wrote: "Well might the Author conceal his Name [because] a more notorious Libel has not been published." Suggesting that the printer had "taken care in the Title-page not to let the World know where or by whom this Pamphlet was printed," Whitefield dwelt

---

[53] Jonathan Dickinson, *A Display of God's Special Grace* (Boston, 1742), i.

[54] George Whitefield, *An Answer to the First Part of an Anonymous Pamphlet, entitled, "Observations upon the Conduct and Behaviour of a Certain Sect Usually Distinguished by the Name of Methodists"* (London, 1744), 125.

on authorship and origins in order to discredit the pamphlet. "It comes into Publick like a Child dropt that nobody comes to own," he concluded, "and, indeed, who can be blamed for disowning such a Libel?"[55]

• Debated the revivals w/ dissenting pastors.
• Used news, media to get the word out & debate others.

RULES OF DEBATE IN THE RELIGIOUS PUBLIC SPHERE

Successful debate in the religious public sphere depended upon close adherence to a set of implicit rules determined by the ultimate panel of judges—the readers. Whitefield acknowledged that in the public sphere readers would exercise their independent judgment. In the preface to his *Journals* the revivalist acknowledged that readers shaped public opinion through exercising common sense. Admitting limitations of his own reasoned appeal to persuade people of the necessity of a new birth, Whitefield wrote, "What reasons I can urge for this persuasion is needless to mention, because few in this case would judge impartially; and what seems a reason to me, may not be deemed so by another."[56] One of Whitefield's strongest supporters, Josiah Smith of Charleston, also appealed to rational, impartial readers. In a testimonial for the Grand Itinerant, Smith penned: "My design in writing this is to shew my impartial opinion." He noted that Whitefield's doctrines were "agreeable to the dictates of reason; evidently formed upon scripture; exactly correspondent with the articles of the establishment." He argued that Whitefield set forth truths no unprejudiced inquirer should miss. Having offered his reasonable defense of Whitefield, Smith invited others to show their opinions with the same impartiality.[57]

An independent, literate audience required supporters and opponents of the Great Awakening to assume the appropriate voice in convincing readers. Writers strove to establish candor and honesty in order to win the minds of the public. In the preface to his autobiography, Whitefield denounced "accounts of good men . . . [when] the writers of them have been partial." He promised to render an honest, accurate depiction of his own life, one that gave "an account of . . . failings as well as . . . virtues."[58] In his antirevivalist writings, Chauncy also responded to public opinion. In a 1742 publication he protested, "You

[55] George Whitefield, *An Answer to the First Part of an Anonymous Pamphlet* 4th ed. (London, 1744), 7, 12.

[56] *Whitefield's Journals*, 97.

[57] See preface of Smith, *The Character, Preaching etc., of the Reverend Mr. George Whitefield.*

[58] *Whitefield's Journals*, 35.

may be ready perhaps to think I have here given you a romantic Representation of Things; but it is the real Truth of the Case without a Figure; yea, this has been the Appearance in all Parts of the Land more or less."[59] Candor was the mark of sincerity.

Although the debate over the evangelical revivals was highly partisan, writers on both sides learned that the reading public demanded reasoned argument supported by evidence. His opponents frequently charged Whitefield with enthusiasm, noting that the revivalist relied on direct divine revelation rather than on Scripture. Whitefield denied such charges, warning against those "Who claim[ed] to have power to work miracles such as restoring sight to blind eyes." Whitefield recognized the importance of reason in discerning religious truth, subscribing to the view that "reason seems to be the faculty given us by God to direct our enquiries in all things." Whitefield warned his auditors that they should "try the suggestions or impressions that [they] may at any time feel, by the unerring rule of God's most holy word: and if they are not found to be agreeable to that, reject them as diabolical and delusive." The itinerant denied charges that he "carried on by an enthusiastick zeal," adding that he "detest[ed] and abhor[red the character] of a blind zealot." He argued that "the quintessence of enthusiasm [was] to pretend to be guided by the Spirit without the written word."[60] Hence, Whitefield depended on rational biblical interpretation as a reliable guide against extravagant truth-claims.

Whitefield's supporters also defended their champion against charges of enthusiasm by insisting that the evangelist's message conformed to the dictates of reason. One supporter wrote, "In opposition to Enthusiasm, he preaches a close adherence to the Scriptures, the Necessity of trying all Impressions by them, and of rejecting whatever is not agreeable to them, as Delusions. He applies himself to the Understandings of His Hearers, and then to the Affections."[61]

Unconvinced, Whitefield's opponents claimed that the revivalist could not be trusted. John Caldwell charged that evangelicals had insulted public reason "from Pulpit and Press" and thereby offended common sense. Caldwell warned, "Let us be careful of such Teachers as are leading us blindfold to their Opinions . . . and also such who are for confining us to the hearing or reading only their Side of the Question in Controversies." Caldwell argued that the revivalists' tendentious strategy "is intended to bypass our judgments, to prepossess us in Favour of their Doctrines, and a tacit Acknowledgment of their Fear

---

[59] Chauncy, *Letter from a Gentleman in Boston*, 17–24.

[60] Gillies, *Works of Whitefield*, 1:50, 5:30.

[61] *South Carolina Gazette*, February 11, 1745.

lest the contrary Opinion would appear probable and better supported than theirs, if Men give them a fair hearing." He concluded by insisting that "if readers were to reach reasoned conclusions, they needed 'Evidence,' not partisan assertion."[62]

Printers as well as writers acknowledged that independent readers would shape public opinion. Refuting antirevivalist charges that "Mr. Whitefield had engag'd all the Printers not to print any Thing against him," Benjamin Franklin promised to publish both sides of the religious debate. He claimed that "when the Publick has heard" from both Whitefield and his opponents, "they will then judge for themselves." However, Franklin continued to face accusations of "great Partiality in favour of the Preaching lately admir'd among us, so as to refuse Printing any Thing in Opposition to it." With growing irritation, Franklin dismissed claims of favoritism as "entirely false and groundless," pointing to numerous antirevivalist works he and other Philadelphia printers had published. Franklin displayed his reverence for public opinion by advocating that all "disputable Points" should be offered "to the Publick." Readers would decide the issue aright "when Truth has fair Play."[63]

Some clergymen addressed readers with great respect, acknowledging the absurdity of any writer's claiming sole possession of the truth. John Sergeant, pastor at Stockbridge, Massachusetts, prefaced his sermon on the causes and dangers of religious delusion by challenging readers to "employ the strictest Severity of their Judgment . . . that they maintain the Candour of impartial Judges." He warned that no individual or sect is infallible, adding that it was "an unreasonable Presumption that Truth is wholly confin'd to a single Party." In the current debate, Sergeant sought a middle way, avoiding "the Extremes of contending Parties" where one finds "the less Truth . . . in Proportion to the Want of Charity." He conceded that not all readers would approve of his discourse, but promised an "impartial examination" of the subject.[64]

The claim to impartiality in public debate required more than mere assertion. Whitefield was particularly annoyed by Charles Chauncy's printed account of the revivals in New England. In a report that circulated throughout Britain as well as the colonies, Chauncy claimed that

[62] John Caldwell, "The Nature, Folly, and Evil of rash and uncharitable Judging. A Sermon Preached at the French Meeting-House in Boston, New England, July the 11th, 1742" (Boston 1742), in *The Great Awakening: Documents on the Revival of Religion, 1740–1745*, ed. Richad Bushman (Chapel Hill, 1969), 159.

[63] *Pennsylvania Gazette*, May 8 and July 25, 1740.

[64] John Sergeant, *The Causes and Dangers of Delusions in the Affairs of Religion* (Boston, 1743), 5–6.

the awakenings had not resulted in an improved state of religion in New England. He charged that they were short-lived and superficial. In his published response, Whitefield suggested that a better title for Chauncy's work would be *The State of Religion Falsely Stated*. He challenged readers to search Chauncy's work for concrete proof to back his scurrilous attack. According to Whitefield readers would discover that "some things are therein asserted without sufficient evidence to prove them, and many more things falsely represented and set in a wrong light." But what was more egregious, Chauncy had attempted to represent himself as an "unconcerned spectator" making unbiased observations. Whitefield would have none of it. "I am one of those readers," Whitefield wrote, "who cannot depend upon all this, merely upon his desiring me to do so."[65] Whitefield invited readers to read Chauncy with a critical eye and decide for themselves.

Revivalists and antirevivalists occasionally resorted to devious practices to present a more persuasive case for impartiality. Countering charges that he misappropriated orphan house funds, Whitefield recognized the difficulty readers faced in judging a debate where opposing sides presented diametrically opposite cases. Acknowledging that readers were the judges of who "is to be most credited," Whitefield warned readers against being seduced by writers' subtle tricks designed to create an appearance of impartiality while disguising their own artful intentions. The itinerant pointed to his opponents' attacks on the orphanage as a case in point. "The compilers . . . in order to make the world believe they have been impartial," Whitefield wrote, "have published a sentence or two, wherein Dr. Colman has written favourable of the orphan-house in Georgia . . . but this is only a disguise." Whitefield appealed to readers to judge a disputant not on how cleverly he constructed his argument but on "what proofs . . . he bring[s]" in support of his claims.[66]

In his attempts to assist readers in interpreting the public debate, Whitefield insisted that his writings be considered in context. Whitefield and his opponents each attempted to discredit the other by lifting isolated passages from published works and suggesting that those snippets accurately conveyed the author's stance. In a printed reaction to a charge of enthusiasm, Whitefield accused his detractor with misrepresenting his theology by quoting from the evangelist's early works. Whitefield appealed to the reader's sense of fairness, asking that he be

---

[65] George Whitefield, *A Vindication and Confirmation of the Remarkable Work of God in New-England, Being Some Remarks on a Late Pamphlet, entitled, "The State of Religion in New-England, since the Reverend Mr. George Whitefield's Arrival There* (Boston, 1742), in Gillies, *Works of Whitefield*, 4:77–79.

[66] Ibid., 79, 88.

judged on his more mature notions rather than those espoused in his youth. "My Journals were some of my most early Performances," Whitefield explained in 1749, "wrote too in the very Heights of my first Popularity (which is apt to make the strongest Head run giddy) in the midst of which, Persons very often do Things, which after Experience and riper Judgment teach them to correct and mend."[67] Whitefield hoped that by providing readers with a context in which to consider his remarks, he would lead them to render a more sympathetic judgment.

Through public acknowledgment of mistakes, Whitefield sought to defuse attacks against him. In his 1744 reply to the bishop of London's accusations of enthusiasm, the evangelical prefaced his rebuttal by admitting his human foibles. "I am a Man of like Passions with others," Whitefield wrote, in what must have been an attempt to evoke reader sympathy and support. He suggested that his inherent weaknesses "may have *sometimes* mistaken Nature for Grace, Imagination for Revelation, and the Fire of my own Temper, for the pure and sacred Flame of holy Zeal." Representing himself as one more interested in truth than reputation, Whitefield wrote, "If . . . upon perusing the Pamphlet I find that I have been blameable in any Respect (as in all Probability I may), I will not only confess it, but return hearty Thanks both to the Compiler and your Lordship."[68] Not all readers responded by lauding Whitefield's openness. As mentioned earlier, John Holmes of Exeter wrote in the margin of his copy of Whitefield's answer, "Oh ho! And how do you know and distinguish your mistakes from verities? . . . Fancies from realities?"[69] Holmes's comment illustrates that despite debaters' strategies to win the contest for credibility, readers had the final say.

Antirevivalists cautioned readers to examine closely the logic Whitefield employed in public debate. The rector and tutors at Yale accused the itinerant of inconsistency in arguing that persons experiencing the new birth should not separate from their congregations while at the same time contending that the generality of their ministers were unconverted and, therefore, unfit. "It seems to us," they wrote, "that your avowing these Principles, and practically encouraging the consequent Effects, and yet denying the Consequence [separation] *in Words*, is acting too much like the Papists." The authors cited John Locke's work on toleration in which Locke pointed to inconsistencies between Catholic statements on papal authority over civil rulers. Locke had noted that

[67] George Whitefield, *Some Remarks on a Pamphlet, Entitled, "The Enthusiasm of Methodists and Papists Compar'd"* (London, 1749), 34.

[68] Whitefield, *Answer to the Bishop of London's Last Pastoral Letter*, 5–6.

[69] Ibid. Holmes's marginal notation found on page 5 of the pamphlet located in the Rare Book Collection, Garrett Theological Seminary, Evanston, Illinois.

Catholics insisted "that the Pope ha[d] Power to excommunicate Kings [and] that every excommunicated King forfeits his Crown and Kingdom; and yet absolutely deny that they hold that the Pope has power to depose Kings." Locke's point was that there were some propositions that, "if nakedly propos'd, would awaken all Mankind to a Sense of their Danger." Hence people disguise their true intentions. The antirevivalists at Yale saw a perfect parallel in Whitefield's teachings against clergymen. They concluded their attack by lecturing Whitefield on the merits of being forthright, suggesting that he would have been more consistent if he had "freely own[ed his] Design."[70]

Some antirevivalists feared that the volume and audacity of Whitefield's self-promotion seduced readers, preempting careful scrutiny of his message. In the June 6, 1739, London *Daily Gazetteer*, one R. Freeman's stated purpose in his front-page attack was a public "Consideration of Mr. Whitefield's Manner of Preaching which hath made so much Notice." He focused first on the publicity surrounding the revivalist. In justifying his efforts, Freeman asserted that "the Accounts [Whitefield] has given of himself, and the Accounts given of him by his Disciples are so extraordinary in themselves, and seem to be intended by them to pass for such new and strange things, as sufficiently warrant the Examination of any publick Writer." Uncritical readers too readily accepted the evangelist's self-portrayal, proclaiming him "another Moses, an Apostolick Man, and true Preacher of Christ's Gospel." Freeman did not fault revivalists for promoting their work. He conceded that evangelicals had "acted very reasonably . . . [in bringing] their Cause before the Publick."[71] But Freeman also insisted that the prorevivalist interpretation be challenged publicly in the press.

Freeman objected most to the public nature of Whitefield's self-promotion. He maintained that because "Doctrines of Mr. Whitefield [were] of a very publick Nature, [they] begot . . . publick Attention." It was true, Freeman acknowledged, that a "Variety of Opinions [were also] published concerning him." Some had expressed the view that Whitefield was inspired, a man of great ability and profound learning. Others had labeled him an enthusiast, a person of very ordinary capacity with very little education. According to Freeman, Whitefield had become such a public figure that he and his message should be subjected to public debate, "critical . . . inquiries. Truth and virtue never suffer," he insisted, "by being examined with the most inquisitive Exactions."[72]

[70] *The Declaration of the Rector Tutors of Yale-College in New-Haven Against the Reverend Mr. George Whitefield, His Principles and Designs* (Boston, 1745), 3–5, 9.

[71] *Daily Gazetteer* (London), June 6, 1739.

[72] Ibid.

Antirevivalists accused Whitefield of constructing and publicizing a favorable interpretation of the revival that contained more hyperbole than substance. One writer whose critique appeared in the *Boston Evening-Post* contended that Whitefield's distortion began when he first arrived in America in 1739. The critic noted that "if we take *his* word, New England's state of religion was *deplorable* when he arrived." Dismissing Whitefield's claims that he sparked a revival of true Christianity, the author pointed to "convincing Proofs that the Revival of Religion so much boasted by Mr. Whitefield and his Followers consisted in *external Appearances*." Now, in 1754, Whitefield had returned to America. Again he proclaimed that the colonies were "in a dead Sleep of spiritual Indolence and carnal Security." And the evangelist promised to "renew the Fire he had formerly kindled."[73] To the writer, it was all a fabrication designed to promote Whitefield.

According to Whitefield's critic, even the revivalist's sermons were exercises in self-promotion, not discourses seeking scriptural truth. He accused the evangelist of filling his homilies with "pretty diverting Stories" that have as their "grand Point . . . to establish Mr. Whitefield's Reputation." The detractor blamed local ministers for setting Whitefield "up as an idol." The results had economic as well as theological implications. "We justly complain of heavy Taxes, and Loss of Trade," the anonymous writer argued, "but the Loss of Time occasioned by Mr. Whitefield's preaching in one Week is supposed to be equal to Ten Thousand Pounds, Old Tenor." He equated Whitefield with other itinerants whose performances people run after to see "juggling tricks" and other popular diversions. As a result of his entertaining sermons, "the People of Boston were so foolish as to be wheedled out of vast Sums of Money . . . fourteen years ago." No doubt, the writer warned, Whitefield in 1754 would again "carry off large Monies."[74]

The *Boston Evening-Post* presented another image of Whitefield, that of a champion of the laity who had long suffered under heavy-handed ministers. The November 19, 1754, edition printed a response to the previous week's attack against Whitefield's preaching "in the Market Place at Cambridge without the Invitation or Consent of the Ministers, as lately also at Charleston." The anonymous writer began his defense of Whitefield's action by reminding readers that the clergy had no "claim [or] power over any Market Place or common Land in any Town or Parish," including meetinghouses "built at expence of the people for their use." Therefore, as Englishmen, New Englanders were free to decide what "Civil and Religious Purposes Meeting-Houses may

---

[73] *Boston Evening-Post*, September 23, 1754.
[74] Ibid.

serve." In the present case, the author declared "that the generality of the People in both those Parishes by their Selectmen invited and desired the Rev. Mr. Whitefield to preach."[75] Far from a self-promoting opportunist, Whitefield was a servant of the people in this public portrayal. By offering religion in the marketplace, Whitefield availed men and women of choice, freeing them from monopolies parish ministers sought to protect.

Readers had to contend with an enormous volume of publications during the evangelical revivals as proponents and opposers contested revivalist messages and methods in the press. At the height of public debate in 1745, one observer complained that "Letters, Sermons, and Pamphlets of every kind are slung in so thick upon us that Persons of the greatest Leisure have scarcely time to give them a Reading." Writers developed strategies with the overwhelmed reader in mind. Thomas Prince, editor of the *Christian History*, "very wisely determined to deal out to his Readers weekly such Portions as he judged they might be able to digest at a Sitting."[76] Chiding the evangelical Thomas Foxcroft for his prolix apology for Whitefield, an antirevivalist scolded that "Numbers might have read your Book, who will now content themselves with looking only on the Title-Page."[77] In the struggle for readers' attention, brevity was a virtue.

Some observers of the religious public debate, representing themselves as neutral, judged the conduct of the disputants rather than their theological positions. Nathaniel Rogers and Daniel Fowle of Boston devoted much of the September 1743 issue of their *American Magazine* to the print war. In reviewing "the many Papers and Pamphlets which have been published," the editors wrote, "the Authors, who are most of them of the sacred Order, [nevertheless penned] sarcastical Pieces that seem calculated rather to make Men merry than wise." Further, the clergy "treated one another with much Bitterness, and have not attended to that Justice, Charity, and Impartiality in their Representations of Men and Things as might be expected from Men professing the Gospel." In other words, the contestants failed to deliver on their promise of impartiality. Rather than a candid and fair examination of substantive theological difference, the debate had degenerated into a spectacle in which readers were asked to give "credit to every accusation that contending Parties think fit to receive and propagate of each other."[78] But readers voiced their response in the marketplace by purchasing pamphlets as soon as they were printed. Whether entertaining

[75] Ibid., November 19, 1754.
[76] Aarand Cleveland, *A Letter to the Reverend Mr. Foxcroft* (Boston, 1745), 4.
[77] Ibid., 3–4.
[78] *American Magazine*, September 1743, 5.

or informative, the debate provided colonial readers with a steady
supply of reading material.

Thus through his vigorous use of the press, Whitefield participated
in creating a new religious public sphere that extended throughout the
American colonies. Indeed, by exploiting the expanding print market
of the mid-eighteenth century, Whitefield had redefined popular religion, fashioning something public and national out of what had been
private and local. In the process he had empowered men and women.
Far from being passive consumers of religious notions crafted by the
clergy—including Whitefield himself—ordinary men and women exercised their independent reason to construct their own meanings of
the revivals in the marketplace of ideas. While Whitefield and others
established the terms of the public debate, readers forced writers to
provide evidence in support of their claims. Whitefield employed a
range of authorial strategies aimed at rendering his intercolonial message authoritative, commonsensical, and impartial, realizing that final
judgment rested with the religious public he had helped create.

CHAPTER 6

The Americanization of Whitefield

ALTHOUGH the Great Awakening had subsided after the public debate in 1744–1745, Whitefield continued to visit America, journeying to the colonies on four occasions between 1751 and his death in 1770 at Newburyport, Massachusetts. While the young evangelist had arrived in 1739 as an important expression of Anglicization—the latest religious fashion imported from England—during his last two decades he became part of a familiar landscape for thousands of colonists. Newspapers continued to report his every move as he traversed the Atlantic seaboard. But press coverage reflected important changes in the evangelist and in America. Accounts depicted Whitefield engaged fully in the fabric of colonial life—no longer an import but an adopted son. In 1751, he realized a long-held dream and became a large-scale slaveholder in Georgia as the new royal officials governing the province sanctioned the institution long opposed by the original trustees. During his return trip in 1754, newspapers took note of Whitefield's involvement in a wide variety of colonial voluntary associations formed to establish colleges and support charities from Boston to Savannah. Then in 1765, departing from his avoidance of political controversy, the evangelist openly expressed his support of colonial opposition to the new British imperial policies. In part, Whitefield engaged in political discussion to maintain visibility during a time when the crisis between England and the colonies crowded religion off the front pages of newspapers.

During Whitefield's last four American trips he witnessed the gradual metamorphosis of the colonies into an entity distinct from Britain. Indeed he was sympathetic with Americans who began to feel that the mother country was trampling on colonial rights. Although loyal to the Crown, Whitefield spoke out against such policies as the Stamp Act, discussing the political struggle in highly moral language before his intercolonial audience. Increasingly, America became the center of Whitefield's world.

Whitefield provides a direct link between the Great Awakening and the American Revolution. Although the intercolonial revivals had long subsided when Britain imposed new imperial measures in the 1760s, through four preaching tours and widely disseminated newspaper accounts Whitefield's message of the new birth as triumph over the tyranny of sin provided an important set of moral metaphors and symbols that many colonists embraced in explaining their revolutionary attitudes and actions. For much of the last twenty years of his ministry Whitefield challenged the authority of the Anglican church in the colonies, first in its efforts to limit the influence of revivalists in Virginia and then in its attempts to restrict his plans to convert Bethesda into a college.[1] In both instances Whitefield exploited the colonial press to publicize his position and, in the process, linked his struggle against ecclesiastical control with the patriots' resistance to political oppression.

WHITEFIELD IN AMERICA AFTER THE GREAT AWAKENING

When Whitefield embarked for Georgia aboard the *Antelope* in 1751, he was a different person from the young minister who had first sailed for America in 1737. At thirty-seven, the evangelist was more given to mature reflection than to the intemperate remarks that had frequently characterized his early publications. Indeed, he was considering an extensive revision of his *Journals* and autobiography, a work that would appear in 1756 with many "exceptionable" passages erased. He wished to craft a different image in the print market, one marked by a softer, more conciliatory tone in his ongoing theological debate with Anglican clergymen.[2] Benjamin Colman had noticed a change in style near the end of Whitefield's last visit to Boston. Whitefield had demonstrated a greater willingness to listen to his adversaries rather than strike out at them with little awareness and regard for their theological positions—a more statesmanlike stance. "Mr. Whitefield seems to grow more and more sensible of ye evil spirit of . . . animosity among us and the worth of our Ministers," Colman wrote of Whitefield's new openness.[3] In his last four colonial visits, Whitefield's public persona was that of evangelical statesman as opposed to partisan warrior.

When Whitefield arrived in Savannah in October 1751, he found a

[1] On December 18, 1764, Whitefield petitioned Governor James Wright of Georgia for a charter and additional land to convert the orphan house to a college. The Georgia Council, headed by James Habersham, and Wright approved the project and forwarded the request to the king with a favorable recommendation. See Gillies, *Works of Whitefield*, 3:469–475.

[2] In 1756, Whitefield published his revision, which erased "many passages that were justly exceptionable." See *Whitefield's Journals*, 31.

[3] See Benjamin Colman to Solomon Williams, April 12, 1745, in the Whitefield Manuscripts Collection, Historical Society of Pennsylvania.

religious climate far different from that of five years earlier. Although revivals flourished in parts of Virginia and in other scattered local communities, the intercolonial phase of the Great Awakening had subsided. The revival's waning can be explained in part by the nature of the awakening. Prior to his visit in 1739, Whitefield and other evangelicals had noted with dismay the low state of experimental religion throughout America. Whitefield had noted in his *Journals* New York evangelicals' complaint that there "a work of God had never been carried on." He observed that in Maryland "religion seem[ed] to be at a very low ebb."[4] And Jonathan Edwards had warned him that even New England, noted for piety, was in a state of religious decline.[5] For five years Whitefield and his associates spread the message of the new birth throughout the colonies so that "there was never such a general awakening and concern for the things of God known in America before."[6] Presses and pulpits testified to the pervasive concern for religious matters. But the revival's success also carried seeds of its decline. Once revived, evangelicalism could not sustain the number of converts that responded during the first year. Moreover, revival opponents became better organized and by 1743 matched Whitefield in adapting commercial techniques to sell their notions, especially through the colonial print trade. Thus, when Whitefield returned to America on his third visit in 1744, he found himself embroiled in a heated, partisan public debate that served more to harden attitudes for and against the revivals than to promote a general awakening. Even during that trip, Whitefield sensed that spiritual fervor had diminished, referring in past tense to the "late revival of religion."[7]

The revivals also suffered a decline because more radical itinerants such as James Davenport brought disrepute to all evangelists including Whitefield. In a well-publicized event, Davenport had called on his followers to symbolize their renunciation of the world by burning their worldly possessions. Leading through example, Davenport began removing his own clothing and tossed garments into the bonfire built for the occasion. With that antic, Davenport found himself thoroughly discredited, forced by other evangelicals to publicly recant his extremist views. When Whitefield next arrived in Boston following the incident, he noted that "all is laid to me as being the *primum mobile*."[8]

---

[4] *Whitefield's Journals*, 488.

[5] See Abelove, "Jonathan Edwards' Letter," 488. After his arrival, Whitefield confirmed Edwards's assessment of New England's spiritual decline. See *Whitefield's Journals*, 483.

[6] See Gillies, *Works of Whitefield*, 1:179.

[7] *Whitefield's Journals*, 517.

[8] Gillies, *Works of Whitefield*, 2:73.

Whitefield found himself on the defensive differentiating his brand of revivalism from that of more radical expressions, hardly a posture for expanding the awakenings.

Viewed within a commercial context, the revivals declined because of a shift in demand. Fickle consumer demand moved away from evangelicalism in particular and religion in general. The trade in religion had become oversold. If Henry Fielding was an accurate gauge of the English book trade, demand for religious works began sliding in the 1740s, after Whitefield had attracted his largest crowds in the late 1730s and early 1740s. In *Joseph Andrews*, Fielding discusses demand for books in a conversation between a bookseller and Parson Adams, who hopes to augment his income through publishing his sermons. "Sermons are mere Drugs," the bookseller explained. "The Trade is so vastly stocked with them," he continued, claiming "that really unless they come out with the Name of *Whitfield* or *Westley*, or some other such great Man," there is no demand. To Adams's disappointment, the bookseller added that he had known publishers to give "a hundred Guineas . . . for [publishing rights to] a Play . . . for they got hundreds by it."[9] Demand had shifted toward the theater and away from the church.

American demand for religious works also fell, although considerably later than the English decline. In his analysis of the colonial book trade, Stephen Botein observed that by the late 1750s the trade in America was "vastly overstocked" with religious works. David Hall, Benjamin Franklin's partner in their Philadelphia bookshop, told William Strahan and other London suppliers that he would not take any more shipments of religious volumes unless from the best-known authors, including Whitefield.[10] In 1739, when Whitefield ignited the intercolonial phase of the Great Awakening, slightly more than one-half of all colonial publications were on religious topics. When he returned to America in 1744 and became embroiled in the print war with antirevivalists, still almost 45 percent of the works coming from colonial presses addressed religious issues. But when Whitefield returned in the 1750s, less than 30 percent of colonial titles referred to sacred matters. And as the number of political tracts skyrocketed in the 1760s, religious works dwindled to only 20 percent of the total. While demand for Whitefield's works remained firm, they appeared in a much weaker market.[11]

After 1751, the number of Whitefield's publications coming off colo-

---

[9] Henry Fielding, *Joseph Andrews and Shamela* (Oxford, 1966), 70–71.

[10] Joyce et al., *Printing and Society in Early America*, 75.

[11] Decline in religious publications calculated from Evans, *American Bibliography*.

nial presses declined sharply. During the first fourteen years of his ministry, ending in 1750, British and American publishers released Whitefield works at the astounding rate of almost one every two weeks. Then in his last twenty years of preaching, output declined by 85 percent to about one every seventeen weeks or just three per year.[12] Any explanation for the drop in annual publication rates must begin with shifting demand within the print trade itself.

The consumer market that had served Whitefield so well, enabling him to reach a far-flung, mass audience now judged the revivalist to be unfashionable. For a long period, Whitefield had been in great demand, the leader of what the impersonal market would call a fad. But as demand for Whitefield's publications dropped from their peak, the marketplace transformed the evangelist from a fashionable commodity to a staple product, no longer capable of spectacular sales, but good for steady numbers. While Whitefield's works continued to appear in booksellers' catalogs, they ceased to be highlighted as current bestsellers and were treated as backlist merchandise. For example, his hymnal, first published in 1753, was a steady seller as Whitefield incorporated evangelical hymn singing into his worship services. Buyers also continued to purchase his *Journals*, especially the 1756 revision, as well as collections of his sermons.

The market alone did not dictate Whitefield's publication record between 1750 and 1770. He himself decided to print less for several reasons. First, with an established reputation, he did not have to flood the Atlantic world with his writings to make himself known. Second, he delayed publishing in hopes of retiring from active ministry and writing more then.[13] Third, he continued to preach the same message. His friend and biographer John Gillies noted that "a uniformity of sentiment . . . runs through all [Whitefield's] sermons and writings after he was thoroughly enlightened in the truth."[14] In other words, after Whitefield became a confirmed Calvinist during his second American preaching tour in 1740, his theology was fixed.

Changes within the colonial print trade also influenced Whitefield's publishing practices. His strongest American ally, Benjamin Franklin, was no longer active in his printing business, having relinquished management to his partner, David Hall. Further, relations between American and British printers were strained during the 1760s and 1770s. In 1775, Franklin penned a letter to his former friend and business correspondent William Strahan. "You as a Member of Parliament, and one

[12] Publications per year calculated from chronological list of titles in Roberts, *Whitefield in Print*.

[13] Cited in *Journals of Muhlenberg*, 1:675.

[14] John Gillies, *Memoirs of Reverend George Whitefield* (Middletown, Conn., 1838), 265.

of that majority which has doomed my country to destitution," Franklin wrote, "are now my enemy."[15] Although Franklin never sent the letter, his sentiments illustrate that shifts in political and economic relationships altered possibilities in the commercialization of religion.

Whitefield did demonstrate occasionally that he could write instant best-sellers, although with much less frequency than during the Great Awakening. In 1753, he wrote a polemic against Count Zinzendorf, a major Moravian benefactor. Viewing the Moravians as competitors and eager to put distance between himself and them, Whitefield attacked the count's antinomian theology and his fund-raising tactics, claiming with no little irony that the Moravian was extracting large sums of money from unwary English men and women. The work appeared in three editions within the year.[16]

Then, in 1756, Whitefield discovered that political topics aroused attention and afforded him a means of maintaining exposure in the public prints. On the eve of the Seven Years War, he struck a patriotic theme in a pamphlet that went through six editions in a single year. The work warned against a possible invasion of England by the Catholic French and denounced French and Indian attacks on British North America. Viewing the war as a struggle between good and evil, Whitefield called on Protestants of all denominations to shield themselves with the safest moral armor: true Protestant principles.[17] One of his last best-sellers appeared in 1763, another polemic that generated sufficient demand in Britain and America to warrant five editions in twelve months.[18]

Although Whitefield's publication rate dropped, he continued to command a great deal of attention in colonial newspapers. Aware of the enormous crowds that continued to attend his preaching services, newspaper publishers provided their readers with coverage matching that of his earlier visits. Even the antirevivalist Thomas Fleet felt obligated to report Whitefield's activities during his fourth visit. With the evangelist preaching in the Lower South, Fleet published "for the Comfort of Mr. Whitefield's Friends in These Parts [Boston]" an account of the evangelist's successes in Charleston.[19]

[15] Cited in *The Annals of America*, 18 vols. (Chicago, 1968), 2:226.

[16] George Whitefield, *An Expostulatory Letter, Addressed to Nicholas Lewis, Count Zinzendorff, and Lord Advocate of the Unitas Fratrum* (London, 1753).

[17] George Whitefield, *A Short Address to Persons of all Denominations occasioned by the Alarm of an Intended Invasion* (London, 1756).

[18] See George Whitefield, *Observations on Fatal Mistakes* (London, 1763).

[19] *The Boston Evening-Post*, April 13, 1752.

WHITEFIELD'S PARADOX OF SLAVERY AND FREEDOM

While Whitefield would establish himself as a true friend of colonial liberty in the 1760s, he began his fourth American visit championing slavery. Paradoxically, he viewed the bondage of African Americans in Georgia as necessary to his success in the competitive Atlantic market. With slave labor, he could finally turn Bethesda into a profitable plantation, exporting rice and timber to the West Indies. Thus, more than revivalism was on Whitefield's mind in 1751 as he prepared for what proved to be his briefest visit to America. Prior to sailing, Whitefield heard the good news that "the time for favouring . . . [Georgia] seems to be come." A result of Georgia's becoming a royal colony, the 'favor' was the legalization of slavery. Whitefield had long advocated slave labor and justified human bondage on religious and economic grounds. First, he held out the possibility that the institution might bring spiritual benefit to the slaves themselves: "Who knows but their being settled in Georgia, may be over-ruled for the great end [of their salvation]?" Second, the legality of slavery posed no problem for Whitefield. "As to the lawfulness of keeping slaves," he reasoned, "I have no doubt, since I hear of some that were bought with Abraham's money, and some that were born in his house." Piling up more biblical evidence, Whitefield speculated that "some of the servants mentioned by the Apostles were slaves." Turning to an economic rationale, the Georgia landholder wondered "how many whites [had been] destroyed for want of [slaves] and [how many] thousands of pounds spent to no purpose." Georgians had too long suffered commercial loss from trading in goods burdened with high labor costs. Whitefield absolved himself of any blame by declaring that while slavery is a "trade not to be approved of, yet . . . it will be carried on whether we will or not." With that he stated with finality: "Now this is done . . . let us reason no more about it."[20]

For Whitefield, slavery on his Georgia plantation illustrated the tension Christians face in a sinful world. He admonished his followers to "be in the world and yet not of it," meaning that they were to use every earthly means to propagate the gospel no matter what their endeavor. To a merchant just before his fourth departure for America, Whitefield wrote, "I am travelling and you are trading for Jesus Christ."[21] He urged people of all callings to "trade for God. Let merchants see by your example," he implored one follower, "that Jesus Christ can make

[20]Gillies, *Works of Whitefield*, 2:401–405.
[21] Ibid., 361.

many saints in a store."[22] Christ could also make saints among Georgia slaves. As he expressed his desire to purchase slaves, Whitefield wrote, "I should think myself highly favored if I could purchase a good number of them in order to make their lives comfortable and lay the foundation for bringing up their posterity in the nurture and admonition of God."[23] He had found a formula that fit his view of living in the world but not of it: take advantage of slavery where it existed but justify it as a means of evangelism.

Events in the colonies seemed to confirm Whitefield's hopes. Just as he embarked on the *Antelope*, he learned of a revival in Virginia among blacks as well as whites. Samuel Davies, a Presbyterian revivalist, had sparked an awakening in the Chesapeake, fanning the flames of piety sparked years earlier in Hanover County as laymen found true Christianity by reading Whitefield's sermons. Davies did not hesitate to preach to slaves, believing they possessed the capacity to understand and accept religious instruction and believing that he had the responsibility to preach the gospel to all people, regardless of race or social condition.[24]

Slaves responded to Davies's straightforward message of the new birth. One slave complained that at the Anglican parish church he attended with his master, "the preaching was above our comprehension," but the Methodists "preached in a manner so plain that the way faring man, though a fool, could not err therein."[25] Samuel Paynter, a slave converted to Christianity in 1770 under revivalist preaching, preferred a fervent delivery of sermons. He wrote that because of the evangelicals' "earnest manner of giving out the text . . . [it] struck [him] that there was something more implied in the words than [he] was aware of."[26] Thirty years earlier, a black woman in Philadelphia had testified similarly to Whitefield's performances. She was convinced that at times the evangelist had been entranced; in her view, "Jesus Christ had told him what to speak to the people, or else . . . he could not speak as he did."[27] In appealing to the heart as well as the head, revivalists struck responsive chords with those who had little education.

[22] Ibid., 137.

[23] Ibid., 404–405.

[24] For a discussion of the Virginia revival, see *Letters From the Rev. Samuel Davies, etc. Shewing the State of Religion in Virginia, Particularly Among the Negroes. Likewise an Extract from a Gentleman in London to his Friend in the Country, Containing Some Observations on the Same* (London, 1757).

[25] Cited in Albert J. Raboteau, *Slave Religion: The "Invisible Institution" in the Antebellum South* (New York, 1978), 133.

[26] "The Experience of Samuel Paynter, a Negroe of Antigua," in *Arminian Magazine* 13 (1790): 307.

[27] Seward, *Journal of a Voyage*, 38.

In 1751, Davies reported that "Ethiopia has . . . stretched forth her Hands unto God," explaining that "there is a great number of Negroes in these Parts [Hanover County, Virginia]; and sometimes I see a 100 and more among my Hearers." He estimated that "more than 1,000 Negroes attended on his ministry" at the different churches he established in Virginia.[28] Davies's preaching sparked a series of revivals that continued for the remainder of the eighteenth century with Baptists and Methodists reaping the greatest gains in membership among both whites and blacks. The Methodist itinerant Francis Asbury indicated that a hundred blacks belonged to an evangelical society near Petersburg, Virginia, and that "fourteen hundred, white and black, [were] converted" in one year in the 1780s.[29]

When they gathered at revival meetings, African Americans responded to the emotional preaching. Unlike Anglican ministers who favored an appeal to reason, evangelicals believed that true religion was experienced in the heart. Noting the reaction of slaves to his preaching, Davies wrote in 1755, "Never have I been so struck with the appearance of an assembly as when I have glanced my eye to that part of the meetinghouse where they usually sit . . . with so many black countenances eagerly attentive to every word they hear, and frequently bathed in tears." The new birth could be a wrenching experience as individuals recognized their sinful condition and inability to escape its consequences. Sometimes lasting for days or weeks, this period of conviction produced powerful feelings of fear, anxiety, and unworthiness. An African American converted under Whitefield's preaching, John Marrant, described his own conviction as "a wounded spirit" producing a "distress of soul . . . [resulting in] three days without any food, only a little water now and then."[30] When conversion followed, it was often accompanied by a great emotional release manifested by ejaculatory cries and shouts. Davies noted that "some . . . negroes have been in great trouble about their souls; their hearts have been broken for sin; they have accepted Christ as their only Saviour; and are Christians indeed."[31]

While African Americans responded to the outpouring of God's Spirit from the pulpit, some also found Christ through the printed page. Indeed, reading was instrumental in the conversion of several

---

[28] Cited in Raboteau, *Slave Religion*, 129–130.

[29] Ezra Tipple, ed., *The Heart of Asbury's Journal: Being the Substance of the Printed Journals of the Reverend Francis Asbury, Forty-five Years an Itinerant Preacher in America and Thirty-Two Years a General Superintendent of the Methodist Episcopal Church* (New York, 1904), 264, 269.

[30] Cited in Dorothy Porter, ed., *Early Negro Writing, 1760–1837* (Boston, 1971), 431.

[31] Cited in Pilcher, "Samuel Davies and the Instruction of Negroes," 300.

blacks who left records of their new birth. James Gronniosaw, a slave converted by the teachings of the Dutch Reformed minister Theodore Frelinghuysen extended his understanding of the nature of the new birth by reading from the works of Puritan writers including John Bunyan and Richard Baxter.[32] One of the early slave preachers, "Uncle Jack" of Nottoway County, Virginia, paid his master's children in fruits and nuts to teach him to read the Bible.[33] And John Marrant shaped his views of Christianity by reading a "small pocket Bible and one of Dr. Watt's hymnbooks."[34]

The Virginia revival among African Americans encouraged Whitefield to believe that his Georgia slaves could find the new birth even in bondage. Their presence on his plantations also meant financial stability for the orphan house. With twenty slaves felling timbers and manufacturing shingles, staves, and boards, Whitefield in the 1750s entered the lucrative West Indian "lumber trade" and found the profitable commerce he had long sought.[35] Although denounced by his Philadelphia supporter, the Quaker Anthony Benezet, and rejected by the German Pietist Johann Bolzius, who also operated an orphanage in Georgia, slave labor represented for Whitefield a market solution, not a moral dilemma.[36]

Whitefield abruptly terminated his fourth American trip and returned to England in March 1752 when he heard that Georgia had indeed become a royal colony. For the remaining eighteen years of his life, the Georgia orphanage would occupy much of his time. The charity had barely survived despite the thousands of pounds Whitefield had poured into it. Now he had an opportunity to put it on sound financial footing. However, any explanation for Whitefield's obsession with the orphan house must go beyond economic considerations. Bethesda took on important symbolic meaning for Whitefield, becoming a visible sign of his view of evangelicalism: faith in action, a voluntary outpouring of charity for distant strangers by a community of believers that transcended denominational and national borders.

[32] James Albert Ukawsaw Gronniosaw, *A Narrative of the Most Remarkable Particulars in the Life of James Albert Ukawsaw Gronniosaw* (Newport, 1774), 19–23.

[33] William S. White, *The African Preacher: An Authentic Narrative* (Philadelphia, 1849), 12.

[34] Porter, *Early Negro Writing*, 433.

[35] Whitefield purchased slaves through an agent, William Brisbane, to start a lumber mill at Bethesda. See William Brisbane to George Whitefield, September 10, 1753. For beginning of timber business see letter from Jonathan Bryan to George Whitefield, July 1753. Both letters are in the Whitefield Collection of the Manuscripts Division, Library of Congress, Washington, D.C.

[36] See Anthony Benezet, *Observations on the Inslaving, importing and purchasing of Negroes* (Germantown, 1759).

BETHESDA: A SYMBOL OF LIBERTY

In one of the supreme ironies of his ministry, Whitefield transformed his slaveholding Georgia plantation into a symbol of disinterested benevolence. In a memorial sermon honoring Whitefield, a Philadelphia Presbyterian minister, James Sproat, recognized Bethesda as a powerful metaphor for Whitefield's charity. "Let the Orphan-House in Georgia," Sproat intoned, "be as a monumental pillar of his ardent love to his fellow creatures in misery, and his Christian . . . desire to relieve their distresses." Sproat praised Whitefield for his selfless devotion to helping poor children in a remote part of the British empire. Had the evangelist chosen to exploit his enormous popularity, he could have gained far greater acclaim by locating his charity in London or Boston. Sproat explained Whitefield's choice as a turning against the world: "He was in a great measure dead to the allurements and vanities of this world, [and disdained] . . . all those fading trifles, those gilded nothings, which the men of the world are apt to call great, rare, and excellent."[37]

Rather than use the marketplace to accumulate wealth, Whitefield employed it to raise funds for charitable and educational projects in England and America. Among the beneficiaries of his fund-raising were persecuted Protestants in France and in Germany, charity schools all over Britain as well as the colonies, ecumenical church buildings such as the one Franklin proposed for Philadelphia, and a long list of colleges and schools including Harvard (to rebuild the library damaged by a 1765 fire), the College of New Jersey, the College of Rhode Island, Eleazor Wheelock's Indian School, Tennent's Log College, and the Philadelphia Academy.[38] Through his fund-raising, Whitefield enabled colonists to engage in intercolonial efforts to relieve the suffering of faraway strangers. They saw that people from disparate colonies could cooperate in voluntary, sacrificial giving—a lesson that would become politicized in patriotic resistance to British imperial measures of the 1760s and 1770s.[39]

Jonathan Edwards saw a strong link between Whitefield's charitable efforts and the evangelical revivals. In his view, "the remarkable blessing that God has given to Mr. Whitefield, may well be thought to be very

[37] James Sproat, *A Discourse Occasioned by the Death of the Reverend George Whitefield* (Philadelphia, 1771), 16–19.

[38] A Boston town meeting acknowledged Whitefield's fund-raising efforts on behalf of the citizens of Boston. See *New-York Mercury*, March 5, 1764.

[39] Charles Royster develops the evangelical ideal of "disinterested benevolence" in *Revolutionary People at War: The Continental Army and American Character, 1775–1783* (New York, 1979), 22ff.

10. Whitefield, benefactor of the Philadelphia Academy.

much owing to his laying out himself so abundantly in charitable designs."[40] Whitefield also viewed charity as a sound investment for donors. First, those contributing would have the satisfaction of knowing
that their gifts "may be the means of bringing one from distress into
flourishing circumstances." But more important, he invited his readers
to consider "how much better [their] account[s] will be at the day of

[40] Perry Miller, ed., *Works of Jonathan Edwards*, 7 vols. (New Haven 1972), 4:528.

judgment" because of their spending on others rather than engaging in self-indulgence.[41]

To Whitefield, Bethesda stood as a symbol of practical Christianity. Although preaching a message of justification by faith alone, Whitefield taught that "faith without works is the religion of every carnal man." Bethesda was his "visible cause," a sacred trust through which evangelicals of all denominations could help "poor children grow up in the fear of God." The Grand Itinerant viewed the orphanage as a test of his faith. It best expressed his oft-repeated claim that he "never had the love of the world, nor never felt it one quarter of an hour in [his] heart." Indeed, he wrote in 1769 of Bethesda: "I might have been rich. . . . I might have had a thousand a year of this place if I had chose it."[42]

Though transformed into a plantation worked by slaves, Bethesda came to symbolize Whitefield's struggle for freedom, for independence from the Anglican church. Whitefield had resisted any fundraising assistance from the Georgia trustees or the Anglican church. Instead, he financed the project through soliciting voluntary contributions from persons of all denominations throughout the Atlantic region. Whitefield fought to maintain control over the institution's governance, especially in the 1760s as he planned to convert the orphan house into a college. He explained to his followers that the archbishop of Canterbury, Thomas Secker, had agreed to grant him a charter if he "should confine it totally to the Church of England." Whitefield refused to accept such a restriction and stated that because "Dissenters and all sorts of people had contributed to it [he] would sooner cut [his] head off than betray [their] trust."[43] In resisting Anglican encroachment in the 1760s, Whitefield linked his fight for liberty with that of the colonists.

During his sixth American trip, Whitefield petitioned James Wright, governor of Georgia, to convert the orphan house into a college. Whitefield hoped that a college at Bethesda would provide "for the education of persons of superior rank who thereby might be qualified to serve their king, their country, and their God, either in church or state." He noted the absence of a "seminary for academical studies as yet founded southward of Virginia." He thought that such an institution would be useful to Georgia, the two Floridas, and even the British West Indies. In order to support his proposed undertaking, Whitefield requested an additional two thousand acres. By "purchasing a large

[41] Whitefield, *Sermons on Important Subjects*, 485.
[42] Ibid., 725.
[43] Ibid., 724.

number of negroes for the further cultivation of the present Orphan-house, and [the] additional lands," Whitefield expected to generate sufficient revenue to fund the project.[44]

Whitefield's proposal met with swift approval. Endorsed by White-field's friend and former orphan-house supervisor James Habersham, now a successful merchant and president of the council, the bill received enthusiastic support. The legislature and the governor concurred that "the endowment of a College" in Georgia was "perfectly sensible" and approved the grant of two thousand acres. With unqualified approbation, Governor Wright forwarded the proposal to the king, who passed it on to the archbishop of Canterbury for his recommendation.[45]

Concerned about the issue of governance, the archbishop insisted that the college conform to Anglican articles of faith. He informed Whitefield that the head of the institution must be a minister of the Church of England and that the masters must subscribe to the daily use of the church's liturgy. Whitefield responded by informing the archbishop of how such policies had worked in other American colleges. The evangelist argued that similar proposals had "greatly retarded the progress of the College of New-York" because most of the colony's residents were Dissenters and objected to the institution's narrow foundation. By contrast, according to Whitefield, "a broad bottom hath as much promoted the growth of the College of Philadelphia." Whitefield maintained that he did not object to the stipulation that the "Provost shall always be a minister of the established church," but he did protest a charter that "enjoined" the trustees to appoint an Anglican.[46] To Whitefield the issue was liberty: the right of the college's supporters to decide its governance.

In a subsequent letter to the archbishop, Whitefield argued that his acceptance of Anglican rule would betray his pledge to donors. White-field informed the archbishop that "by far the greatest part of the Orphan-house collections and contributions came from Dissenters, not only in New-England, New-York, Pennsylvania, South-Carolina, and Scotland, but . . . in England also." Moreover, he had repeatedly assured contributors that the intended college was to be founded "upon a broad bottom, and no other." He had made such promises because of the "unconquerable attachment of Americans to toleration principles as well as from the avowed habitual feeling and sentiments of my own heart." Thus Whitefield tied his proposal into the larger strug-

[44] Gillies, *Works of Whitefield*, 3:470.
[45] Ibid., 471–472.
[46] Ibid., 475–476.

gle between colonial America and Britain. He, as an Anglican minister, discovered that all were not equal within the British empire. He had judged incorrectly that he was protected by "the known, long established, mild, and uncoercive genius of the English government."[47] The Georgia orphan house had become part of the larger constitutional question of home rule, thus connecting Whitefield to American patriots from Boston to Savannah.

In early 1768 Whitefield made his case public through the colonial print trade. After concluding that the archbishop was inflexible on the subject of governance, Whitefield informed the Anglican head of his decision to suspend his plans to convert the orphanage into a college. The evangelist decided instead to pursue a more modest goal: the creation of a public academy at Bethesda. More important, Whitefield told the archbishop he intended to make the entire matter public. "I intend to lay before the public a draught of the future plan," Whitefield wrote in a 1768 letter to the archbishop, "and as the letters which I have had the honour of writing to your Grace contain most of what I have to say on this subject, I suppose your Grace can have no objection against my publishing those letters, together with the answers returned, and the issue of the correspondence." Whether the archbishop responded to Whitefield's letter is unknown and unimportant because Whitefield had announced his intentions, not requested permission, to publish. He did indeed publish in England and America all his correspondence regarding his college proposal. Whitefield portrayed himself as the servant of colonists who had voluntarily contributed to a public cause; he depicted the archbishop as summarily dismissing the request and insisting on the established church's rights in the colonies. With that publication, Whitefield joined other pamphleteers in documenting a growing case against arbitrary British actions.[48]

As mediator of the growing political debate over British rule, the Patriot press linked Whitefield with his former rationalist opponents in a pamphlet war waged against Anglican power in the colonies. While Whitefield was fighting Anglican control of his proposed college, anti-revivalists such as Jonathan Mayhew and Charles Chauncy were locked in a print war against Anglican missionaries who advocated a larger role for the Church of England in the colonies. In 1763, after England defeated France in the French and Indian War, the question of Anglican governance in America resurfaced. East Apthorp, SPG missionary at Cambridge, Massachusetts, initiated the press battle in a pamphlet addressing the "question whether by maintaining episcopal churches

---

[47] Ibid., 481.
[48] Ibid., 482–483.

in settled towns and villages missionaries had misapplied funds for the conversion of heathen." Mayhew and others charged the Anglicans with violating the SPG charter, which targeted "Africans and Indians" as objects of missionary activity. Apthorp argued that the charter was never so restrictive and that the purpose always included "benefit[ing] *English* subjects." Indeed he saw new opportunities for the SPG: evangelizing in the "extensive country just won to the British empire" through the Treaty of Paris.[49] The prospect of an expanded role for the Anglican church renewed colonial fears of a resident bishop in America.

In his reply to Apthorp's pamphlet, Mayhew viewed the SPG's history in America as an encroachment on colonial liberties. Rather than focusing on those people "destitute of God's word and sacraments or the means of grace," Anglican ministers had invaded "those parts where the administration of God's word and sacraments is provided for after the congregational and presbyterian modes." Mayhew pointed out that the gospel flourished in New England from its founding and that "there neither is nor has been any Occasion for the Society to support missions and schools here." Yet in 1761, the SPG had thirty missionaries in New England and none in the West Indies "where there are many thousands of Negro Slaves in total ignorance of Christianity." Moreover, Anglican missionaries called for greater uniformity and conformity in church discipline and petitioned for a bishop. Mayhew urged the "people of New-England to stand fast in the liberty wherewith Christ hath made them free, and not to return under that yoke of episcopal bondage which so miserably galled the necks of our Forefathers."[50] Although at the opposite end of the theological spectrum, Mayhew and Whitefield waged a common war in colonial papers against threats of Anglican infringement of American liberties. Having opposed each other in the public debates of the 1740s, revivalists and antirevivalists made common cause in the 1760s.

Five years later, in the midst of the Tea Act controversy and after Whitefield's death, Americans read Whitefield's correspondence with the archbishop as a reminder of how arbitrary authority undermined liberty. His dispute had become part of the proof that British leaders conspired to subvert colonial liberties. On July 30, 1773, the *New London Gazette* reprinted Whitefield's insistence that the proposed Georgia college "be put upon a broad bottom and no other . . . [because the]

[49] East Apthorp, *Considerations on the Institution and Conduct of the Society for Propagating the Gospel in Foreign Parts* (Boston, 1763), 7–9, 24.

[50] Jonathan Mayhew, *Observations on the Charter and Conduct of the Society for the Propagation of the Gospel in Foreign Parts; Designed to Shew Their Non-Conformity to each Other* (Boston, 1763), 13, 29–30, 52–53, 104–105, and 175.

greatest part of the Orphan-house collections and contributions came from Dissenters." The anonymous writer presented the reprint in light of recent events showing "how George Whitefield's intentions have been trampled upon." The reporter related an incident in which a Dissenter had asked the Georgia Academy's chaplain, a Mr. Eccles, if she could have a spot reserved in the orphan-house cemetery that she might be buried next to her husband. Although Eccles saw no reason to deny the request and thought the academy's Anglican president, Rev. William Piercy, would not object, Piercy ruled that the woman's wish could not be granted. Piercy wrote the woman: "You are not unacquainted of the College being established on the Church of England plan . . . [and therefore] no Dissenter may be permitted to bury or perform any ceremonial ordinance."[51] What Whitefield had feared had occurred: the Church of England would subvert colonial Dissenters' rights. Three years after the evangelist's death, Whitefield had become a powerful symbol in the colonial fight against tyranny. And the orphan house stood as a metaphor for liberty, even in newspapers a thousand miles away.

To realize his plan to convert the Georgia orphanage into a college, Whitefield had solicited support from his admirers and followers throughout the colonies. One of those Whitefield approached was Henry Laurens, a wealthy Charleston merchant. Laurens received the evangelist warmly in March 1770, perhaps as much for Whitefield's role in the Stamp Act's repeal as for the merits of the proposed college. Whatever the reason, Laurens pledged to "do every thing in my narrow circle to serve him." In a letter to James Habersham, Laurens expressed his admiration for Whitefield: "I am intirely of your opinion that the plan & design of this good Man is eminently generous and disinterested."[52] The key word "disinterested," recurrent in contemporary political and religious discourse, suggests a motivation aimed at advancing public rather than private interests. Merchants were being called upon to forgo profits by refusing to trade with the English. In Laurens's view, Whitefield refused to realize his private dream at the expense of the community of faith that had contributed to the orphanage.

REVIVALISM AND REVOLUTION

On September 16, 1775, a group of Continental Army volunteers gathered at the First Presbyterian Church at Newburyport, Massachusetts.

[51] *New London Gazette*, July 30, 1773.

[52] George C. Rogers and David R. Chesnutt, eds., *The Papers of Henry Laurens*, 10 vols. (Columbia, S.C., 1979), 7:241.

About to embark on an expedition against Quebec under the command of Benedict Arnold, the soldiers paused for spiritual refreshment. After listening to an extemporaneous sermon delivered by Chaplain Samuel Spring, some of the soldiers desired to see the tomb of George Whitefield, which they knew lay in the crypt beneath the altar. After the sexton opened the coffin, the officers began to cut off small pieces of Whitefield's collar and wristbands. As they marched off on a dangerous mission, they carried with them amulets taken from the body of one whose life and ministry had become a symbol of hope and salvation.[53]

This anecdote illustrates how Whitefield became a part of American popular culture during the Revolutionary period. It invites us to examine further how the evangelist constructed a public persona that would serve as a powerful image for Americans struggling against the tyranny of British rule in the 1760s and 1770s. Much of Whitefield's image building took place in colonial newspapers after the Great Awakening, during the four trips he made to America in the twenty years before his death at Newburyport in 1770. During his journeys of 1751–1752, 1754–1755, 1763–1765, and 1769–1770 Whitefield continued to travel throughout the colonies conveying his message of the new birth on a continental scale. More than anyone else, Whitefield popularized the evangelical tradition that provided a moral framework and vocabulary permitting thousands of ordinary men and women to conceptualize and discuss revolutionary events. Alan Heimert, Patricia Bonomi, Charles Royster, and other historians have suggested that the Great Awakening provided a cluster of ideas which informed revolutionary discourse.[54] Indeed they argue that most men and women explained revolutionary issues to themselves and others more through evangelical than Enlightenment language. They indicate that ordinary people knew their Whitefield and Edwards better than they knew their Locke and Montesquieu. The tyranny of sin, the corruption of worldly clergymen, the fallibility of ecclesiastical hierarchies, the empowerment of righteous (i.e., converted) individuals, the necessity of evangelical community, and the sacrificial relief of suffering strangers served as a moral standard for judging imperial acts and colonial resistance. The soldiers' pilgrimage to Whitefield's tomb bears testimony to the itinerant's centrality to a powerful evangelical culture that could be easily politicized.

Just as it had during the Great Awakening, the colonial print trade mediated Whitefield as symbol to the American people. Although the

---

[53] Cited in Royster, *Revolutionary People at War*, 24.

[54] See Alan Heimert, *Religion and the American Mind: From the Great Awakening to the Revolution* (Cambridge, Mass., 1966); Bonomi, *Under the Cope of Heaven*; Royster, *Revolutionary People at War*.

itinerant published far fewer books and pamphlets during the 1750s and 1760s than he had in the 1740s, newspaper coverage continued to be extensive, reporting his ministry to every colony. Through the press Whitefield warned against not only the tyranny of sin but oppression in all its forms: the Catholic French and Spanish, the hierarchy of the Church of England, and imperial measures such as the Stamp Act. Upon his death, merchants commercialized Whitefield as an important American symbol through paintings, verses, hymns, sermons, and wax figures. His 1739 arrival in America had prompted a flood of publications from the colonial press; his death in 1770 represented a final expression of self-fashioning.

In addition to voicing his support for rescinding the Stamp Act, Whitefield articulated his fear that the Anglican church, like Whitehall, was extending its authority in the colonies. In 1751 he had publicized Anglican opposition to the "great awakening [in Virginia], especially in Hanover County, and the counties adjacent." Noting that the revival had begun "by reading of [his] books," Whitefield further indicated that "at the instigation of the council a proclamation was issued out to prohibit itinerant preaching." Underscoring his belief that the church was behind the restriction, Whitefield wrote, "The commissary is one of the council, and with the rest of his brethren, I believe no friend of the Dissenters." Realizing that most of his American audience consisted of Dissenters, his charges were calculated to link the fortunes of revivalism and liberty. Echoing the sentiments of colonists who increasingly demanded equality as English subjects, Whitefield contended that Virginians wanted "no other privileges than what dissenting protestants enjoy in our native country."[55]

Samuel Adams and other patriots echoed Whitefield's warnings against Anglican encroachment on American liberties. In a series of articles published in the *Boston Gazette* and signed "A Puritan," Adams sought in 1768 to awaken his fellow countrymen to the British threat of religious tyranny. "I confess I am surprised to find," he wrote, "that so little attention is given to the danger we are in, of the utter loss of those religious rights, the enjoyment of which our good forefathers had more especially in their intention." The object of his fear was the establishment of an Anglican episcopate in the colonies. Anglican missionaries had long advocated the appointment of a resident bishop to ordain new ministers, maintain church discipline, and promote Anglicanism among Dissenters. Adams saw any expansion of English civil and religious authority as nothing less than "popery." He promised to oppose "those *artful* men who have come into our country *to spy out*

---

[55] Gillies, *Works of Whitefield*, 2:418–419.

our liberties; and who are restless to bring us into *bondage*." He warned that colonists are most likely to lose their liberties when "people are in a deep sleep." What he feared most was that Americans had become so dependent upon and enamored with English manufactured goods that their growing love of luxury undermined their defense of liberty. "The more I know of the circumstances of America," he lamented, "the more reason I find to be apprehensive of Popery. Bless me! Could our ancestors look out of their graves and see so many of *their own* sons, decked with the worst of *foreign superfluities*, the ornaments of the *whore of Babylon*, how would it break their sacred Repose!"[56] Like Whitefield, Adams employed the language of goods to preach against the seduction of the world. But both had politicized the language of goods as they warned that overconsumption and overspending would lead to a loss of freedom.

Adams was particularly concerned about how Virginians viewed the proposal to establish an episcopal see in America. In Virginia, the Church of England was already established, supported by taxes imposed by the burgesses. In a 1771 letter to Arthur Lee, a native Virginian, Adams expressed his relief that Virginia had joined with other colonies in a "wise and well timed opposition." Adams's ideas indicate how closely connected were the notions of religious and civil liberty. Applauding "the protests of diverse patriotic clergymen in Virginia against an Episcopate in America," he contended that "the junction of the Canon and the feudal law . . . has been fatal to the liberties of mankind." To grant episcopal authority would be counter to the original Puritan settlers' intentions. "The design of the first settlers of New England," Adams reminded Lee, "was to settle a plan of government upon the true principles of liberty in which the clergy should have no authority. It is no wonder then that we should be alarmed at the designs of establishing such a power."[57] Whitefield's staunch public resistance to Anglican control of his proposed college could only have further endeared the minister to Adams.

Whitefield's most stinging attack on the Anglican church's plans to establish an American bishopric came in a 1768 publication printed on both sides of the Atlantic. The event that precipitated his writing the pamphlet was the expulsion of six students from Edmund Hall, Oxford University, because they persisted in "extempore prayer." Whitefield charged that their expulsion violated English law, which protected all religious societies except those "composed of seditious persons . . .

[56] Norman Cousins, ed., *In God We Trust: The Religious Beliefs and Ideas of the American Founding Fathers* (New York, 1958), 346–347.
[57] Ibid., 350.

[who] plot against the state." But he saw even graver implications for the American colonies. He viewed the incident in light of a letter dated March 29 from the head of the SPG resolving that no missionaries should be sent to America except "such as have had a literary Education, and have been bred up with a design to dedicate themselves to the Ministry." To Whitefield, that meant only Anglicans would qualify, and it represented the first step toward Anglican dominion over America. He reminded his readers that "the establishment of Episcopacy in our Islands and Plantations" had long been under consideration. Whitefield warned that what had been "a Society [the SPG] which since its first institution hath been looked upon as a Society for propagating the Gospel hath been all the while rather a Society for propagating Episcopacy in foreign Parts." Like Adams and other Patriots, Whitefield viewed the Anglican hierarchy as part of a conspiracy to undermine fundamental colonial rights. He predicted that by countenancing the students' expulsion the archbishop would "increase the prejudices of our Colonists, both in the Islands and on the Continent against the establishment of Episcopacy."[58] By politicizing his attack against the established church, Whitefield found a voice that Americans wanted to hear. And Samuel Adams's newspaper articles confirmed the accuracy of Whitefield's prognostication.

Whitefield's influence on the Virginia revivals and his protest against Anglican restrictions on itinerants linked him to Patrick Henry, whose political oratory in the cause of American liberty paralleled the evangelist's theological rhetoric. Indeed Henry waged his first public protest of British oppression in Hanover County in a case involving the special privileges of the Anglican church. Samuel Davies had fanned the flames of dissent that Whitefield's printed sermons had sparked in Hanover County. From the outset, Henry resisted clerical efforts to secure a law requiring the licensing of itinerants. Although his uncle was an Anglican clergyman, Henry opposed the privileged position of the church, especially its financial support by taxes levied on every Virginia taxpayer including those who belonged to dissenting congregations. His opposition served the defense of officials who had reduced clerical salaries through the Two Penny Tax.[59] In selecting a jury in the so-called Parson's Cause, Henry placed among them "three who were 'New Lights,' and therefore dependable for the right verdict." Like Henry, those evangelicals, who subscribed to Whitefield's experimental

[58] Whitefield, *A Letter to the Reverend Dr. Durrell*, 11–5, 19–20.

[59] The Two Penny Tax was a measure that capped the price of tobacco for purposes of calculating pastoral salaries, resulting in clerical incomes well below the windfall clergymen would have realized in a market of prices inflated by drought-induced shortages.

religion, believed that Dissenters should be able to speak freely about religion "without the license of those whose sanction they considered worthless."[60] Although Henry lost the case, he discovered a message and rhetorical style that made him an intercolonial spokesman for patriots, especially revivalists.

Whitefield extended indirect and direct support to Americans in their struggle against what they characterized as British tyranny in the 1760s and 1770s. His entire ministry stood as a testimony against oppression in its various forms. Central to his gospel message was that sin corrupted hearts and produced spiritual slavery. In a typical expression of slavery as a metaphor for unredeemed sin, Whitefield asked, "Have you not resolved many and many a time [to stop sinning], and have not your corruptions yet dominion over you? Are you not bond-slaves to your lusts, and led captive by the devil at his will?"[61] The language of revivalism paralleled that of revolution: sin flowing from a corrupt nature enslaved individuals just as tyranny deriving from corrupt Whitehall ministers enslaved the colonies.

In a consumer society the corrupting influence was often unbridled desire for marketplace baubles. Whitefield warned his followers that "happiness . . . doth not consist in the things which [one] possesseth." For a person to expect fulfillment from goods was vanity. Whitefield reasoned, "Might not the poor slaves in the galleys as reasonably be wedded to their chains?"[62] People lost their spiritual freedom by selling out to the world. "Woe unto you who sell your consciences," he wrote, "and pawn your souls for a little worldly wealth or honour."[63] Overconsumption and luxury resulted in the loss of independence. The Devil ensnares men and women by tempting them with the things of the world. "It is true the devil is tempting us continually," Whitefield warned, "and our evil hearts are ready to join with the tempter to make us fall into sins, that he thereby may obtain a victory over us, and that we . . . may be his subjects, his servants, his slaves; and that by-and-by he will pay us our wages, which will be death temporal and death eternal."[64] The political consequences of becoming dependent on British merchants were just as dire.

For at least one slave, spiritual bondage was to be feared more than physical bondage because it extended throughout eternity. Upon learning of Whitefield's death in 1770, a young Boston slave, Phyllis

---

[60] Cited in Jacob Alelrad, *Patrick Henry: The Voice of Freedom* (New York, 1947), 24.
[61] Cited in Downey, *Eighteenth Century Pulpit*, 174.
[62] Whitefield, *Sermons on Important Subjects*, 131.
[63] Ibid., 187.
[64] Ibid., 196.

Wheatley, penned an elegy memorializing the evangelist who had died on September 29. Although in bondage herself and no doubt aware that Whitefield was a slaveholder, Wheatley viewed the itinerant as a friend of those in bondage. "Take him ye Africans," she wrote, "he longs for you; Impartial Saviour is his title due." In verse, the poet extolled Whitefield's efforts to bring the new birth to all people, regardless of race or condition of servitude. To Wheatley, who had undergone a conversion experience, eternal redemption from the slavery of sin was of infinitely greater importance than deliverance from the temporal chains of chattel slavery.[65]

Increasingly, Whitefield's message took on political meaning. As colonists resisted British constrictions of colonial liberties through nonimportation and nonconsumption, Whitefield railed against the "Vanity and Emptiness of earthly Pleasures." He contended that marketplace baubles and worldly diversions were "insufficien[t] . . . to make [people] completely happy." After listening to Whitefield on the subject, one auditor wrote "that People of Rank and Condition should be distinguished by the Choice of their Satisfactions, and not by Dress and Equipage."[66] When Whitefield toured the colonies in the mid-1760s, that message had become politicized as patriots expressed their opposition to new imperial taxes through boycotting English consumer goods. Now wearing homespun and eating simple fare was both morally and politically correct. The language of goods that Whitefield had appropriated in preaching the necessity of the new birth became a powerful vocabulary for patriots. According to one historian, "the artifacts of a consumer culture took on new symbolic meaning . . . , and before long it was nearly impossible for Americans to speak of imported goods without making reference to constitutional rights."[67]

When, in 1770, Whitefield toured the colonies for the last time, he preached against the corrupting influence of consumption, a lesson that the colonists were applying to their deteriorating relations with Britain. Having piled up huge debts in their insatiable appetite for English manufactured goods, colonial consumers found themselves at the mercy of their creditors. As English merchants restricted new sales and called for payment on old ones, Americans realized that their former assumptions regarding trade were mistaken. Instead of buying and selling as equals in the Atlantic market, colonists in the 1770s learned that British merchants viewed them as poor credit risks. Colo-

---

[65] [Phyllis Wheatley], *An Elegaic Poem, On the Death of that Celebrated Divine, and Eminent Servant of Jesus Christ, the Reverend and Learned George Whitefield* (Boston, 1770).

[66] *Boston Gazette*, September 9, 1746.

[67] Breen, " 'Baubles of Britain,' " 91.

nists responded through the language of goods, which, thanks to the preaching of Whitefield and others, carried a strong moral message.[68] Early in 1770, colonists retaliated through nonimportation and nonconsumption of English goods. By refusing to purchase English merchandise, colonists lessened their dependence on the British, and by preferring homespun over imports, they reclaimed some of the virtue dissipated in their spending orgy. Those colonial merchants who violated nonimportation were publicly excoriated for their selfish, immoral behavior.[69]

Colonists conceived of their opposition to Britain as a moral struggle. Patriot leaders challenged Americans to virtuous living in a struggle pitting good versus evil. In a consumer society, virtue and consumption were closely related: luxury bred vice; frugality promoted virtue. But morality was also a matter of conscience. Voices like that of Abigail Adams urged Americans to reclaim the religious zeal that had characterized early New Englanders. Sounding much like Whitefield, whose sermons she attended, Adams feared that in 1771, religion was "only a negative virtue, and that [Americans] are only a less vicious people." However, she found solace in the last sermon she had heard Whitefield preach. As Whitefield had assured that audience, "he had been a great traveller, yet he had never seen so much of the real appearance of Religion in any Country as in America." By contrast, religion in England languished. "In London Religion seems to be periodical," Adams wrote, "like an ague which only returns once in Seven Days, and then attacks the inhabitants with the cold fit only, the burning never succeeds in this Country."[70] Through comparing religion in America and England, Adams satisfied herself that the colonists possessed a powerful advantage through a comparatively deeper moral reservoir.

Whitefield extended direct assistance to the colonists during the Stamp Act crisis in 1765. On his sixth American visit when the act went into effect, the itinerant communicated to Samuel Adams through a mutual friend, Jonathan Mason, his "Desires to serve [American] civil as well as religious Interests." A leader of the Boston Sons of Liberty, Adams appealed to Whitefield by reminding the evangelist of New

[68] See T. H. Breen, *Tobacco Culture: The Mentality of the Great Tidewater Planters on the Eve of the Revolution* (Princeton, 1985).

[69] See for example, *Pennsylvania Chronicle and Universal Advertiser*, January 22, 1770, and *Boston Gazette*, March 19, 1770. Though the language of goods had become politicized, we should avoid glamorizing the colonists' willingness to sacrifice. Imports reached record highs almost everywhere in 1771–1773, even though the duty on tea remained in force.

[70] L. H. Butterfield et al., eds., *The Book of Abigail and John: Selected Letters of the Adams Family, 1762–1784* (Cambridge, Mass., 1975), 50–51.

England's religious heritage. "We need not inform you that we are the Descendants of Ancestors remarkable for their Zeal for true Religion & Liberty," Adams wrote, adding that the Puritans had "transplanted themselves at their own very great Expence into the Wilds of America . . . [and] resolved to set up the Worship of God according to their best Judgment, upon the Plan of the New Testament." King Charles I had blessed the mission by entering into a "Contract between the King & the first Patentees . . . that They & their Posterity might enjoy such & such Privileges." But with the Stamp Act King George III was depriving New Englanders of rights "manifestly founded in Compact."[71]

In soliciting Whitefield's assistance, Adams laid out a very specific role for the itinerant. Adams wanted Whitefield to plead New England's case before "some eminent Personages." Frustrated that British officials had not received accurate reports from the colonial placemen, Adams wanted Whitefield to persuade such persons as the earl of Dartmouth, a Whitefield supporter, that New Englanders bore "the warmest Sentiments of Duty & Affection to his Majesty & his illustrious House."[72] Whitefield could open doors inaccessible to American Patriots, and he could provide Whitehall with an accurate, that is, Patriot, firsthand report.

Although Whitefield's actions supporting the colonists' opposition to the Stamp Act are unknown, he became a public advocate for the American position. Whitefield had accompanied Benjamin Franklin to Parliament in early 1766 and listened to Franklin's representation of colonial grievances. In a letter to the Philadelphia merchant and land speculator Samuel Wharton, Whitefield extolled Franklin's performance. In an extract from the letter reprinted in the *Pennsylvania Gazette*, Whitefield reported that "Doctor Franklin spoke very heartily and judiciously in his Country's Behalf when at the Bar of the House of Commons."[73] Whitefield's private expression of joy at the act's repeal matched his public exuberance. He recorded his elation in his letter book: "March 16, 1766, Stamp Act repealed, Gloria Deo."[74]

Whitefield's opposition to the Stamp Act won approval from the most radical colonial preachers who railed against British tyranny. One of the most outspoken Patriots was Nathaniel Whitaker, pastor at Salem, Massachusetts. Calling for a "Calvinistic crusade" against monarchical oppression, Whitaker's "pulpit diatribes closed the door on

[71] Harry A. Cushing, ed., *The Writings of Samuel Adams*, 4 vols. (New York, 1904), 1:33–34.

[72] Ibid., 34–35.

[73] *Pennsylvania Gazette*, May 1, 1766. See also Labaree, *Papers of Banjamin Franklin*, 13:176.

[74] Gillies, *Memoirs of Whitefield*, 233.

all compromises."[75] After Whitefield's death in 1770, Whitaker said of the evangelical itinerant, "He was greatly concerned for the liberties of America, and under God it was in no small measure owing to him, that the Stamp Act [was] . . . repealed." Whitaker added that Whitefield "was loyal to his king, and paid him all due honour, yet he had a quick sense of the liberties of his fellow subjects." Citing the tribute paid Whitefield by several New England newspaper publishers, Whitaker agreed that the Anglican evangelist was a "real patriot."[76]

In September 1769, as Whitefield prepared to depart on his final American voyage, he received an ominous report on the deteriorating relations between Britain and the colonies. Franklin wrote that "the sending [of] soldiers to Boston . . . appeared to [him] a dangerous step." He saw nothing good coming from a confrontation between two groups who viewed each other with suspicion and distrust. He noted that "soldiers [were] taught to consider Boston in rebellion, [and] Bostonians [thought] themselves injured and oppressed." Drawing on an explosive simile, Franklin likened the situation to "setting up a smith's forge in a magazine of gunpowder." Franklin and Whitefield had discussed the growing colonial resistance to imperial measures and agreed that American affairs were "not well managed by . . . rulers here below." Unlike Whitefield, Franklin was less confident that matters were "well attended to by those above." Rather, he suspected that "our particular little affairs are perhaps below notice, and left to take the chance of human prudence or imprudence."[77] After receiving Franklin's letter, Whitefield confided in his letter book: "Poor New England is much to be pitied; Boston people most of all. How grossly misrepresented!"[78]

In his farewell sermon before embarking for the colonies in 1769, Whitefield expressed deep concern that British soldiers would trample on colonial religious as well as civil liberties. He denounced "the great mischiefs the poor pious people [of Boston] suffered lately through the town's being disturbed by the soldiers." Specifically he denounced soldiers' actions that disrupted worship. He related to his audience and readers a report that he had received from a correspondent in Boston concerning disturbances at the meetinghouse of revivalist Joseph Sewall: "the drums were beating before the house of Dr. Sawall, [*sic*] one of the holiest men that ever was, when he was sick and dying, on the sabbath day, by his meeting, where the noise of a single person was never heard before, and he begged that for Christ's sake they would not

[75] Cited in Charles W. Akers, *The Divine Politician: Samuel Cooper and the American Revolution in Boston* (Boston, 1982), 134.

[76] See Nathaniel Whitaker, *A Funeral Sermon* (Boston, 1771), 34.

[77] Labaree, *Papers of Benjamin Franklin*, 16:192.

[78] Gillies, *Memoirs of Whitefield*, 249.

beat the drum: they damned and said that they would beat to make him worse." To Whitefield the soldiers had become more than instruments of Whitehall; they had become tools of Satan. "This," he wrote, "is not acting for the glory of God."[79]

Tories as well as Whigs sought to interpret Whitefield's 1770 Boston visit as supportive of their position. After returning to the town on August 14, Whitefield preached at least once daily for three weeks, attracting "crowds nearly as large as those of the 1740s." Clearly he had a message for the 1770s. General Sir Thomas Gage applauded the evangelist's call for "Obedience to Government and Laws," no doubt welcoming the diversion Whitefield's sermons provided from the almost incessant unrest that had prevailed since the Boston "Massacre" in March. But Whigs—including the Sons of Liberty, whose annual festival coincided with Whitefield's arrival—"reported from his sermons whatever they could interpret favorable to their cause."[80]

Many Patriots recognized Whitefield as a supporter of their cause. Phyllis Wheatley cited the evangelist's friendship to the colonists in her elegy. Referring to his expressions of sympathy and denunciation of violence following the Boston Massacre in March 1770, Wheatley wrote: "When his Americans were burden'd sore; / When streets were crimson'd with their guiltless gore! / Unrival'd friendship in his breast now strove: / The fruit thereof was charity and love / Towards America."[81] Others praised Whitefield for his patriotism, meaning by that term his unflagging support of the Americans in their resistance. To them he had condemned imperial tyranny with the same eloquence he had employed against the oppression of sin. In a struggle that many considered a moral test, individual sin and national wrongdoing were closely connected.

Colonists viewed Whitefield as a symbol of American patriotism not only for his outspoken support but for his selfless service to suffering people. They recognized him as one who extended himself for community rather than personal benefit, citing the thousands of pounds he had raised and given to charities. In 1770, how one spent his or her money was a measure of patriotism. In a typical plea for nonconsumption, the *Connecticut Courant* contended that by "REFUSING TO PURCHASE the baubles brought from the Island of Britain . . . [Americans would] save their money and their country at once." A writer to the *New London Gazette* presented Whitefield as a true Patriot, one who placed communal good over personal gain. "Let Britain, let America, let all the friends

[79] Whitefield, *Sermons on Important Subjects*, 712.
[80] Akers, *Divine Politician*, 113–114.
[81] Wheatley, *An Elegaic Poem*.

of Liberty and Mankind," the author wrote, "pay the tribute so justly due to this shining PATRIOT. Compar'd with him, how low, how vile, how despicable, the Wretch, who for sordid gain, and empty sound, blown from the servile breath of cringing Slaves, would sell his Country's richest blood!" History would never forgive those who would "enslave the rest to feast themselves. When all this vile Herd are struck off the list of time, and hurled in one ignominious throng, down oblivion's stream!—WHITEFIELD's name, unimpaired by time, will shine like a brilliant Star in Heaven's eternal Sphere!"[82] Whitefield had been transformed from the Pedlar in Divinity to an exemplar of nonconsumption.

Long after his death Whitefield stood as a symbol of liberty. In their lengthy correspondence in the early nineteenth century, John Adams and Thomas Jefferson exchanged views on a wide range of subjects but never strayed far from the idea of liberty. Both saw a close connection between political and religious liberty. They agreed that denominational differences promoted tyranny in religious leaders who sought to control their adherents by prescribing denominational orthodoxy while labeling other creeds heterodox. Adams expressed his disgust with interdenominational bickering: "Howl, snarl, bite, ye Calvinistic, ye Athanasian divines, if you will. Ye will say I am no Christian. I say ye are not Christians, and there the account is balanced. Yet I believe all the honest men among you are Christians, in my sense of the word." Adams wrote, "I know of no philosopher, or theologian, or moralist, ancient or modern, more profound, more infallible than Whitefield" in his ecumenical conception of believers. He then repeated for Jefferson Whitefield's oft-cited description of the inhabitants of heaven. Inquiring of Father Abraham who occupies the celestial city, Whitefield asked in turn about Catholics, Protestants, Churchmen, Dissenters, Presbyterians, Quakers, and Anabaptists. Whitefield concluded that heavenly citizenship did not depend on subscription to a creed or membership in a denomination but fell upon each "who feareth God and worketh righteousness."[83] For thirty-three years, Whitefield had proclaimed in the Atlantic presses and marketplaces a catholic, experimental religion whereby individuals, not institutions, underwent the new birth. He became an enduring symbol for what religious and civil freedom would mean for individuals in the new republic.

[82] *Connecticut Courant*, August 27, 1770; *New London Gazette*, October 26, 1770.
[83] Cited in Cousins, *In God We Trust*, 252–253.

Legacies

AFTER Whitefield's death in 1770, control of the Georgia orphan house passed to the countess of Huntingdon under terms of the evangelist's will. The patron's generosity had helped support Whitefield's enterprise since its 1740 inception. However, Lady Huntingdon failed in the management of Bethesda because, unlike Whitefield, she "overlooked the fact that Georgians were hustling materialists, little interested in charitable and religious goals."[1] She turned her attention almost exclusively to converting Indians and slaves, ignoring the orphanage's links to the market that had helped it survive. Whitefield had never lost sight of the need to sell Bethesda as contributing to Georgia's economic development as well as to the colony's moral improvement. Although Lady Huntingdon donated more than twelve thousand pounds to the orphan house, its affairs drifted in a state of confusion under poor management. After the countess's death in 1791, a board of trustees held the property until a fire, followed by a hurricane, destroyed the institution. In 1808, the board sold its assets, and Whitefield's "house of mercy" ceased to exist.[2] The itinerant's legacy would not include the one organization for which he had labored throughout his thirty-year ministry.

While Whitefield did not leave a new denomination or even a lasting institution, he left an indelible imprint on American society. The itinerant's most durable contribution to American society was his conception and practice of mass evangelism, emulated by succeeding generations of revivalists. In 1835, the evangelist Charles Grandison Finney acknowledged Whitefield's legacy in a treatise, *Lectures on Revivals of Religion*, a handbook for promoting revivals. He believed that awakenings could be promoted, and encouraged ministers to employ proven "measures" to attract crowds. Finney referred to advance publicity, female prayer meetings, and lay exhortation as effective tools to prepare people for a "protracted meeting," a series of preaching services held over five or six consecutive days in a single community. He cited forerunners who had "in Divine Providence been set forward as prominent *in intro-*

---

[1] Mollie C. Davis, "The Countess of Huntingdon and Whitefield's Bethesda," *Georgia Historical Quarterly* 56 (Spring 1972): 72–82.

[2] Ibid.

ducing these innovations." First, the apostles had paved the way by breaking down "the Jewish system of measures and root[ing] it out." Then Luther and the Reformers had introduced "new modes of performing the public duties of religion," challenging the authority of the Roman Catholic church in the process. From the Reformation, Finney jumped to the first Great Awakening in the mid-eighteenth century, focusing on George Whitefield, "an innovator" whose "new measure[s]" raised an "astonishing opposition" throughout the colonies, especially among the clergy. Whitefield commercialized religion, "preaching out of doors and any where . . . seeking out ways to do good and save souls."[3]

In the 1830s, Finney and other evangelicals such as Lyman Beecher led a revival that spread from New England westward into the rapidly expanding Northwest—a religious stirring often referred to as the Second Great Awakening. Finney's view of Whitefield as an innovator in propagating the gospel and a progenitor of his own revival techniques suggests greater continuity between the first and second great awakenings than most historians have allowed. By focusing more on theological differences than methodological similarities, some scholars have cited Finney, not Whitefield, as the "father of modern revivalism." That distinction resulted from the assertion that the two revivals were indeed different not only in degree but in kind. According to the widely held interpretation, God's providence was the primary force inspiring the eighteenth-century revival, electing those he had predestined to salvation. Adhering to a strict Calvinism, Whitefield was a passive instrument who proclaimed what God was doing, leaving little room for human agency. The second awakening represented a sharp break. Men and women became the main actors, shaping the revivals through publicity and persuasion. Preaching an Arminianism emphasizing the free will of people to choose salvation, Finney and other itinerants promoted the great religious stirrings of the early nineteenth century.[4]

Although Whitefield preached Calvinist tenets throughout his ministry, his was an evangelical Calvinism, one that emphasized the universal need for preaching. While adhering to predestination, Whitefield also believed that human means—including newspaper publicity, outdoor sermons, public debate—constituted vehicles by which God mediated his grace. And because no one could be certain of election, all needed to hear or read God's word.[5] Thus the emphasis in Whitefield's

---

[3] Charles Grandison Finney, *Lectures on Revivals of Religion*, ed. W. G. McLoughlin (Cambridge, Mass., 1960), 250–276.

[4] Ibid., 12–13.

[5] See letter from George Whitefield to John Wesley, June 26, 1739, Methodist Archives, John Rylands University Library, Manchester.

revivals was on attracting people to services and declaring the message of the new birth to them. Whitefield taught that conversion itself, wrought by divine initiative, involved human agency including the use of reason. Suspicious of enthusiastic claims of direct revelation, the itinerant insisted that God chose to operate through people's rational powers as a means of dispensing salvation. Hence, Whitefield appropriated such means as those offered by the marketplace to reach the widest possible audience.

Acknowledging Whitefield as an innovator in promoting revivals, Finney minimized their theological differences. Indeed he expressed sympathy for Whitefield's Calvinistic preaching in the 1740s because "then the churches in New England had enjoyed little else than Arminian preaching, and all were resting in themselves and their own strength." Whitefield, therefore, offered them choice, laying before audiences such doctrines as grace, divine sovereignty, and election, which many clergymen no longer offered. Unfortunately, according to Finney, New Light ministers following Whitefield preached nothing but a narrow Calvinism, claiming the same sort of exclusivity in the marketplace of religion as Arminians had before the Great Awakening.[6] Thus, in Finney's view Whitefield presented men and women with the opportunity to choose, empowering them to make up their own minds concerning which clergymen they would follow and what teachings they would believe.

Although Whitefield left no lasting structure, his legacy included an organizational model for revivals that barred ecclesiastical control, a paradigm followed by his successors in mass evangelism. Refusing to submit to restrictions the bishop of London sought to impose on him and declining invitations to join dissenting churches, Whitefield appealed directly to his audiences for support. Through appeals in person and in print, the itinerant secured the financial independence that enabled him to criticize religious leaders with impunity. His was a loose-knit organization, depending on voluntary assistance of evangelical pastors and laymen to help him publicize his services. Through his letter-writing network, Whitefield had, for example, enlisted the support of most of Boston's ministers prior to his first New England visit in 1740. For months before his arrival, pastors had prepared their parishioners for Whitefield's coming, reading accounts of his successes to congregations. Hence, with church members mobilized to attend his services, Whitefield was assured of large crowds. Finney, Dwight L. Moody, Billy Sunday, and Billy Graham built on that model of sending

---

6 Finney, *Lectures on Revivals*, 203–204.

"advance teams" to evangelical churches, ensuring success before revival services began.[7]

In adapting commercial techniques to attract and persuade audiences, Whitefield developed close associations with merchants. Indeed,
his emergence as the leader of the mid-eighteenth-century revivals,
surpassing even his mentor, John Wesley, stemmed from Whitefield's
willingness to accept the advice of a promoter who treated the evangelist and his message as commodities. When William Seward advertised
Whitefield's revival services in London newspapers as part of a sustained publicity campaign, he took an important first step toward modern revivalism. American evangelists who have led national religious
awakenings have, albeit sometimes unwittingly and even reluctantly,
accepted and then relied upon assistance from savvy businessmen.
Finney maintained close ties with the New York merchant Lewis Tap-
pan. Moody benefited from the backing of such moguls as Cyrus
McCormick. Billy Graham became a national figure when William
Randolph Hearst instructed his editors to "puff Graham" and his anti-
communist message.[8]

Advance publicity, especially newspaper advertising, represents one
of Whitefield's greatest innovations and most enduring legacies. While
clergymen were reluctant to promote religion through the press,
Whitefield discovered it to be an effective pulpit, reaching thousands
he would never preach to in person.[9] Whitefield's imitation of merchants in publicizing his message paved the way toward mass evangelism, one Finney would perfect. For Finney, the immediate inspiration
to employ the press came from Jacksonian politicians. He urged revivalists to do as those running for office did: "They get up meetings,
circulate handbills and pamphlets, blaze away in the newspapers, send
coaches all over town with handbills . . . all to gain attention to their
cause and elect their candidate."[10] Like Whitefield, Finney had learned
from the secular culture he criticized the art of advance publicity.

As Whitefield's success resulted in part from such innovations as
newspaper advertising, unknown to his evangelical predecessors,
nineteenth-century revivalists employed media unavailable to the
Grand Itinerant. Technological advances enabled Whitefield's successors to propagate the gospel more efficiently. Moody, who preached
to mass audiences in the last quarter of the 1800s, exploited both the

[7] See W. G. McLoughlin, *Modern Revivalism: Charles Grandison Finney to Billy Graham*
(New York, 1959), 422, 495.

[8] Ibid., 79ff, 225, 489.

[9] *Connoisseur*, November 13, 1755.

[10] McLoughlin, *Modern Revivalism*, 87.

secular and the religious press, but unlike Whitefield, who inspired the first evangelical magazine, Moody promoted his revivals in "four hundred religious journals in the country then looking for copy."[11] And while Whitefield had publicized the results of previous meetings to promote subsequent services, Billy Graham perfected the same strategy through electronics. Whitefield had recorded statistics measuring his successes—size of crowds, amount of collections, and number of sermons—in newspapers, magazines, journals, and pamphlets. Graham, like Finney, Moody, and Sunday before him, also kept a numerical barometer of his revivals. In 1950, during a "crusade" in Portland, Oregon, Graham went beyond statistical measurements, making a "documentary color film of [a] revival from start to finish . . . to help arouse interest in preparation for [forthcoming] Graham revivals."[12] Although separated by technological advances, Whitefield and later revivalists shared a common vision that evangelicalism was a prize commodity which should be sold in the most creative ways to the widest audiences.

Through bold promotion Whitefield limned the self-portrait he desired: a divine instrument producing remarkable results. Although remaining in the Anglican church, Whitefield refused to be bound by the hierarchy's wishes. Therefore, he faced the task of establishing his own authority through self-advertising. Contemporaries testified to his effectiveness. Jonathan Parsons, pastor at Lyme in Connecticut, wrote an eloquent testimony to Whitefield's publicity before his 1740 arrival in New England. Parsons testified that "the news of Mr. Whitefield's rising up with great zeal for holiness and souls, had great influence upon my mind: God made use of frequent accounts about him to awaken my attention, to humble me for past deadness, and rouse me up to see my own standing, and sound an alarm in some poor sort, to a drowsy, careless people."[13] Before Whitefield ever preached in New England, Parsons was prepared to accept him as an emissary of God's providence.

Perhaps Whitefield's greatest legacy was his ability to bend the same powerful market forces that he preached against to his own designs. His appropriation of commercial strategies resulted from a series of negotiations with the market. At first, Whitefield was timorous, uncertain about using the press for self-promotion. Seward's initial advertisement on Whitefield's behalf produced embarrassment for the evan-

[11] Ibid., 219.

[12] William G. McLoughlin, *Billy Graham: Revivalist in a Secular Age* (New York, 1960), 61–62.

[13] Cited in Alan Heimert and Perry Miller, *The Great Awakening: Documents Illustrating the Crisis and Its Consequences* (New York, 1967), 40.

gelist before demonstrating a powerful new vehicle for propagating the gospel. Whitefield sat for his first portrait only because detractors had sold an unflattering likeness representing him as a grasping papist. After seeing the dramatic results in attendance stemming from newspaper coverage, Whitefield consented to sustained publicity in the metropolitan and colonial press. However, when his opponents also filled the papers with antirevivalist articles, Whitefield feared that his message had become just one commodity among many offered to the public. Therefore, by 1742 he sought to withdraw from the secular press and confine his publicity to media he could control—evangelical magazines and the letter-writing network. Even as Whitefield molded the market to suit his own designs, he maintained a steady assault on its excesses. He was a Jeremiah calling on his followers to adhere to a traditional message while leading them into modern mass evangelism.

Index

Wadsworth, Daniel, 157

Watts, Isaac, 207

Wedgwood, Josiah, 54, 58

Weekly History, 70–74, 81–82, 88, 91, 141, 157, 179, 167, 187

Weekly Rehearsal, 99

Weller, Samuel, 127–128

Wesley, Charles, 11, 50, 54, 144

Wesley, John, 11, 15, 17, 19, 24, 50, 52, 54, 58, 71, 141, 143–144, 150–151, 229

Wesley, Samuel, 50

Wharton, Samuel, 222

Wheatley, Phyllis, 219–220, 224

Wheelock, Eleazor, 103, 208

Whiskey Rebellion, 135

Whitaker, Nathaniel, 222–223

Whitefield, Elizabeth (mother), 36–37

Whitefield, Elizabeth (sister), 36

Whitefield, George: and advertising, 54; advertising of, 5, 68, 82; assesses books, 117; and auction, 39, 110, 112; autobiography of, 11, 13, 16, 25, 37, 81, 101, 120, 122, 130, 144, 157, 184, 189, 199; baptism of, 16; as book distributor, 90, 122; and book sales, 76–77, 122–123, 128; as bookseller, 91; boyhood of, 16; as business, 110; caricature of, 6; as commodity, 112, 128; his conception of audience, 14, 96; on consumption, 8, 44–45; conversion of, 9, 11, 13–15, 18–20, 22, 44, 142; criticizes Anglicans, 16, 22–23, 25, 62, 164, 180; death of, 3, 198; defends advertising, 108–109; defines mission, 14, 63; denied pulpit, 64; on denominations, 21; diary of, 50; and distribution of books, 86; as Dr. Squintum, 5, 46; on dress, 49; as editor, 89, 146; estimated number of sermons of, 3; and first colonial preaching tour, 92; and first printed sermon, 84; fundraising of, 6, 57, 58, 176, 180, 182; *Journals* of, 58, 62–63, 66, 68, 75, 77–81, 83, 85–86, 88–89, 101–102, 107, 110–111, 113, 122–123, 125–126, 128, 130, 134, 144, 147–148, 155–158, 161, 163–164, 171–172, 174–175, 184, 189, 193, 199–200, 202; letters of, 89; lineage of, 36; manufactures news, 171; merchandising techniques of, 6, 80, 93, 200, 228–230; on negative publicity, 83; as news, 103; and newspaper publicity, 108; open-field preaching of, 62, 64, 92, 160, 166; as "pedlar in divinity," 47, 93, 179, 225; portraits of, 5, 49, 86, 231; preaching tours of, 3; and predestination, 15; and preparation for priesthood, 24; as publisher, 145–146; on reading, 17; reading habits of, 18, 37, 45; as reporter, 120; 1739 American arrival of, 3, 95; as text, 5, 129, 155

Whitefield, James, 32, 36, 38–39, 45

Whitefield, Richard, 16, 36–38

Whitefield, Thomas, 16, 36–37

Wigglesworth, Edward, 131

Wilkes, John, 76

Willard, Samuel, 114

Williamsburg, Va., 98, 121, 126

Wilmington, Del., 106

Windham, Conn., 133, 183, 186

Winthrop, John, 43

Wollaston, John, 5

Wright, James, 210–211

Yale, 83, 193–194

Zinzendorff, Count Nicholas von, 162, 203